AF378598

THE ULTIMATE TEST

Also by Richard Evans

Whineray's All Blacks
Match Point (with Marty Riessen)
Nastase
If I'm The Better Player, Why Can't I Win? (with Dr Allen Fox)
McEnroe: A Rage For Perfection
Tales From The Tennis Court: An Anthology
Open Tennis: The First Twenty Years
McEnroe: Taming The Talent
Vijay (with Vijay Amritraj)

THE ULTIMATE TEST

RICHARD EVANS

PARTRIDGE PRESS

LONDON · NEW YORK · TORONTO · SYDNEY · AUCKLAND

TRANSWORLD PUBLISHERS LTD
61–63 Uxbridge Road, London W5 5SA

TRANSWORLD PUBLISHERS (AUSTRALIA) PTY LTD
15–23 Helles Avenue, Moorebank, NSW 2170

TRANSWORLD PUBLISHERS (NZ) LTD
Cnr Moselle and Waipereira Aves,
Henderson, Auckland

Published 1990 by Partridge Press
a division of Transworld Publishers Ltd
Copyright © Richard Evans 1990

The right of Richard Evans to be identified
as author of this work has been asserted in accordance
with sections 77 and 78 of the Copyright Designs and
Patents Act 1988.

All scorecards kindly supplied by *The Cricketer* magazine

British Library Cataloguing in Publication Data
Evans, Richard
   Black & white.
   1. Cricket. English teams. Test matches. Biographies
   I. Title
   796.35865092

   ISBN 1–85225–132–8

Printed in Great Britain
by Mackays of Chatham, Chatham, Kent

Contents

Introduction

After being raised on a diet of Compton and Edrich and my mother's sandwiches at Lords, there was never any doubt that cricket would play a part in my life, albeit for many years a distant one.

The opportunity to become immersed in the game again, as I was when I began my career in sports journalism with Reg Hayter's agency, proved irresistible once the dates for the rebel tour to South Africa and the England tour to the West Indies were announced. I realized that it would be possible to cover the important moments of both tours and, in so doing, try to examine the extraordinary way in which cricket permeates people's lives in a cultural and political as well as a sporting sense.

Both tours, of course, turned out to be even more fascinating than had been expected, and I have simply tried to chronicle each day as events unfolded, writing without the benefit of hindsight. The temptation to go back and tinker with what was written in the heat of the moment has been resisted because there is no point in trying to appear cleverer than you are. Sooner or later you get found out!

The emphasis in the South African section is placed more off the field than on because cricket, inevitably, started to play second fiddle to the momentous events that erupted around us. In the West Indies, the cricket took over and how riveting it was!

I am indebted to everyone who took time to talk to me and especially those colleagues in the press-box who suffered stoically under the barrage of technical questions I flung at those, like Jack Bannister, Mike Selvey, Vic Marks, Robin Marlar and David Gower, who could speak from the experience of having been out there in the middle. Also to Tim de Lisle of the *Independent on Sunday* for the statistical data he always had at his fingertips and Peter Lashley of Cable & Wireless for his help and hospitality.

I am also grateful to Graham Morris for his action photos and *The Cricketer* for supplying so much statistical data.

It was a long and often arduous three months and those personal friends in South Africa, Jamaica and Barbados will know how much they helped me survive.

Finally a special thank you to my editor, Debbie Beckerman, who possesses the rare ability of remaining calm and unfussed when one of her authors disappears for weeks at a time. Confidence at home base can be very reassuring when one is writing on the run.

RE
London
April 1990

viii

Arrival in
South Africa

30 January

I arrive with my prejudices firmly in place. I am prejudiced against the elders of a nation that calls itself Afrikaans which, in 1948, passed into law a method of government that was an affront to civilization. They called it apartheid and wondered why the world recoiled in horror. Racism is practised by groups and individuals in almost every nation on earth, but nowhere else have people been condemned at birth to an inferior way of life because of the colour of their skin. Nowhere else will a court of law, the law of the land, pass judgement based on pigmentation.

We know the reasons, of course. By virtue of his upbringing and religion, the post-war Afrikaner was taught to believe that he had a divine right to govern the great country his race had cultivated any way he chose. But, hidden behind that arrogant façade was a deep-seated fear that if the black man was not kept in bondage he would rise up and demand his democratic right: the right of the majority. It was as abhorrent as it was ultimately unworkable. Yet for two decades even many English-speaking South Africans considered it to be a normal way to exist. White people were educated and in charge. Non-white people were dumb, docile and subservient. It was the way of the world. Until the world came knocking at the door and told them it wasn't.

At the beginning of the seventies, the winds of change with which Harold Macmillan had released so much of Africa from colonialism were beginning to build up around the kraal. At first they went unheeded but then, when the liberalized world began instigating sanctions, deep in the veldt something stirred. The sanctions were economic, cultural and sporting, and of the three nothing made the Afrikaner sit up and take notice quicker than a sudden denial of his right to flex his muscles in the international sporting arena. South Africa is a sports-crazed nation and sport to the Afrikaner means rugby football. When the Springbok pack was mothballed, the Boer bled.

But it was not just rugby. Soon there were no Olympics, no Davis Cup, no Test matches for South Africa. The sports' boycott bit hard at the nation's psyche, partially because most sports' organizations were run by decent human beings and partially because no segment of society was hit more dramatically by the boycotts than sport. Yet tennis and cricket gradually began to lead the way in removing the more hideous effects of apartheid. Many years later, even rugby had moved so far from its entrenched position among the white minority that Dr Danie Craven, who was Mr Rugby in South Africa even before the Avril Malan tour of Britain that I covered in 1960, actually went and talked to ANC leaders in Zambia. I had to read that twice when I saw the item in *The Times*. Finding Margaret Thatcher enjoying a quiet beer with Arthur Scargill in a pub in Huddersfield would have been less of a surprise.

So if sport was taking the high road and showing the rest of South Africa that no fatal disease set in if you shared a locker room with a black man, was this appreciated? Even rewarded, perhaps? As a friend of mine would say, 'you cannot be serious!'

Following the same kind of justice the Afrikaner had been handing out to the black man, sport was singled out as the means by which South Africa would be taught a lesson. Forget that it had shown how much good it could do. Forget that soccer was not only fully integrated but run by a black federation or that athletics, boxing and tennis had also made the colour of a competitor's skin an irrelevance in winning races or matches. The politicians were not interested in that. What they wanted was what sport so clearly offered – a soft target, a cheap and easy headline extricated at the expense of simpletons who knew how to dummy or serve but who wouldn't have picked a political googly in a hundred balls. Every time sports' federations tried to say all the right things about an individual's right to free expression, their Governments told them to shut up. Tut-tutting noises were heard when those on high were confronted with evidence of economic sanctions being broken or some smart businessman selling more tear-gas canisters to South African police. But let a cricketer or a tennis player stray south of Victoria Falls and listen to the howls of condemnation that rain down on his head and echo round the parliaments of the 'free-thinking' world.

Do I reveal my other prejudice? Second only to my revulsion at policies based on racism, is a feeling of disgust for politicians who use hypocrisy, humbug and brazen opportunism to fan the fashionable political breeze of the moment. I have known a few truly sincere politicians, Robert Kennedy, Margaret Thatcher, Helen Suzman . . . The list is not long. Whether or not one agrees with their point of view has nothing to do with it. An honest opinion, honestly expressed, is what one searches for, often in vain.

So I fly in to Jan Smuts Airport in a tricky position. Unequivocally set against apartheid, I am held back from fully condemning Mike Gatting's team by a feeling that, mercenaries though they may be, few can be as bad or as blatantly dishonest as some of the people who speak out against them with such sanctimonious indignation. On apartheid I am black but, on the question of this tour, for the moment at least, I must admit that my colour is grey. We shall see.

The English papers, thoughtfully provided on the Air Zimbabwe flight that brought us down from Harare, showed me what kind of press the rebels were getting back home. Even in Australia, where I have been covering the tennis at Flinders Park, Gatting's foot going into his mouth after the demonstrations during the first match at Kimberley had not gone unnoticed by the media. But the British tabloids were really giving him some stick. No-one had needed to tell him he was going to earn his money the hard way.

After we landed, I stood in the immigration line thinking how long it had been since my last visit – just over thirteen years. I had been here twice, in 1973 and 1977, when the country on the other side of that barrier in front of me was a very different place. Judging from what President F.W. de Klerk had been hinting at, I had a feeling the differences could accelerate over the next few weeks. South Africa could change under my feet.

But, as I watched a couple of children play by the side of the queue, I wondered if it would change quickly enough for them to grow up on a basis of true equality. They were two little girls of about three. Almost exactly the same height, with very similar bows in their hair, they started to swing in unison on a low metal barrier that was positioned perfectly for some elementary gymnastics. Because they were so pretty and having such fun, everyone in the queue was watching them and few could have missed the symbolism. Even now, in de Klerk's South the law would treat them differently as soon as their parents took three more steps and passed through passport control. For one was blonde and very white and the other very black.

Frances Forbes was there to meet me when I passed through, unquestioned, with my loose-leafed visa. 'I'm sure you don't want one of our stamps in your passport, man,' the gentleman at the South African Consulate in Sydney had said. Very perceptive.

Frances and her husband, Gordon, are dear friends who will be my hosts whenever the tour passes through Johannesburg. Gordon Forbes, a former Davis Cup player, is also the author of the sporting classic, *A Handful of Summers*, a book which is as delightful, gentle and humorous as the man himself. Grudgingly, I suppose I have to admit that he deserves a woman as splendid as Frances.

I was aware that the beautiful smile I received as I came through customs presented me with a very different kind of welcome from that which had greeted the English team when they arrived ten days before. The first anti-tour demonstration had been large and noisy and the idiot police, reacting like the trained assassins they are, waded in with clubs and tear-gas, spilling blood and breaking bones and presenting to the world precisely the kind of image President de Klerk was trying to eradicate.

'FW', as people call him here, has given the police chiefs a stern lecture since then, telling them that it is no longer their business to become politically involved but they must simply keep the peace. That must have come as a nasty shock. But peaceful demonstrations are now being allowed and the police apparently have been kept on a tighter rein in Kimberley.

With Gordon away in London tending to his Greenset tennis-court business, Frances takes me to an Italian restaurant for dinner where we are joined by Forbes' long-time doubles partner, Abe Segal and his girl-friend. Abe runs a sportswear manufacturing company here in Johannesburg and, at weekends, teaches kids of all sizes and colours at Sun City in Bophuthatswana. Abe, a big, brash, open-hearted man, has lived most of his life at full throttle and shows no immediate signs of changing gear. When I tell him I am off to Bloemfontein in the morning, he gives one of his gruff laughs.

'Hah, be careful when you go out in the evening,' he says. 'You might get killed by boredom.'

Not this time, I suspect. Not this time.

Bloemfontein

31 January

It does not take long for the new arrival to discover this is not a normal tour. But then we have been warned often enough over the years about not being able to play normal sport in an abnormal society.

The abnormality begins at breakfast at the otherwise splendid Landrost Hotel. If you want the black waiter to bring you a pot of tea it is necessary to convince him you are not a member of the English cricket team. The team are in an alcove around the corner, near the self-service buffet, cordoned off from the main, multi-racial dining-room. The irony is not easy to miss. Apartheid at breakfast.

After passing through the road blocks on the way to the ground, I find there is apartheid in the press-box, too. After just one previous stop at Kimberley, the British and South African Press are already at each other's throats. They sit at opposite ends of the small, glassed-in press-area, eyeing each other with suspicion and resentment.

'Hello, welcome to our happy little tour!'

It is Malcolm Folley of the *Daily Express*, greeting me with his caustic grin. Normally, Malcolm would have been with me at the Australian Open in Melbourne but, as a sports writer with an increasingly wide brief, has been diverted to cover a tour which always promised to produce what journalists like to call 'good copy'.

Picking up the papers on my way here through Sydney, Perth, Harare and Johannesburg, I noticed there had been no shortage of it during the first week. With Mike Gatting as the fall guy, how could there have been? So far poor old Gatt has been a sitting duck for the tabloid hounds. There are only two categories of people the popular Press is interested in portraying – heroes or villains. Black or white. There is no time for shading in the other colours. And what the victims, understandably, find a little hard to understand, is that it is nothing personal. The two are inter-changeable. Villain one day, hero the next. A single edition of a newspaper has a life span of about twelve hours. And a memory just about as long. And before anyone starts getting too critical of the editors, just remember it is the public who buy these papers in their millions every day who are the real culprits.

So, at the moment, Gatting is the villain. How could he be anything else? A fallen hero at home after shouting at an umpire in Pakistan: later sacked, ostensibly, for picking up a barmaid during a Test match at Trent Bridge and now a mercenary captain in the land of apartheid. He set himself down in a minefield and the explosions have started already.

After one of the demonstrations during the first match in Kimberley, Gatting described the demonstrators as having had 'a good song and dance'. As the black people who turned up both at Kimberley and here in Bloemfontein do, indeed, sing and dance, it was quite an accurate observation. But, of course, the connotations were very different and Gatt had made his first gaff.

It had not been an easy start for him which would have come as no surprise. But if the beard had a couple more strands of grey in it when he emerged from the dressing-room to meet me, there was no other visible change in a man whose squat body would seem to have been built for the duties of an England prop forward rather than an England cricketer. Outwardly, at least, Gatting is not the kind of man who comes apart at the seams.

Even when Malcolm Marshall smashed his nose into nasty little pieces of broken bone on a lethal track at Sabina Park, Gatting managed to rejoin the England team in the West Indies after a very necessary nose job in London. That was before he was offered the England captaincy by the indelicate Peter May in a lavatory at Lords, while an unsuspecting David Gower tried to defend himself from the Press upstairs. The same Peter May, who had seen fit to cow-tow to the tabloid Press and fire Gatting two years later after his romp with the barmaid, was splashed across the front pages of the *Sun*. Gatting had been bumped around in the night by the selectors on so many occasions – Gower had to plead for his inclusion on the tour to India where he went on to score a double century in Madras – it was hardly surprising that he eventually resorted to a little nocturnal bumping around of his own.

There hadn't been a position in the top seven of the batting order that Gatting hadn't been asked to fill as he tried to establish himself in the team during the early eighties and, like the honest, dedicated pro that he was, he had done so without complaint while others moaned if they were switched from four to five. For years England had had no more loyal servant.

But loyalty has its limits and there was no doubt that Gatting became disillusioned with the whole England set-up after he was stripped of the captaincy and hauled over the carpet because of his book which dealt, partially under the cover of a ghost writer, with the incidents in Pakistan. During that insane summer of 1988 when any halfway decent cricketer who walked through the Grace Gates at Lords was liable to be offered the England captaincy, Gatting told me what he thought of the people running English cricket when we were attending a function in the Lords' banqueting-rooms. Then he went off to huddle behind a screen with someone who appeared at the time to be an unlikely conspirator. Chris Cowdrey's family pedigree in cricket is, after all, as long as Gatting's is short, but when Cowdrey, too, was thrown on the growing refuse heap of England captains after just one Test later that summer their commonality of experience and later, of purpose, became apparent.

As a result of what I had gleaned through incidents like this, Cowdrey's was the name that surprised me least when Ali Bacher released the list of sixteen players who had agreed to go to South Africa. But those of Philip DeFreitas and Roland Butcher stuck out like sore, black thumbs. Just how sore was made quickly apparent within a few days when both DeFreitas and Butcher withdrew, lamely excusing themselves on the grounds that they had not realized how much opposition they would face as black players in a rebel side touring South Africa. Did the ABC of the problem really have to be spelled out to them all over again? Didn't they ever read the papers? The proverbial ostrich had nothing on these two.

Even though I was aware of the extent of Gatting's disenchantment with the game's establishment, it still came as a bit of a shock to see him named as the rebel captain. And when Graham Gooch was confirmed as captain of the England team to tour the West Indies, one groped in despair to find some speck of logic or justice in the whole situation.

Gooch was the man who had connived behind Keith Fletcher's back when his own county captain was leading England in India in 1982, gathering about him a team he would lead a matter of hours after returning home on the first English tour to South Africa – a tour that would earn him and his colleagues a three-year ban from Test cricket. Gooch was the man who had wanted to quit the England tour of the West Indies four years later, because he had become the focal point of the anti-apartheid campaign against any England players in the team with South African connections. And, when the selectors blindly – or, according to some cynics, deliberately – talked him out of a contract to play for Western Province so that they could appoint him captain of the team to go to India in 1988, Gooch was the man whose presence in that tour party got the whole thing cancelled. According to the logic at Lords these, apparently, were just the sort of credentials required for an England captain on another tour to the West Indies.

No matter that Gatting had been putting body and soul into the cause of English cricket all these years. Forget the smashed nose (all in the line of duty, old boy); forget the more important things like leading Middlesex to championship and cup-winning triumphs while Gooch resigned the captaincy of Essex because he didn't like the job. Forget, too, the team spirit Gatting had forged during the Ashes-winning series as England captain in Australia, or the three one-day victories over the supposedly invincible

West Indies immediately prior to that fatal frolic at Trent Bridge. Mike Gatting had done something Gooch would never have had the spirit to do, he had shouted at an aggressive Pakistani umpire of dubious honesty. Of course he was wrong to do it. Of course he should have been censured more heavily than he was at the time. But how does a three-minute loss of temper in a dire situation stack up against an act of outright duplicity; an entire tour spent in a mood of such morose introspection that it affected the morale of the entire team; and, later, a flatly-stated preference for spending another winter in South Africa rather than touring India? Oh, Gooch changed his mind on the last count, all right, soon after the possibility of being appointed captain hove into view. But since when did someone have to be *persuaded* to captain his country?

Even after he was sacked, Gatting wanted the job back and, from everything I have heard, the majority of his team wanted him to have it back. More interestingly, so did Ted Dexter, the newly appointed chairman of the England selectors, as well as the manager, Micky Stewart, at a time when English cricket was supposed to start with a fresh slate, prior to the visit of the Australians last year. But Ossie Wheatley, the third member of the panel, was invested with the power of veto and used it. Wheatley, who unlike Dexter and Stewart, had never played Test cricket; had never toiled for England through the heat and dust of the sub-continent, is evidently not a forgiving man. He would not forgive Gatting for the incident in Pakistan and insisted that his minority view held. It was that undemocratic act which set in motion the chain of events that would lead Gatting to a land which, up to then, had also believed in the power of the minority – South Africa.

To make it worse, Wheatley's veto was kept secret so that Gower spent his second and most disastrous term as captain believing he had been Dexter's first choice. Even when Gower resigned after losing the Ashes series and Gooch, showing a little more enthusiasm for the honour this time, agreed to take over, Gatting was still holding out some hope that England would want him in some capacity, even as Gooch's deputy, for the 1990 West Indies tour.

Like all the others here in Bloemfontein, Gatting had known

players were being signed up all through the summer, but he had been one of the last to be approached and had made no firm commitment when Micky Stewart drove out to Uxbridge to talk to him during one of Middlesex's county matches in August. Gatting and Stewart, both Londoners from the same kind of social and cricketing backgrounds, had formed a close bond during the period of Gatt's captaincy; too close, in the opinion of those who felt Stewart should have exercised a more detached form of discipline in Pakistan. But that bond did little for Gatting now.

'I sat down and had a long talk with Micky,' Gatting told me when we met in the Tavern at Lords a couple of weeks later. 'I asked him to send me some signal, any kind of signal from the selection committee that there was a place for me in the England set-up. I told him about the South African offer and said that I was still looking for reasons not to sign. But I never heard a word.'

Not a word back from his great mate Micky; not a phone call from Dexter who had wanted him to be captain before Allan Border and his men ripped Gower's team to shreds; not even a hint through a third party that Gatting's vast experience and proven courage would be considered an asset to a team that was obviously going to be short on old hands, both for the one-day Nehru Cup matches in India in November and the full West Indies tour.

Gatting had stated publicly that he was available for India, but that family commitments would prevent him from going to the West Indies for three months. What he might have said in private had the signal he was looking for come through is another matter. Gatting's rejection had come about because he had been over-zealous in the commitment to the cause. Whatever the old school ties at Lords think about the importance of discipline and good manners, there are worse crimes than that. In the days of the Raj, desertion was considered a bigger crime than shouting at a black man. Gooch had deserted, had been given three years and was now being promoted to the highest post of honour in the game.

Even if the TCCB had been offering more than the appalling sum of £2,500 a man for the six-week Nehru Cup series in India as compared to the £50,000 (almost double for the captain) Bacher was offering for six weeks in South Africa, Gatting could have been excused for needing a little coaxing back into the fold. Not unnaturally he felt he had served his time. It was not as if England had prospered without him. Precisely one Test – against Sri Lanka at the Oval – had been won since he was sacked during which time four captains had been tried. Surely someone would tell him he was wanted. But no one did.

So was it surprising that the better part of £200,000 for two six-week tours of South Africa seemed so appealing? What if he never got selected for England again? Would his Middlesex salary of about £20,000 a season have been adequate compensation for unappreciated loyalty?

'I owed it to my family to accept the South African offer,' Gatting told me. 'This can secure their future. I know there are going to be problems and we are all going to get criticized for going but, as far as I am concerned, this does not mean I am condoning apartheid. I don't know much about how it works at the moment, but one way to find out is by going there. I'll learn and I'll listen to anyone who wants to tell me about it.'

Nigel Felton, a cape coloured who was in the Northants side that had been playing Middlesex that day, joined the discussion in the Tavern and immediately started enlarging Gatt's knowledge on the subject. Then Greg Thomas, who had spent many winters playing and coaching in South Africa, entered into a spirited discussion while giving no hint that he would sign up a week later as DeFreitas' replacement.

'Actually I was rather sorry DeFreitas and Butcher pulled out,' said Gatting. 'It would have been a good test as to how we would be treated as a team. Any attempt to discriminate against them in restaurants or anything like that and I would have brought the side home.'

He would have done, too, because that's the sort of person he is. You don't get to become a respected leader of a county team that contains five regular black players if you condone any kind of racial discrimination. But Gatting, unaware that petty apartheid was virtually a thing of the past in South Africa, never got the chance to take a stand like that. Instead it would be the blacks who would do the discriminating by refusing to serve his team when they checked into the Sandton Sun Hotel in Johannesburg and the Landrost here.

'You've been getting some fearful stick in the Press back home,' I told him as he stopped to look out on to the picturesque Springbok Park ground from the doorway of the press-box. 'Has it been worse than you imagined?'

'All part of the job,' he replied, instinctively playing the dead bat. 'Some of your colleagues haven't helped, mind you, picking on some of my remarks and trying to make out I don't care. We're all against apartheid. We all want to see it abolished. If I've learnt one thing so far it is that the whole thing is so much more complicated than I believed possible.'

We watched John Emburey, Gatt's vice-captain, try to perfect his unique falling pull-shot against one of the South African Universities' spinners and achieve nothing other than to fall over. Embers is not a man to be deterred, however, when he feels he is on the right track. The very next delivery, the front foot went to mid-off; the body and the bat to square leg and this time the ball followed. All the way past square leg, in fact, for four. Emburey studied his handiwork from a prone position at the crease with the air of a professor well satisfied with his latest experiment. There has never been a batsman quite like John Emburey. Several have looked as bad as he does, but none of them have scored 1,540 runs in Test cricket for an average of 21.69 with eight fifties.

'It's a question of not getting the leg across,' Gatt explained, sticking out a stubby limb by way of illustration. 'If you plant the leg there, pointing at mid-on, you can pull and keep your balance. But if you plant over to the off as Embers does, the only way you can pull properly is to let your body go with the shot and fall if necessary.'

Gatting, master of the reverse sweep, is not unacquainted with unorthodoxy. Nor is he troubled by it. Within minutes he was curled up on the treatment table that stood in the narrow corridor outside the dressing-room, fast asleep. Rod Laver used to be like that. 'Just going to have a bit of shut eye, mate,' the great Wimbledon champion would say and ten seconds later he'd be out like a light. Gatt obviously has the same knack. This tour isn't getting to him yet.

Colin Bryden, the tour's PR man, has arranged for me to say hello to Dr Ali Bacher, the driving force behind this whole enterprise. It would be reasonable in a reasonable country to assume that Dr Bacher would be the kind of figure the black activists could hate with impunity – a conservative member of the white establishment who had arranged this tour in defiance of anyone other than his own little interest group. But, of course, none of that is right. Assumptions here rarely are.

Ali Bacher, the last man to have captained South Africa in a Test match, is a Jewish liberal who, by South African standards, is quite left wing. He can talk to the ANC because his thinking isn't very far removed from theirs. There are not that many white South Africans who would explain the situation in South Africa to a visitor by saying, 'The National Party wouldn't talk to the ANC in the old days so they decided to start fighting people which was reasonable enough. Then Gorbachev arrived on the scene and told them that he had got a problem in Afghanistan and couldn't help them any more. And the whole picture changed. The Nats knew the country's economy was bleeding and the ANC found their funds drying up. Everybody had to start talking. There was no alternative.'

We were talking in the members' enclosure of the spanking new stands at Springbok Park, a pleasantly designed structure of grey brick trimmed with red railings. In fact the whole ground is less than two years old, having been claimed from land adjoining tennis courts and other sports facilities to create a modern head-quarters for Orange Free State cricket. Behind us we can hear the chants of the demonstrators bussed in from the nearby townships, while in front of us, sitting in the shade of the big scoreboard on the far side of the ground, there are a group of a few hundred blacks, also bussed in, clutching free tickets and lunch boxes. Apparently they were lured here by the idea of a pleasant after-noon outing. Many of them are young girls and, judging by their reactions, few have much clue of what is happening on the field.

'A local community club, the Eagles, phoned up a couple of weeks ago and asked to buy some tickets,' Bacher explained. 'We don't know anything more about it than that.'

Everybody, it seems, is trying to score runs off this tour for some political purpose or another.

At the end of the day's play I come across yet another group of young blacks who come trailing across the ground from the scoreboard they have been operating. There are only half a dozen of them but, amazingly, they turn out to be the real thing, genuine black cricketers.

Later I learn they are members of the Rocklands Township team that has been put together by Henry Matthews, Director of Cricket Development for the Orange Free State Cricket Union. Matthews plays in the team with a couple of other whites and, proudly, they head their league.

The boys watch the last of the demonstrators drift off to the buses and start chatting. Zebbie Makoena is, at twenty-one, the oldest of the group and is the side's fast bowler. Brian Maloisane opens the batting and, although he has only just turned sixteen, has already been on a Nuffield tour of England as one of only two blacks in the side. He is rated as one of the most talented black cricketers in South Africa and recently did his reputation no harm by scoring a half-century off an attack that included Allan Donald, the native Free Stater who bowled as fast as anyone in English county cricket last season while playing for Warwickshire.

Inevitably, I asked them what they thought about the tour.

'It's not good for us,' said Zebbie. 'It's great to watch good players like this, but we are afraid of what it will do to our own cricket. Already we are getting threats from people in the townships. If we have anything to do with the English cricketers they say they will burn our houses down.'

There is no bitterness in his voice. He just seems to accept this sort of senseless barbarity as part of life.

'It's a pity because we could do with some better coaching,' says Brian Maloisane. 'We only have two players of Test level in the Free State team, Omar Henry and Allan Donald, and Donald hasn't been around here much. Omar coaches us occasionally and last week I had a day with Bob Woollmer who helped me a lot. But he lives too far away and I don't know when I'll get to see him again.'

Woollmer, the former Kent and England batsman, has spent many years coaching at all levels in South Africa and remains one of the diminished band of first-class cricketers from England who are still helping out in South Africa now that the penalties for doing so have become so harsh, primarily because his own career is over. But he can't be everywhere.

So who, I want to know, are the boys' heroes?

'Curtly Ambrose,' replied Zebbie with predictable admiration for the great West Indies fast bowler.

But Brian proves himself colour blind and names Hansie Cronje, captain of the South African Universities XI who, the previous day, had hit a fluent 104 off an English attack that included Graham Dilley, Neil Foster and Paul Jarvis.

Upstairs I seek out Henry Matthews who is keen to tell me all about his programme and the progress his youngsters have been making in multi-racial cricket.

'The boys get to play cricket every day here,' he says. 'They earn some money doing jobs around the ground and we have set up some facilities for them to practise near their homes in the townships, too. But right now the tour is creating political problems and things are a bit tense.'

Nevertheless, Matthews, who was brought up in Pretoria and is happy to describe himself as left wing in terms of South African politics, has found Bloemfontein more open to new ideas in the three years he has been here.

'People think of Bloemfontein as the heart of Afrikanerdom, but it is changing fast,' he tells me. 'There are more mixed marriages here between the Afrikaner and the English, and that is helping to create more liberal attitudes.'

Change, everyone talks of change, but will it come fast enough for the boys I have just been talking to? I found them to be very realistic about their lot.

'I'd love to play for the state team, but I think I'm too old to make the grade now,' Zebbie said, wise beyond his twenty-one years. 'Most of us have only been playing the game for three years. Everyone's trying to help us, but we came in too late. Maybe the eleven year olds who are starting out in the programme will have a better shot at it.'

Hopefully they will if the political activists don't burn their houses down.

Back at the hotel this evening, Gatting's team were helping themselves to the buffet and carrying their dinner back to their little cordoned-off enclave while the black *maître d'hôtel* was checking our room keys to make sure we weren't members of the official England party. When I was here seventeen years ago with Arthur Ashe, we visited Alan Paton, author of *Cry, the Beloved Country.*

'We are a very odd nation,' he told us with a wry smile. 'Very little that happens here makes any sense.'

To that extent the place has not changed. There is still some crying to be done.

1 February

The crying was not long in coming. There is a press release from Henry Matthews lying on our desks when we return to Springbok Park. All matches for Rocklands and other teams in the development programme have been cancelled for the remainder of the summer.

'I'm just numb,' says Matthews when I find him in his office. 'But really we had no option but to cancel. It happened in Transvaal when the team arrived in Jo'burg and it's going to spread. The pressure in the townships is building all the time. You won't see Zebbie and the boys back here today. Last night they were told their houses would be burnt down if they came back to work the score-board. It's sickening, but what can we do?'

Matthews had been eagerly awaiting Rocklands first-ever match against an Afrikaans school the following Saturday. But there would be nothing now. Zebbie and the boys would be lucky if they got a net in the coming weeks, let alone play a match. They had become the first really innocent victims of the tour. Even the demonstrators who had been beaten up at Jan Smuts Airport had gone there with full knowledge of what the South African police might do to them. But Zebbie Makoena, Brian Maloisane, Eric Nkukane, William Maleke and the rest had been trying to do nothing more provocative than play cricket. But cricket was the white man's sport and now cricket must be used as a tool with which to assert black independence; to hack away at the conscience of the faltering proponents of apartheid.

'I was for this tour to start with,' said Matthews. 'I really thought it would stimulate interest in the game with all groups and give the boys a chance to watch some great players in action. But how can I be for it now? My whole programme is ruined.'

Matthews was hoping that, once the team left Bloemfontein, things would calm down and that, within a few weeks, reason would prevail. But, for the moment, there would be no black cricket.

When I told John Emburey what had happened he looked shattered. It is easy to say if he had stayed away it wouldn't have happened. But nothing as vicious as this had happened before, not during the tour he made under Gooch's captaincy in 1982, nor the subsequent ones undertaken by Sri Lankan, West Indian and Australian sides.

No one had even demonstrated against those tours. But it had been a different South Africa Emburey had known before. Demonstrations had been illegal then. More to the point, they had been illegal ten days ago. But F.W. de Klerk had changed all that and now cricket was making history of a dubious kind. It was becoming the focal point of the first-ever legal demonstrations ever allowed in the Republic. Suddenly cricket could be used for political purposes as it had never been used before.

'That's terrible,' said Emburey. 'Why is it necessary to do that sort of thing? We wanted to help those kids with a bit of coaching, not hinder them.'

Emburey is not a naïve man, but he and his colleagues still have a lot to learn about harsh political realities.

Later, as the visitors' top order batsmen tried to work their way into some kind of form chasing a near impossible target in the fourth innings, the view from the roof, looking back over the road, seemed marginally more interesting than what was happening on the field. It was thought that there would be no demonstrators today as the trade union funds had only stretched to two of the three days play in Kimberley. But that did not prove to be the case here. Although smaller than the previous days, a crowd of some 200 had shown up by lunchtime, armed with their inevitable placards reading, 'English Team Go Home!' or 'Gatting is a Racist' and had settled quickly into their footstomping chants.

From our vantage point, a motley collection of police officers, journalists of varying persuasions and cricketers could look down on the mobile police HQ and across the 50-yard strip of reddy-brown earth to where a single rope marked the point beyond which the demonstrators were not allowed to go. A few of the leaders, daring the police to make a move, did slip under the rope and begin their dance – toy-toying as the blacks call it – in no-man's land. The police, trying to remember the restraints their president had placed on them, fidgeted and did nothing. It was all very new to them, this business of legal demonstrations. Very new and very irritating.

There were a lot of young women in front, pressing up against the rope, linking hands and soon the singing started, growing louder and swelling in an evocative way.

'It's really rather moving,' said Emburey who appeared at my elbow, pads on, cup of tea in hand. On his way up from the dressing-room, he had been ribbed by Bill Athey. 'They've only come to see you bat,' Athey laughed.

On my left there was a large Afrikaner who reacted immediately to Emburey's arrival.

'They call that a peaceful demonstration,' he said, keen to ingratiate himself with the visitors. 'There's no such thing as a peaceful demonstration, man. They should be kept away.'

I looked at Emburey. 'They're all right as long as the police stay away from them,' he said. 'But I tell you what, they've got a lot of stamina. They were out here for hours yesterday in that hot sun. It's not easy pumping your legs like that. I don't know how long I'd last out there.'

'But you could hear them on the field, couldn't you?' asked the man on my left, now less certain of his ground.

'Oh, yes, you could hear them,' said Emburey. 'They sing pretty well.'

'And they've got great rhythm,' I added.

'Oh, yes,' the man agreed eagerly, sensing he had been on the wrong tack. 'They've got great rhythm, man, great rhythm.'

It was unfair, really. I'd set him up and he had fallen for it with embarrassing ease. Unfortunately he was not going to be the last person who was going to get hooked today.

Suddenly, it started to rain, but the singing continued. A couple of umbrellas went up, a few placards were held over heads but as the cloudburst swamped them, no one moved.

'You've got to hand it to them,' said Emburey and disappeared downstairs to take his pads off.

Word came through just before the scheduled tea interval that the anti-tour leaders wanted to present Mike Gatting with a petition. From the word go, Gatt had said he would meet anyone representing factions opposed to the tour and he intended to carry out that pledge. So the police were told to let a delegation come up to the roof where Gatting and the tour manager, David Graveney, would meet them. Naturally the Press were informed and a core of hard-nosed British scribes – John Jackson of the *Daily Mirror*, Paul Weaver of *Today*, John Etheridge of the *Sun* and Folley amongst them – were waiting to witness the ceremony when Gatting and Graveney appeared. So, too, were Graham Morris and some of the other photographers.

Three men had been allowed through the police cordon, although one of them looked no more than a boy. That was deceptive because John Sogoneco was actually twenty-five, but then the whole business was a bit of a deception. As the petition was handed over, Sogoneco's shirt was pulled off and Gatting found himself confronted by an area of the man's back that had been peppered with buckshot as a result of police action in the townships a couple of nights before.

It was a picture set-up and the cameramen got precisely the shots the anti-tour leaders intended them to get – the English captain staring at direct evidence of the violence the presence of his team was generating.

Gatting reacted badly. 'Did that happen at the ground?' he asked.

'No, in the township.'

'Then it's nothing to do with us,' Gatting replied. 'We can't be held responsible for anything that happens away from the ground.'

Gatting knows his limitations and is inhibited by them. He can attack with a bat and manoeuvre himself about a cricket field but, in a battle of words, he is blunt and defensive. Graveney is altogether more articulate but it is Gatting who is in the firing-line and, at the moment, he is getting shot to pieces. This unhappy incident has provided just another example of how soft a target sportsmen can be for wily politicians. This team of cricketers are completely out of their depth. They are being outwitted at every turn.

Downstairs in the corridor outside the press-room, Gatting and Graveney are called to one side by Richard Streeton of *The Times*, Frank Partridge of the BBC and a couple of other journalists whose job does not require them to deal in simplistic headlines, and they are told bluntly that they are going to get another mauling in the British tabloids.

'We understand you were caught unawares by what happened up there but you reacted badly,' Gatting is told. 'You had better prepare some sort of a statement.'

Gatting seems resigned to his fate, but Graveney takes the advice to heart. 'Right, then we'll call a press conference back at the hotel and try to clarify our position,' he says.

Later we all assemble in the captain's suite at the Landrost. Gatting and Graveney face the television cameras while vice-captain Emburey sits on a sofa looking glum. Gatting makes a brave attempt to explain how shocked he had been to see the boy's condition and how he hadn't meant to sound as if he didn't care, but stuck rigidly to his line about refusing to be held responsible for every incident that might take place in the townships where violence was commonplace.

Richard Streeton, a veteran cricket writer and a kindly man, suggests that, as 'the boy' was actualy twenty-five, might it not be better if Gatting referred to him as a man. In the current climate, it is a valid point and Gatting, looking grateful, readily agrees. 'Gatting calls shot black man "boy".' It would have made another juicy headline.

But, despite this rear-guard action, the stories are already winging their way to London; the pictures have already been wired and nothing that was said here is going to reduce the size of the print.

It is announced that the team will get out of town and on the road to Pietermaritzburg that night instead of the following morning so as to give everyone more time to relax before the match against a South African XI starts on Saturday.

'There is nothing sinister about this,' Graveney says, smiling. 'We don't want you guys to think we are slipping away in the night.'

Some of my colleagues looked unconvinced. On this tour every move is regarded with suspicion.

While the gear is being brought down into the lobby, I reintroduce myself to Chris Broad whom I saw last when he visited our BBC radio commentary team at Wimbledon in the summer. After gaining a reputation for being 'difficult' – partially deserved, I suppose, after the well-publicized rows with his county captain at Nottingham and the incident which I witnessed when he took a swipe at his stumps after being dismissed in a Test match at Sydney – Broad became another prime candidate for this tour when he fell out of favour with the Establishment. But he is an open and pleasant person to talk to and it is sad to think that England will have to do without him for five years now. Ambitious, highly competitive openers with an average of 39.54 and six centuries in twenty-five Tests are not thick on the ground.

Emburey wanders over to join us and is obviously chafing at the bit.

'That's the third press conference I've been to and I haven't said a word yet,' he complains.

Emburey is not impressed by Gatting as a communicator.

'He should let Graveney do the talking,' Emburey says. 'Gatt has never been any good at making public statements. The ideal thing for England would have been for David Gower to do the speech making and press conferences and leave Gatt to lead the team on the field.'

'I'm not sure about David's speeches,' says Broad. 'I think cricketers are too down-to-earth to understand half of what he's on about. But I've got a great deal of respect for Gatt. He's a good captain to play for.'

The captain himself appears.

'How was I?' he asks.

'Better,' I reply. 'You almost kept a straight bat this time.'

Gatting allows himself a little smile and waddles off to

supervise the departure for Pietermaritzburg where the Zulus await us.

The rain, which stopped play before tea, ensured the match finished as a draw. I am beginning to think it will be a miracle if this tour gets stopped by nothing more than rain.

En Route
Bloemfontein – Pietermaritzburg

2 February

The vast, brown landscape skims by once we hit the motorway to Natal. Great flat-top mountains erupt at intervals of twenty to thirty miles. Everything seems so vast one almost expects some giant to plonk down a 200-foot garden chair, spread a table cloth two miles wide and eat his lunch off one of those mountains. It is Gulliver country and our little bus, smaller and more rickety than we had expected, scurries along like a beetle, dwarfed by everything around it.

It will take us six hours to reach Pietermaritzburg, a thought which deterred some members of the party and they have decided to fly via Johannesburg. With the kind of security the team have been put through at airports, the bus seems like the line of least resistance even though there were a couple more defections when the actual vehicle turned up at the hotel. The big luxury coach we had been promised is only to go as far as Bloemfontein Airport with the South African team.

'The Press go in that one,' said the coach company official with finality. 'We are sorry about the air-conditioning, but that's the way it is.'

When we got on board it wasn't the air-conditioning that we were so concerned about. Open windows took care of that. It was the bloody radio. That didn't work either, and so, when President de Klerk made his speech which turned South Africa into a different country we were skirting Lesotho and within striking distance of Ladysmith, surrounded by echoes of the past but unable to catch the words that would change the future.

It was not until we decided to stop for a bite to eat at a Wimpy bar in Harrismith that we heard the news. Graham Morris, one of cricket's ace photographers, had been following us in a hire car with a radio that worked.

'De Klerk's unbanned the Communist Party as well as the ANC; suspended all executions and promised that Mandela's release is imminent,' said Morris.

We didn't choke on our cheeseburgers or feel the earth move, but no one would have been surprised if we had. As we learnt more details from the speech, it became clear that de Klerk had gone further than anyone had expected. It seemed that he had become intent on turning himself into the Gorbachev of the southern hemisphere.

The change that has overcome F.W. de Klerk since he succeeded P.W. Botha as president has stunned those who knew him as a loyal and largely unquestioning member of the National Party's cabinet. Some of my liberal friends here have been telling me that he has 'seen the light', not realizing how close they were to describing de Klerk's own explanation for the dramatic change in his thinking.

I have heard, from what political correspondents would probably call an unimpeachable source, that de Klerk has told a couple of friends in recent weeks that he literally 'saw the light' on his knees in church. Apparently he said that he had a vision of a new South Africa which released him from the agonies of indecision with which he had been wrestling and allowed him to set out on a straight forward path that would lead, ultimately and inevitably, to black rule 'even if that means I will no longer be president'.

My source, who has known de Klerk for years, was staggered by this revelation because the President is a Dopper, a term used to describe those who belong to the most conservative branch of the Dutch Reform Church and attended a strictly orthodox Afrikaner university at Potchefstroom, some seventy miles west of Johannesburg in the heart of the Transvaal. A sudden conversion to liberalism in middle age would be virtually unheard of and an incomprehensible occurrence for anyone with this background.

Those who do not believe in religious experiences will point to Vimpy de Klerk, FW's very liberalized brother as a more likely source of inspiration. But no matter from where it comes, de Klerk seems intent on a pace of change that is going to leave everyone scrambling to keep up.

No mention was made of the cricket tour in the speech which is surprising only in that it is continuing to provide the only negative international publicity at a moment when de Klerk is trying to convince western leaders that normalization is on the way. Privately the Cabinet must be cursing Bacher for having brought the cricketers here at this time but, for the moment at least, they are refusing to interfere.

We clamber back aboard our little bus, Tony Millard who is covering for the *Daily Telegraph*, chattering away; Richard Streeton deep in thought; Frank Partridge and Mark Baldwin of the Press Association jotting down notes as the vehicle jolts back on to the highway which takes us past Ladysmith and on into Pietermaritzburg.

The Capitol Towers Hotel is situated in the centre of town and, being a considerably older establishment, is bereft of the modern luxuries on offer at the Landrost. However it is the other things that are missing which concern us more. Like the English cricket team.

'Someone phoned last night to cancel their reservations,' the manager told us and promptly filled in a few more interesting titbits of information, such as the fact that the cancellation had come too late to save them from having to pay in full. So the SACU, or whoever their unnamed financial backers are, will have to cough up the 7,000 rand this accommodation would have cost (about £1,700), plus whatever they are now paying at the more luxurious accommodation they have found one hundred kilometres away on the beach near Durban.

So Graveney was only being half truthful. The quick getaway from Bloemfontein had also included a late change of hotel so as to give them at least twenty-four hours respite from the British newshounds. Clever stuff.

The South African Press had been tipped off, of course, so we are spared their presence in the bar tonight. But if we expected that to improve the atmosphere, we were being too optimistic. One of the South African journalists who had decided not to make the long haul to Durban proceeded to exceed his normal intake of alcohol and was soon berating John Etheridge for something he was supposed to have said to a black waiter at the Landrost. Etheridge defended himself quite plausibly but our South African friend, a big, bull-necked man, was not interested in listening to reason.

The booze, as it so often does, was turning a normally quiet individual bellicose. He was looking for a target and when Etheridge turned out to be rather a poor one, he quickly resumed his attack on Dumile Mateza, a black broadcaster whom he had evidently been baiting during dinner.

'One more word out of you and you'll hear from my lawyers in the morning,' were the first words Mateza uttered as he walked into the bar.

Frank Partridge and I exchanged apprehensive looks and wondered where all this was going to lead. The fact that the protagonist proceeded to attack Mateza along increasingly racial lines just minutes after accusing Etheridge of being rude to a black waiter did not worry him at all. Stirred or not, alcohol and logic do not make a compatible cocktail.

The argument became increasingly unpleasant and for a moment I thought it was going to turn into a brawl; the burly journalist started pushing Mateza down the bar with his shoulder in the nearest approximation of physical assault you can manage without actually laying a hand on someone.

'That's just what you'd like, isn't it?' sneered Mateza. 'You'd love me to hit you. But I'm not going to give you that satisfaction.'

The scene was becoming bizarre. Here was Mateza, demonstrating by his very presence the extent to which petty apartheid is now ignored in South Africa, being taunted and pushed around by a drunken, English-speaking South African who apparently liked to think of himself as a liberal. Every day something happens to remind me of those words of Alan Paton, 'We are a very odd nation.'

Possibly because Frank and I made some soothing noises and engaged Dumile in conversation, our drunken colleague eventually went off to sulk down at the other end of the bar. I had been interested, however, by one of Mateza's retorts when his adversary had been trying to lecture him on the origins of integrated cricket in South Africa.

'That's bullshit, man,' Mateza replied to something that had been said. 'Don't tell me about who integrated cricket in South Africa. Marshall Lee integrated cricket by going off and playing for a coloured team. That was proper integration. Not this rubbish of having white teams play black teams. What's integrated about that?'

As Marshall Lee and his wife Kate are two of my best friends, the sudden injection of his name into the argument obviously caught my ear. I knew all about Marshall's radical idea of persuading a former Springbok, Colin Wesley, to join him in offering their services to a coloured team back in the early seventies, but it was interesting to hear that his exploits were still remembered.

Soon after my second visit here in 1977, Marshall, who, like Kate, had been a columnist for the much-lamented Rand *Daily Mail*, decided South Africa was no longer a place in which they wanted to raise their three children and had emigrated to England where, for a time, Marshall presented sport on *Newsnight* for the BBC.

When I had mentioned Marshall's name in introducing myself to Ali Bacher, he, too, had recalled the moment when Lee and Wesley had dared to flout the accepted law of the land by batting and bowling side by side with non-white cricketers.

'You have to understand what a courageous move that was at the time,' Bacher told me. 'They left themselves open to charges of being communists and God knows what. My inclination was to do the same thing but, I'll tell you honestly, I didn't have the courage. I was just too shit scared.'

So at least this evening's unpleasant little scene in the bar had established that Marshall Lee's pioneering role in the development of multi-racial cricket in this country is secure. And so it should be. Not many people have the vision and guts to act on the quote that Senator Robert Kennedy was so fond of using during his presidential campaign in 1968, 'Some see things as they are and ask "Why?", others see things that never were and ask "Why not?"' But Marshall picked up his bat and asked 'Why not?' and, in doing so, defied the customs of a nation that had never wanted to answer any questions that could possibly promote progress or change. Had more people followed him, change would have come a lot sooner and Gatting's tour, under a different guise, might have been enjoying legitimate status.

Pietermaritzburg

3 February

At 11.30 a.m. in President de Klerk's new South Africa, the Jan Smuts Cricket Ground looked as peaceful as Tunbridge Wells on a sleepy summer's day. Apart from a hideous stand that is the sort of structure we can expect to see being erected in the name of progress at some English Football League ground, the rest of the scenery is all green with tents dotted around the grass perimeter and families beginning to assemble for picnic lunches under umbrellas. But the tranquillity did not last.

By midday reality had re-asserted itself as the vanguard of 5,000 demonstrators spilled out on to the hockey fields facing the front gates. They were an hour late, one of the organizers told me, because the buses had needed to make two runs into the townships to collect everyone who wanted to assemble in Churchill Square in the centre of town. From there they walked to the ground, six or seven abreast, a predominantly black contingent of Zulus, sprinkled with Indians, coloureds and even a few elderly white sympathizers.

Unlike the demonstrations in Kimberley and Bloemfontein which had needed the eleventh-hour interjection of Ali Bacher to make them legal – he had applied for sanctions on their behalf whether they liked it or not – this well-organized protest had seen to its own legality and was bigger and better marshalled than anything we had seen before. A loud speaker was set up right next to the wire fencing that circled the ground and a rallying cry could be heard clear across the pitch where the English XI were toiling under a hot sun against some obstinate South African Invitation XI batting.

'Mike Gatting, we are the masses of Pietermaritzburg and we have arrived,' said a rally leader. 'We do not want you in our country!'

Earlier I had talked to one of the anti-apartheid committee, an Indian called David, who like most of his colleagues was wearing a 'Gatting Out!' T-shirt. He gave me a quick insight into how politicized non-white sport in South Africa has become.

David had played cricket and other sports under the banner of SACOS, the radical organization that had made the first moves to prevent blacks and coloureds being sucked into the white system while apartheid generally was still in place.

'SACOS must move ahead now and look at the broader picture,' said David. 'If that means everyone being incorporated under the ANC, so be it. I am a teacher at a blind school and SACOS wouldn't affiliate our team because we did not compete against other SACOS approved schools. But how could we when there were no other blind athletes for our runners to compete against? That sort of thing is stupid.'

An ice-cream vendor walked by and one of the other organizers jokingly warned David not to buy one. By a weird coincidence the name of the ice-cream was Gatti.

'Nevertheless,' David continued, 'SACOS has made sacrifices that may not sound like much, such as refusing to send their children to private schools; refusing to allow just a few to have the privilege of using white sports grounds until everyone can; of not going to Sun City. You have to respect that especially as South Africa's white cricketers have never made any sacrifices. Proctor, Pollock and Barlow have all said they are against apartheid, but saying it is one thing and doing something about it is another. The only player who stuck his neck out and actually went and did something about it in the townships was Vince Van der Byl. The rest just talk.'

This was the view from the other end of the pitch; the one with the slope leading upwards; the one that is too often cordoned off by political action of one kind or another and left to rot in the sun while the white players stare down, tut-tutting sympathetically. It is easy for the white world to say, 'Come and join us, we'll help some of you now.' But there is a thing called pride and another called dignity which will not allow the dispossessed to be picked off in twos and threes to be offered special favours while the masses watch and wait. Almost as soon as sport began trying to break down the barriers so the ranks closed and the cry went up, 'All or nothing!' In preservation of that pride, it was the only card they had to play.

So although it was exasperating to have offers of assistance refused, one could only respect David's point of view and make allowances for his militancy. You cannot subjugate a people and expect them to remain amenable for ever.

Had the police presence not been so well organized, David's committee would have had little hesitation in stepping up their opposition to the tour.

'Bacher offered us 500 seats and we thought about accepting so that we could get inside the ground and invade the pitch,' he said. 'But the security is too tight. We don't want any injuries. They won't even let the white kids play on the field during the lunch interval.'

Before he went off to join his colleagues, David admitted that he, like most of the others, had been surprised by de Klerk's speech. 'He went further than any of us expected,' said David. 'Now he must press on and stop looking back over his shoulder to see what the conservatives are saying. He's a bold man.'

So, too, later in the day was Mike Gatting, bolder and braver, in fact, than was ever reported in the Press back home, partially, it must be said, because this was a Saturday and the Sunday papers, with their early-edition times, are not as geared to making space for late breaking stories as the dailies.

Not that Gatt was concerned about journalistic technicalities when he filed through the main gate at the tea interval, with Bacher leading the way and Emburey and Graveney bringing up the rear, to receive yet another petition. There was a waist-high brick wall right outside the turnstile which provided an obvious safety barrier for the players who were immediately faced with the somewhat disturbing sight of an unbroken mass of black faces as the crowd surged forward. The committee, mostly Indian but led by a black man in a red shirt with a megaphone, insisted that Gatting and his party come out from behind the wall. Bacher looked very reluctant but after a little persuasion Gatting moved forward a few paces out into the body of the crowd which included, of course, the inevitable posse of newsmen and camera crews. A three-minute conversation followed in which it became clear that the committee wanted Gatting to receive the petition on the podium they had erected by the fence all of 150 yards away.

'Come, come with us,' said the leader. 'Safe in, safe out. We guarantee it.'

I am sure he was sincere but in effect there could be no such guarantee. A crowd of demonstrators is a volatile entity that can be controlled up to a point, but not past the point where something unforeseen happens – a stumble that leads to a fall and ensuing panic; a wrong remark that ignites a torch of anger or simply a random rumour running wild. Nor was this particular crowd unacquainted with violence. They came from the townships around Pietermaritzburg where tribal killings were being numbered in the hundreds per month. Gatting knew this and so did Bacher and the look on Ali's face told all one needed to know about how safe he thought it would be for the English captain to walk out through a crowd of 5,000 people, all of whom were shouting his name, all of whom were hot, tired and angry.

'Gatting Go Home! Gatting Go Home!'

There were two police officers standing on either side of Gatting, but once he decided to run the gauntlet and move into the body of the crowd, there was no way they or their colleagues, who were standing off to the side, following the new orders on how to handle legal demonstrations, would have been able to intervene had he been set upon. It is impossible for someone to be plucked from a crowd that size in time to save their life. In a very real sense Gatting was putting his life on the line and he must have known it.

But he had said he would listen to anyone and receive any legitimate protest petition and he is not the sort of man who goes back on his word. If walking out into a crowd of 5,000 Zulus was not quite the way tea intervals are usually spent at Lords or Uxbridge then so be it. When in Natal . . .

And so we set off. Gatting and Bacher in front, Graveney and Emburey – his hand firmly clasped in that of an elderly black man – following behind. The path was cleared by an avenue of marshals, mostly young Indians who linked hands and kept the hordes at bay. They were our safety net and they were superb. Earlier they had surrounded a policeman who had foolishly got into an argument with some blacks and escorted him out. They could teach the police a thing or two about crowd control.

Seeing Gatting in their midst also had a salutary effect on the crowd. Many looked amazed at the sight of their target walking amongst them, so close, so vulnerable and so outwardly unafraid. I stopped and asked one of the young Indians what he thought of Gatting.

'He's a very brave man,' said the marshal. 'But I still think the tour should be stopped.'

Gatt was helped up onto the podium and stood there looking glum while speeches were made and petitions handed over. It lasted about four minutes and then it was another 150 yards back to the main gate. One hundred and fifty yards can be a long way in those circumstances. And it seemed longer when some people behind the marshals started lobbing stones in the direction of the cricketers. A few Coke cans followed and Michael Cockerell, who was with his camera crew behind Gatting, said he saw one bounce off the skipper's shoulder. I was in front on the return journey, elbowing my way backwards through the throng, but I never saw Gatt change expression. Nor did he break stride when he finally made it back inside the ground. Marching straight into the dressing-room, he picked up his hat and called out, 'Come on, lads, time to go.'

And then he bowled the second over after tea.

For an old-fashioned example of British stiff upper lip, it wasn't bad. Bacher, who was a bag of nerves by the time it was all over, made no bones about how he felt.

'I am very emotional right now,' he admitted. 'That was one of the most courageous acts I have ever seen by a sportsman off the field of play. You guys have vilified Mike for making a couple of silly remarks about the situation here after being in the country a few days. White South Africans say stupid things every week after living here all their lives.'

There was no denying that. Much cleverer people than Mike Gatting have put their foot in it on the question of apartheid but, if his critics could be persuaded to admit it, he had learnt that deeds were often better than words in situations like the one he had just faced and he had emerged with honour.

On the way back to the press-tent, I ran into a hot and sticky Graham Morris, weighed down by his cameras but as ready as ever with the quick quip.

'Question: What did you do in the war, Daddy? Answer: I went on tour with the English cricket team.'

It was almost a surprise to see some cricket being played out in the middle after all that and, after doing a quick piece over the phone for Paddy Feeney's BBC World Service sports programme back at Bush House, I started filing a front-page story for the Dublin *Sunday Tribune*. The press-tent was a makeshift affair with spectators sitting a couple of yards in front of us, obviously able to hear every word.

Not for the first time that day, I heard some caustic comments being passed and then a man with a northern British accent turned round and said, 'Demonstrations? You wouldn't know a demonstration if you saw one. Why don't you write about the cricket?'

It wasn't a particularly intelligent remark to make to a group of reporters who had recently been in the middle of some tense demonstrations, but it was typical of an expatriate who had made his bed and was determined to call it comfortable even if he did suffer the odd nightmare. Later, when he had calmed down a bit, the man tried to persuade Frank Partridge to drive up to his factory where, he insisted, he could produce a hundred coloured workers who were all in favour of the tour. As his factory turned out to be two hours' drive away, Frank declined. There was no shortage of people wanting to paint their own vision of South Africa and foist it on a visitor as the real thing. Don't listen to those nasty blacks outside, come and see my tame ones. Watch the cricket, man! Even Gatting wasn't that myopic.

Later Christopher Morris of Sky Television passed on to me a copy of the petition Gatting had been handed. It was a well-written and detailed document that deserved more than a cursory glance.

The petition was primarily aimed at showing the inadequacy of sporting facilities for non-whites in the Pietermaritzburg area. It read, in part:

'The purpose of this study is to disprove claims that government "reforms" over the last fifteen years have brought South Africa to the position where sport can be considered "normal" or "non-racial" . . . suffice to say that such pillars of apartheid as the Group Areas Act and the Population Registration Act are still on the statute books. Thus there exist laws in South Africa which determine, on the basis of race alone where a person may live; where a person may play sport (the President of the anti-apartheid South African Council on Sport was recently arrested for being in a black area without a permit) and the type of education and medical facilities that a person has.'

The study then listed the sporting facilities available to the various races as laid out below:

	Whites	Indians and 'Coloureds'	Africans
Population Served	53,000	63,000	260,000
Bowling Greens	17	1	0
Hockey Fields	11	1	0
Rugby Fields	8	1	0
Soccer Fields	9	11	8
Squash Courts	18	8	0
Swimming Pools	3	3	0
Tennis Courts	44	8	6

A similar chart detailing facilities available to schools in the area showed that, while blacks had more soccer fields than white schools – 14 to 5 – no black schools had a swimming-pool; a hockey field; a rugby field; a gymnasium or either squash or badminton courts. White schools had sixty-nine tennis courts compared to the total of two each available to blacks and Indians.

The cricket facilities were dealt with separately and the comparison was even more stark. According to the study,

'The White schools surveyed (containing 11,567 pupils) have thirty-two cricket fields of which twenty-two have turf wickets. The Indian and Coloured schools (13,608 pupils) have one cricket field and this has an inferior matting wicket . . . As a result of this lack of cricket facilities, these schoolchildren have to share the adult facilities of the Maritzburg District Cricket Union.'

No-one I spoke to suggested that these figures were incorrect. They stood as a damning indictment of the discrimination that still exists in South African society no matter how much progress has been made in recent years. Sport, remember, has made greater strides than most other sections of the community, but with imbalances as great as these, who would dare say that the demonstrators did not have a right to use the cricket tour as a means of airing their legitimate anger? But at least the presence of Gatting and his team had given the under-privileged majority an opportunity to make its voice heard and place these shameful facts and figures before an international audience.

It is no use having a message if you cannot get it across. A demonstration through the streets of Pietermaritzburg on a Saturday afternoon to complain about lack of sporting facilities would have attracted a little local attention and, if they were lucky, a passing mention in the world's Press. The English crick-eters would claim no credit for the vast amount of international publicity the anti-apartheid demonstration received, nor should they. Their reasons for being here were hardly altruistic. But the fact remains that if Gatting's team had not been here, neither would we. And it was the media whose attention David and his friends wanted to attract, not Gatting.

4 February

At breakfast this morning there were more black families in the dining-room than white – the clearest indication I have seen yet of the extent to which social segregation is a thing of the past. Just getting Arthur Ashe through the portals of the Elizabeth Hotel in Durban without a porter's cap on his head had been a miracle in 1973 and petty apartheid lasted long after that. But no longer.

The local *Sunday Times* was also an encouraging sight, not merely for a huge colour picture of 'leggy Jane Riley' who has apparently taken over as hostess for some TV quiz show but, rather more seriously, for the front-page 'Opinion' column, written by the editor. Extracts are worth quoting.

'. . . This week, in an act of Gorbachevian boldness, President de Klerk put an end to the evasion. With courage and statesmanship, he declared that if the status quo was untenable, the future need *not* be apocalyptic. Since victory (whatever that means) is impossible for any party, compromise is inescapable for all parties.

'Citizens also bear a heavy responsibility in the days ahead. People who share the same country but so little else, will have to find each other; yes, even learn to love each other.

'The world will be watching us as we edge apprehensively towards reconciliation. That same world should also examine its own conscience and its approach to our hideous dilemma. If sanctions ever served a useful purpose (which we doubt) they should be reconsidered. Statesmen who display courage deserve encouragement not suspicion . . .

'As Churchill said at another time, also at a moment when the forces of light had scored a modest triumph: This is not the end. It is not even the beginning of the end. But it is, perhaps, the end of the beginning.'

It will take Churchillian deeds to lead the South African ship of state, with all its precious cargo, through the squalls and tempests that lie ahead, but at least the editorial gave a balanced viewpoint and did not pretend it would be easy. God knows, it is going to be anything but that.

By the time I got to the ground I had been given another lesson in how dangerous it is to make assumptions in this country. If you didn't stop to think it through, it would seem reasonable to assume that right wingers here would be predominantly, if not exclusively, white. But let my Indian taxi driver offer a clue to another kind of thought process.

'No demos yet,' he said glancing towards the main cross-section where they had gathered yesterday. 'Got to get the beer in them. Then they start to think all wrong and act stupid. They shouldn't attack sport anyway. Sport is good for people. And anyway, anyone who breaks the law should be shot. Just break off the strain, man.'

Had I come across the one Indian in South Africa who veered more towards Genghis Khan than Gandhi? Not a bit of it. There are plenty of right-wing Indians who are terrified of the day when the blacks will gain the upper hand because, quite apart from the fact that the blacks don't like them, it will push them down from No. 2 on the social totem-pole to No. 3 or worse. But at least that was an attitude one could understand. Yesterday, after the drama at the tea interval, I had wandered over that section of the ground which backed on to the demonstrators' platform. A young woman had just started singing and, as I turned to listen, I noticed a big, blond guy in his twenties standing next to me.

'She'll be the first one to get raped if anything happens here,' he sneered.

I almost asked by whom but thought better of it. The tone of contempt in his voice had been so strong that I knew I would get into a terrible argument if I opened my mouth. So I walked away. Now, thinking back on that and my conversation with the taxi-driver this morning, I remember the editor's line about learning to love each other. In this climate, there's an awful long way to go before we can start talking about love. How about beginning with respect?

Despite a little humidity, it is a gloriously sunny day and as there is some cricket being played, maybe it might be soothing to sit on the grass and watch it. Gatting's answer to yesterday's traumas could not have been more typical. A belligerent 50 before lunch as the English XI set about replying to the South African total of 305–2 declared which included an undefeated 150 from a compact and well-organized opener called Mark Rushmere. Kent's Roy Pienaar had weighed in with a stylish 63 and the English batsmen had needed a positive knock from their captain to stay in the match.

But Gatt got bogged down after lunch, possibly mesmerized by the sight of Robinson in a torpor at the other end. Later the Nottinghamshire captain contributed eight in an hour, but Gatt had departed by then and I caught up with him just before he scaled the television scaffolding so that he could get a bird's eye view of what the track was doing, which wasn't much.

I knew he had prepared himself for just about anything on this tour, but had he, I wondered, ever envisaged himself being surrounded by 5,000 reasonably hostile Zulus?

'Not really,' he smiled. 'I hadn't quite seen that one coming. But if they had been Buthelezi's Zulus it wouldn't have been so bad. I understand they are pretty moderate and are not so opposed to the tour. Anyway, it was an interesting experience.'

So much for Gatting not knowing anything about apartheid. This titbit of information hardly qualified him to write a thesis on the subject, but at least he was doing some reading, learning some names and beginning to make sense of some of the complexities which only multiply in close up.

The rest of the afternoon was made enjoyable by the sight of Omar Henry, Basil d'Oliviera's successor as the best coloured cricketer in South Africa, tossing up his left-arm spinners, tempting the batsmen with the kind of attacking slow bowling that one-day cricket has done so much to kill. How easy it is to get lost in those delicious technical complexities of which cricket is so full and forget those other problems, of which C.L.R. James would have been so aware, beyond the boundary.

By the time I accepted a ride to Durban Airport with Christopher Morris of Sky Television, all manner of records were in the process of being broken at Jan Smuts Stadium, most of them by Mark Rushmere. Not content with 150 not out in the first innings, the Eastern Province opener hammered an English attack consisting of Foster, Thomas, Graveney, Ellison and Barnett for 151 not out in the second. Having scored 41 on Sunday, Rushmere proceeded to add another 110 before lunch today, most of them scored in a stand of 150 with Roy Pienaar who also threatened to smash a ton before the interval until he was caught by Robinson off Ellison for 81.

Unlike Pienaar, Rushmere is not a classic, free-flowing stroke maker, but he is merciless with a bad ball and has that happy knack of knowing how to keep a scoreboard ticking. Apart from creating some sort of a record in first-class cricket in South Africa by being on the field every minute of the three days' play, he also joined an élite group of batsmen who have scored a century in each innings for South African teams – 'Pom Pom' Fellows-Smith in 1959/60; Johnny Waite in the same domestic season and Brian Whitfield in 1979/80. None of them, however, managed 150 in each innings.

Even allowing for the fact that Gatting's attack has been somewhat less than frightening here, the concentration required to accumulate 301 runs without being out suggests that this composed twenty-five year old, who spent the 1983 season with Sussex, has a temperament made for Test cricket. Yet his name is not among those selected for the first 'Test' at the Wanderers later this week. The selectors, already embroiled in controversy over the exclusion of Clive Rice, who was expected to have continued in his role as captain, have opted for the thirty-seven-year-old Henry Fotheringham as opening partner for the new captain, Jimmy Cook. Rushmere, however, will be hard to overlook in the future.

The Rice affair seems to have blown up over some remarks the former Nottinghamshire all-rounder made on behalf of the Players Association concerning Kepler Wessels' eligibility to play for South Africa. Wessels, it will be remembered, left South

Africa to spend several seasons with Queensland, during which time he qualified through residence to play for Australia, for whom he opened in numerous Tests. In recent years he has returned to his native land and now wants to play for South Africa again, an idea that does not appeal to many of his colleagues who have battled on in isolation. Although Rice has stressed that he was only dutifully reporting other people's opinions in his role as player representative, he seems to have suffered the fate of so many bearers of bad tidings. However the local papers are full of dark hints that Rice's rebellious nature and fondness for driving in motor rallies instead of playing cricket also had much to do with his dismissal. At least this is one nice, juicy controversy that has nothing to do with the colour of a person's skin. In South Africa one is thankful for small mercies.

Rain was merciful towards the English XI today when the target the South African Invitation XI had set them – 329 in 220 minutes plus twenty overs – had proved beyond their capabilities despite useful contributions from Tim Robinson (41) and Alan Wells (48). With forty minutes play remaining, the visitors were 198–5.

Johannesburg

6 February

Mike Gatting found himself pushed out of the headlines this morning and replaced by someone whose by-line usually appears underneath them – Paul Weaver, sports columnist for the *Today* newspaper. Along with an IRN radio reporter who was trying to cover the tour without a working visa, Weaver was confronted by two large policemen when he opened his bedroom door at the Sandton Holiday Inn at 10.00 a.m. and handed a piece of paper which told him to be out of South Africa by midnight.

Weaver had been told that the heavy brigade were looking for him when he arrived after a long drive from Pietermaritzburg late last night. But resident correspondents, who are accustomed to the way the police work here, felt that he was in for nothing worse than a warning over the sensational and highly critical tone of an article he had written about the bloody battle between police and demonstrators at the airport when the team arrived three weeks ago.

'I found it hard to believe that the Government had taken so long to react to a piece written such a long time before,' said Weaver, who found himself giving a full-scale press conference by the pool before heading for the airport. Weaver was shown on South African television that night but everything he said was voiced over by SABC's own reporter.

So, just a matter of days after President de Klerk's conciliatory and optimistic speech, the right of the individual to express himself in public was still being suppressed and the freedom of the Press was still subject to the whims of State censorship. No matter how virulently anti-South African Weaver's piece had been; no matter that he should have stated more clearly that he had not actually witnessed the horrific beatings he had described so graphically, the fact remained that the expulsion of a foreign reporter ruined much of the image that President de Klerk was trying to create.

Yet, as Weaver discovered when he got to the airport, this was not a low-level decision. The plane he wanted to take to Harare was full and British Airways offered to put him up at a nearby hotel for twenty-four hours until seats became available. From past experience, airline officials felt that this would be acceptable as he would be, in effect, on stand-by for deportation. But on phoning the minister who had signed the expulsion order, they were told that Weaver was to be put on the first plane out, irrespective of its destination. This hard-line attitude suggested that government policy was still rife with contradictions.

So Weaver was put on a flight to London, ten hours flying time past his preferred destination. Strangely, he left behind several colleagues, such as John Jackson of the *Daily Mirror*, who had been just as critical of the tour, the police and South Africa itself as well as others like Frank Partridge of BBC Radio who had been forced to extract apologies from SABC after totally erroneous allegations had been aired about his having incited demonstrators in Bloemfontein by carrying anti-tour placards in his car on the way to the townships. And this was supposed to be a cricket tour? I have covered political rallies in places like Birmingham, Alabama in the days of the racist governor, George Wallace, that were less confrontational and antagonistic than this.

7 February

When Gordon and Frances Forbes moved a few years ago, they were clever enough to buy a new home in a town house complex

300 yards from the Wanderers, one of the world's most impressive sporting clubs that not only boasts the famous Test ground
but, on the other side of the main road, two other lovely cricket
fields, several tennis and squash courts, the imposing red-brick
clubhouse and, in an adjoining building, the headquarters of the
South African Cricket Union. So for the next few days I can walk
to work.

Mike Gatting was leading his team for a run round the practice
field this morning, an exercise that soon left Graham Dilley and
Neil Foster lagging far to the rear. In his best sergeant-major
style, Gatt had words with his two fast bowlers about this. He
would have been a terror on a parade ground.

Generally, however, the spirit in the team seems to be good.
Bruce French, mountain climber and fitness fanatic, takes charge
of the fielding practice, throwing balls wide to each player in turn
so that he can swoop on to it and hurl in a return to French
standing behind imaginary stumps. The athletic Yorkshireman,
Paul Jarvis, receives applause from his team-mates for his efforts
while a misfield from Greg Thomas elicits ribald laughter and a
stern command from French to try again. 'And watch the ball this
time, boy-o!' The Welshman obliges.

When the team for tomorrow's Test is announced there are no
surprises. Dilley is palpably unfit; Graveney will not be required
to assist Emburey in the spin department and neither Chris
Cowdrey nor Matthew Maynard have been able to seize their
strictly limited opportunities to produce any kind of form. At the
end of practice, Gatting goes over to Cowdrey for a consoling
chat. It's tough enough being on this tour as it is without being
left out of the action.

The demonstrators will be back tomorrow, drawn this time
from the nearby Alexandria township. The local council has
decreed that, legal or not, they will be barred from congregating
en masse outside the gates of the Wanderers due to lack of space
and the disruption it would cause to traffic. It is a convenient
excuse but valid to some degree. Even a thousand people would
bring everything to a standstill in this heavily populated area.

SOUTH AFRICAN XI v ENGLISH XI
Played at Wanderers, Johannesburg, on February 8,9,10, 1990.
South African XI won by 7 wickets. Toss: South African XI.

ENGLISH XI

B.C. Broad	c Jennings b McMillan	48	c Jennings b Donald		0
C.W.J. Athey	b Donald	3	lbw b McMillan		16
R.T. Robinson	c Snell b McMillan	31	c Jennings b McMillan		17
M.W. Gatting*	c McMillan b Snell	22	b Kuiper		0
A.P. Wells	b Snell	4	c Wessels b Donald		11
K.J. Barnett	c Fotheringham b Donald	0	c Donald b Snell		24
B.N. French†	c Jennings b Donald	1	c Jennings b Donald		0
J.E. Emburey	c Jennings b Snell	1	c Jennings b Snell		2
R.M. Ellison	b Donald	6	c Cook b Rundle		12
N.A. Foster	c Rundle b Snell	11	c Jennings b Donald		21
P.W. Jarvis	not out	1	not out		0
Extras	(b 4, lb 17, nb 7)	28	(b 4, lb 11, nb 2, w 2)		19
TOTAL		156			122

SOUTH AFRICAN XI

S.J. Cook*	c Robinson b Ellison	20	c & b Gatting		15
H.R. Fotheringham	lbw b Jarvis	8	lbw b Ellison		38
K.C. Wessels	st French b Emburey	1	lbw b Gatting		2
P.N. Kirsten	c French b Jarvis	4	not out		17
R.F. Pienaar	c French b Ellison	13	not out		1
A.P. Kuiper	b Foster	84			
B.M. McMillan	b Ellison	0			
R.V. Jennings†	c Emburey b Ellison	23			
D.B. Rundle	c French b Foster	23			
R.P. Snell	c French b Jarvis	7			
A.A. Donald	not out	7			
Extras	(lb 7, nb 1, w 5)	13	(w 3)		3
TOTAL		203	(3 wkts)		76

BOWLING

S. AFRICAN XI	O	M	R	W	O	M	R	W
Donald	21	10	30	4	18	5	29	4
Snell	22.5	11	38	4	15	5	28	2
McMillan	15	2	41	2	11	6	18	2
Kuiper	6	1	21	0	14	4	23	1
Rundle	1	0	5	0	5	2	9	1
ENGLISH XI								
Jarvis	22.5	7	71	3	6	2	25	0
Foster	21	6	54	2	4	0	20	0
Ellison	15	6	41	4	7	1	13	1
Emburey	14	5	30	1				
Gatting					6	1	17	2
Athey					1.1	1	1	0

FALL OF WICKETS

	E	SA	E	SA
	1st	1st	2nd	2nd
1st	15	33	2	56
2nd	96	28	33	56
3rd	106	40	34	71
4th	118	40	42	—
5th	119	77	69	—
6th	123	77	73	—
7th	132	148	78	—
8th	138	180	85	—
9th	152	189	122	—
10th	156	203	122	—

Umpires: C. Liebenberg and J.W. Peacock.

A 'Test' match

8 February

The first ball Allan Donald bowled to Bill Athey pitched on middle stump and had wicket keeper Ray Jennings leaping, Shilton-style, high to his left to pluck it out of the air. It was that sort of wicket and, like the day, it didn't get any better. Heavy clouds brought rain; a new organization called Freedom in Sport brought a bunch of blacks who sat obediently watching the cricket but plainly understood little and colleagues returning from scouting expeditions brought bad news from the townships. Teargas had been used, truncheons raised and a CBS TV camera crew briefly arrested. Police had used force against a group of National Sports Congress supporters who were demonstrating outside the British Consulate in Commissioner Street. I wonder if Goochy and the boys are having a nice time in St Lucia?

With the famous Wanderers, always packed for Test matches in the days of Nourse, McGlew, Goddard and even Pollock, less than a quarter full, chill winds hastening three interruptions for rain and a couple of late wickets falling after Broad and Robinson had added 81, Gatting must have really wondered by the time stumps were drawn at 5 p.m. if this whole exercise was worth it. Sunshine would, of course, have put a brighter complexion on things, but the weather gods do not seem to like this tour, either.

From the moment Gatting hooked Richard Snell's rising delivery down Brian McMillan's throat at square leg to depart for 22, the odds were heavily on this being a bitch of a day for the English XI and so it proved. A total of 156 all-out was meagre even on this track and Jimmy Cook showed what he thought about it all by thrashing Paul Jarvis for three fours in his first over. Jarvis improved after that which was more than could be said for Neil Foster whose left arm – the balancing factor in his last delivery stride – is falling away so drastically that he is starting to bowl like a combination of Devon Malcolm and Syd Lawrence on one of their less-accurate days, but not as fast as either.

Nevertheless, it must be said Foster was unlucky in the fourth over when Henry Fotheringham – 'Fothers' to one and all – played a defensive prod and watched aghast as the ball rolled on to his stumps. But the bail did not budge. Lucky? Of course. But all sportsmen will tell you luck evens itself out. Let's try another dangerous assumption – lightning never strikes twice. Offer that one to Jarvis after he had produced a lovely in-cutter to remove Fothers lbw. With old stick-in-the-mud himself, Kepler Wessels, prodding forward in his crab-like sort of way, damn me if the ball didn't roll on to his off-stump, too, and, once again, fail to topple the bail. No one in the press-box could remember that happening twice in a day's play and one began wondering if an errant groundsman hadn't used that convenient little indentation on the top of the stump as a receptacle for his chewing gum. Sticky wickets were one thing. But sticky bails?

At lunchtime, I sought out Peter Celliers, an Afrikaans businessman who has started up the Freedom in Sport movement, seemingly off his own bat. He insists that his fledgling organization which he and his wife run from home, is strictly non-political and that he had never heard of a certain John Carlisle MP – who happens to run something very similar with very right-wing connotations in England – until a few days ago.

'The similarity in name is a complete coincidence,' says Celliers who tells me that he has been an aerobatic pilot and has had problems competing in glider championships in West Germany because of his nationality.

'I made a big fuss about that, I tell you, man. I want to stand up and protect the feeling I have as a South African to compete internationally in sport. I want to protect the right of the individual on a totally non-racial, non-violent basis.'

Celliers said most of the money that pays for the biplane which circles above our head with a 'Freedom in Sport Welcomes Gatting' flyer trailing in the sky comes from his own pocket or sympathetic commercial sponsors but he admitted paying for the black spectators who turned up yesterday.

'Yes, I paid for their tickets. You know why? I wanted them to see how we whites enjoy an afternoon playing our kind of sport. I wanted them to see that it wasn't threatening to them and that maybe they could learn to enjoy it, too. What's wrong with me buying blacks tickets? What's the difference between that and some school bringing all their white kids here in their uniforms for an afternoon at the cricket, like you saw today? The kids didn't pay for their tickets, somebody else did.

He had a point there, did Mr Celliers. He was a bit zealous about it all as converts tend to be when they suddenly wake up one morning and discover what is right and what is wrong. But, even if his tactics were a little over the top, at least he was erring on the correct side of the line that still divides this country.

The division was rather unpleasantly apparent when I walked over to the front gate a little later and found myself standing on the inside looking out, over the shoulders of a line of police, at a small group of demonstrators who had been given their fifteen minutes of demo-time in which to prove that South Africa was now tolerating free speech.

All that would have been fine had I not found myself mixed in with a small group of about twenty young whites who immediately started hurling racist abuse at the demonstrators. 'You're just a bunch of gorillas, man!' yelled an over-weight swarthy individual who closely resembled an ape. 'You want to come in? Hey, let them in so we can show them who's boss around here!'

This prompted more shouts of, 'Yea, let 'em in! We'll give 'em a demo they won't forget!'

It's very easy to play the big man when you are secure behind bolted iron bars and a row of armed police and I suppose on a revulsion factor this lot rated no higher than the brainless louts you can find at many English football grounds on a Saturday afternoon. Around about a nine, I would say. But, after the demonstrators had been led away and the gates opened, I noticed a revealing little incident that indicated very clearly where the sympathies of the police lie. A tall young policeman who had been standing immediately in front of us, trotted over to the ringleader of the anti-demo mob, patted him on the back and said, 'Well done, that was great, man.'

F.W. de Klerk is going to have to watch his police force. The rank and file still like nothing better than to go black bashing and if a few get killed here and there, tough shit. God, they are unpleasant people.

But the unpleasantness wasn't over yet. News was coming in from London of scenes on television being shown there – but not, of course, here – of men, women and children being beaten with batons after leaving a church in downtown Johannesburg. Apparently a happy crowd of worshippers had been told to disperse when they congregated in the square outside the church and had failed to do so with the immediacy that the police felt was appropriate. So they had waded in.

Having just heard the news I mentioned it to Greg Thomas and the team's 'minder', a sallow-skinned, black-haired man whose chest and bicep measurements spoke of long hours in the gym. Greg introduced me as someone who was covering the tour for the *Melbourne Sunday Age* which was, indeed, one of the papers I was writing for and that gave him the opening he needed when I started complaining about police behaviour.

'And what about the aboriginals, man? You think Australia treats them properly?'

I got three minutes on how badly treated the aboriginals were as if that, in some perverse way, justified the way South Africa deprived the black majority of its rights. It is always the first line of defence you get here. 'We're not the only country that practises racism.' Quite true. But it happens to be the only country where racism is *law*.

At any rate, the team's minder who, of course, turned out to be a senior police officer seconded to Gatting for the tour, got very hot under his collar when I objected to police beating up women and children. 'They were breaking the law. If you break the law, you deserve what you get.'

After he stormed off, I regretted getting into it. You can't argue with a mind like that.

'Oh, he's a good bloke, really,' said Thomas. 'He's got a job to do and he looks after us well.'

I like Greg. He's one of those members of the team who takes the trouble to think about what is going on down here and, after eight or more winters spent playing for Border and Eastern Province and coaching in the townships, he knows a fair bit about it. But I think we differ on the definition of a 'good bloke'. In my book, anyone who condones institutionalized violence against defenceless people fails to make the grade.

Wearily, I take the short cut Gordon has shown me, through the hole in the wire fence and down the path by the side of the Wanderers that leads to his little complex of town houses which nestles next to a bird sanctuary. The Forbes household is a sanctuary after a day like this; a little haven of warmth, love and humour where one can try to forget the way people make such a big deal about their differences and hate each other for them.

I have turfed Jamie Forbes, who is seven, out of his room, but he doesn't seem to mind sleeping downstairs. He only minds when we all go out to dinner and leave him alone. He thinks that's a bit unfair even though he has Phina to look after him. Phina is a tall, quiet, dignified woman who has worked for Gordon for twenty years and, like so many black domestic servants in the northern suburbs, is considered one of the family.

Even though her flat is actually in the house itself, she sits in the living-room after Jamie has gone to bed if everyone is out to dinner and Frances gets a terrible conscience about staying out after midnight. Sometimes she will find Phina nodding off, but still sitting bolt upright in the armchair when we return. She would never leave her post.

10 February

A five-day 'Test' match has ended in three days with a seven-wicket win for South Africa. On a pitch like this, no one is particularly surprised. It is embarrassing, nonetheless, and Ali Bacher was furious about the way the wicket had been prepared when I spoke to him at lunch. Adrian Kuiper, with a magnificent 84 in South Africa's first innings, was the only batsman on either side to pass 50 and Gatting, while conceding that his team had been well beaten, said that Headingley was the only other place where he had come across a comparably difficult wicket prepared for a five-day game.

The bare bones of it were that the English XI, 67 behind on first innings, were shot out for 122 in their second, with Kuiper, indisputably the man of the match, ripping out Gatting's off-stump for nought with a sharp delivery that cut back off the seam.

Only a brave 37-run stand for the eighth wicket between Richard Ellison, the visitors' best bowler incidentally, and Neil Foster prevented complete humiliation. Foster ended up the second highest scorer behind Kim Barnett with 21.

After Cook and Fothers had sprinted away to 56 in no time before Gatting caught and bowled his opposing captain, there was never any danger of South Africa struggling to get the 76 they needed for victory even on this track and it was all over with time to spare on the third evening.

In his new role as columnist on the *Sunday Star,* Clive Rice commented, 'I felt sorry for the batsmen out there. Many of them were made to look like fools, but with the ball seaming around all over the place it was hardly of their own making.'

Gatting had prepared himself for the fact that his team were still a couple of matches short of the practice they needed before tackling such talented opposition, but even so he had been shocked at the form of one or two of his key players.

'I've never seen Neil Foster bowl like that,' he admitted. 'Having seen the pitch and knowing how he can bowl under those conditions, I would have put money on his getting ten wickets in the match.'

In fact, Foster's aggregate average was 2–74 off twenty-five overs which would hardly have pleased him on a good batting strip, let alone this minefield.

For different reasons, Ali Bacher was equally displeased.

'I've had words with the groundsman,' he said after ordering a coffee for me in the members' dining-room where familiar faces like Jackie McGlew, Mike Proctor and Vince Van der Byl were dotted around the tables. 'I know our boys wanted a wicket with a bit of life in it, but that was ridiculous. That strip was barely fit for a three-day game. Never, in all the times I've played on this ground, have I seen a Wanderer's wicket behave like that.'

Casting aside, for a moment, the rights and wrongs of the political aspect of the tour, one could not help feeling sorry for the many admirable people involved with South African cricket of whom Bacher is probably the most impressive. For well-documented reasons, they have seen precious little cricket of international standard for the past two decades and now, when the chance comes, the whole thing is turned into a lottery by a poorly prepared pitch. And, in addition, there is the problem of lost revenue for a tour that is already costing a fortune now that two days' gate money has been wasted. Peter Hain would tell you that it is no more than they deserve and if they had listened to his warnings, they could have saved themselves the trouble. True enough but it is equally true that Bacher, Van der Byl and men like them are not actually responsible for apartheid and have done more than most to try to overcome it.

Bacher, in particular, finds himself in an agonizing position. I asked him if he regretted organizing the tour now that his township cricket programme which he has done so much to nurture, has been so badly affected.

'Obviously that's a terrible blow which I did not foresee,' he replied. 'But I still feel that the kids still have to have heroes to look up to and to do that one has to keep in touch with the international game.'

After the waitress had brought the coffee, he leaned forward and continued, 'Listen, the ANC are telling me, "Come and join us now and you can have international cricket tomorrow." But I am resisting that even though it would mean we could have South Africa playing at Lords next summer if a date could be found. I can't have South Africa play abroad under the ANC banner, stamped and approved by a political party. Sport cannot become that closely linked with politics. It has to retain some kind of independence, if only for its own dignity. But, as you know, my thinking is not that far from the ANC's and there may be other ways to bring it about sooner than some people think.'

Despite the misjudgements that have been made about this tour, it would be wrong to underestimate Ali Bacher. Unlike the armchair critics, he is a mover and shaker, a man who puts himself in the firing line and expects to get hit by the short-pitched stuff occasionally. But that will not deter him. If South African cricket has any immediate future, it must surely rest in his hands.

11 February

Nelson Mandela is free. More than an hour after the scheduled release, this tall, handsome man emerged from Victor Verster Prison on the outskirts of Cape Town with Winnie at his side, offering the black power salute and a warm smile to the hundreds of supporters who had been standing in the burning sun all afternoon. Television viewers around the world saw more than we did, sitting in Johannesburg, because the SABC coverage was appalling, quite the worst prepared and poorly presented outside broadcast of a major event I have ever seen, anywhere.

Later, when the main evening news came on, SABC did not trust themselves – or, rather, Mandela – to take his speech live and excused themselves by saying that there were 'technical problems' due to bad light, and that excerpts from the speech would be shown at the end of the programme.

The light was certainly fading fast as the world's most celebrated prisoner addressed a crowd of over 80,000 people crammed into Cape Town's Grand Parade less than four hours after his release from twenty-seven years incarceration. But Mandela's seventy-one-year-old eyes dealt rather better with the prepared text of his speech than SABC's cameras. Psychologists will tell you that people who have been shut away for a long time have difficulty adjusting to large groups of, say, a dozen or more people and that they need time to acclimatize. Yet here was Mandela, his voice ringing out to a multitude of 80,000, strong and clear and unwavering.

'First let me say, I do not come to you as a prophet.'

It needed to be said. Newspapers in London were already

talking in terms of a 'second coming' and there was no doubt at all that the incredible media attention his release had attracted, had elevated Nelson Mandela to the hopeless position of a new Messiah who would be expected to perform miracles at every turn. Just seeing him there, a free man, unbowed and seemingly in control of the media circus, the like of which he had never known, appeared to be enough of a miracle on its own.

How different it all might have been had 'Plan One' of how to deal with the Mandela problem not been aborted more than two years before. Over dinner a couple of nights previously I had heard a remarkable story which I have no reason to doubt. It was told by a person who has no particular axe to grind nor propaganda to push. The person in question has a long record of knowledge-able contact with senior members of the National Party and no record of planting duff information. This then is the story:

In the South African winter of 1987, virtually the entire cabinet, including the then president, P.W. Botha, were sitting round a camp-fire in the veldt after enjoying a day's hunting. It was a Saturday night. Halfway through the meal, another senior Cabinet Minister arrived, brandishing a sheet of paper which he handed triumphantly to the president.

'We've got it,' he said. 'All the judges have now signed. It's legal. We can let him go.'

The document was a presidential order to the effect that the political prisoner, Nelson Mandela, should be released forthwith. The additional signatures were those of the High Court judiciary whose approval was needed to make it law.

'Great!' someone exclaimed out of the darkness. 'Now we can push the little kaffir out on to the station at Robben Island with his suitcase and send him on his way before anyone realizes what's happening.'

The guttural guffaws of Afrikaans laughter erupted round the fire. That was the way to handle the situation. Do it quick, before anyone could make a fuss.

'Right,' said President Botha. 'It will be nine o'clock Monday morning, then.'

And so it would have been had not a deputation of the most senior officers in the Army and police arrived to see the president as dawn broke on that Monday morning. In very menacing terms, they told Botha that if Mandela was released they would resist the move with force. It was not necessary to spell out what they were talking about. Botha knew he was facing the threat of a military coup.

So Mandela stayed in jail and, from what I understand, the intervening years were spent offering several senior military officers early retirements with fat pensions and nice farms in the Cape.

'And those that have risen to the top since, think very differently now,' my dinner partner added. 'By Afrikaner standards, there really is quite a lot of enlightened thinking in the Army now.'

It would, of course, have been so much better from the National Party's point of view to have avoided the long build up of anticipation and the inevitable fanfare that greeted Mandela's eventual release. But all that is past history now. No one could have believed, even six months ago, that Mandela would have been released into a country with the kind of president that F.W. de Klerk is turning out to be. If Mandela can establish himself as the real leader of the ANC, which is far from evident just at the moment, then there must be a real chance that some genuine progress can be made when he and de Klerk talk face to face. Like a growing number of people in this country, they both want a new and better South Africa.

12 February

Mandela handled his first press conference brilliantly today. Gordon shuddered when he mentioned nationalization which not surprisingly is an anathema to the South African business community, but generally the man is incredibly impressive. The world's leading interrogators, real pros like David Dimbleby, Ted Koppel, Tom Brokaw and Dan Rather, were peppering him with questions, but he hardly stumbled and actually answered each question on its merits instead of fudging around the issue as so many politicians do in Britain and America now that they have been professionally prepped on how to get in their two cents' worth. Mandela is close to achieving the impossible. He is almost living up to his advance publicity.

Meanwhile Gatting's team did mundane things like throwing cricket balls around at the Wanderers. They, like most cricket fans, were disappointed that Bacher had decided not to stage a one-day game tomorrow to make up for the prematurely ended 'Test'. Ali issued a statement yesterday, which did actually see the light of day despite rather more momentous happenings, to the effect that logistical problems would prevent a match being staged. Coming from a 'can-do' sort of guy that seems a bit strange to me.

Less strange is the news that Kepler Wessels has withdrawn from the Cape Town 'Test' at Newlands which is due to start in a couple of days. Peter van der Merwe, the chairman of the selectors, has issued a statement which says, 'The controversy that has raged in relation to the Clive Rice Affair has taken a massive mental toll on Kepler and he feels totally drained and demotivated by it all. Due to this pressure, he feels he cannot fulfil his role as a Springbok cricketer to his best ability.'

Now that Wessels has gone, will Rice return? There are still a lot of unanswered questions about the next match, not least those surrounding the security arrangements. A bomb went off in the Newlands clubhouse a couple of nights ago. No one was hurt but the omens are not good. Bacher has been more concerned about the Cape Town 'Test' than any other match from Day One and the anti-tour lobby seem determined to fulfil his fears.

Abraham Adams, who is president of the Western Province Cricket Board as well as leading the Anti-tour Forum, was quoted in the *Star* today as saying that he would not be applying for a permit to demonstrate.

Mr Adams seems to be one person who refuses to play by the obtuse and contradictory rules of the game. 'We reject any idea of a permit,' he said. 'It ridicules the whole concept of protest action and our intention of wanting the tourists out of the country.

'How do you apply for a permit from the very system you object to in the first place? If that makes sense or is in any way moral, I must be living on the moon.'

Alan Paton would have understood perfectly what Abraham

Adams was on about. I should imagine André Brink, author of the powerful *Looking on Darkness* would, too. He is one person I want to track down when I get to the Cape.

13 February

There will be no Cape Town as far as this tour is concerned. It's been curtailed, if not exactly cancelled. I heard the news this morning when I phoned Francois Vedemans of the SACU to see if he could take me out to look at some of the cricket facilities in the townships. 'There will be a press conference this afternoon,' he said.

So that was what it had all been about, I thought, as I climbed the wide staircase in the Wanderers' clubhouse to find everyone crammed into one of the meeting rooms, bathed in television strobe lights. Obviously things had been moving too fast behind the scenes for an extra match to have been played today.

Ali Bacher, David Graveney and Mike Gatting were sitting behind a long table and the questions came thick and fast. But not all the answers were forthcoming.

Bacher, in particular, was evasive about the 'third party' who had apparently telephoned from abroad last Saturday to plead with the SACU to 'find some compromise solution to ensure that other problems in the country would not be affected' as Bacher put it.

This 'third party' had evidently been so influential that Bacher and Krish Naidoo, the lawyer who heads the National Sports Congress, had got together and thrashed out a deal over the weekend. Stressing that events had overtaken the tour and that wider implications that go far beyond cricket had to be taken into account, Bacher said that it was 'a time for compromise, a time for reconciliation.'

The compromise amounted to this: the Cape Town 'Test' would be scrapped and the seven remaining one-day internationals would be reduced to four, none of which would be played in Cape Town, East London or Port Elizabeth where protest was expected to be strongest. In return, the NSC which, basically, is the new sporting wing of the ANC, would call upon its supporters not to demonstrate at the remaining matches.

Bacher insisted that the South African government had played no part in the new arrangements and, later in the day, Education Minister Dr Gerrit Viljoen, probably the most liberal member of the Cabinet, answered questions at a press conference by saying, 'The South African government has not and is not exerting any pressure on the SACU in regard to its decisions on the tour. We are really serious about depoliticizing sport.'

So it would seem because, as I have noted earlier, nothing has proved so embarrassing to the de Klerk government at this highly delicate time than a bunch of cricketing mercenaries running around the country attracting angry demonstrations at every turn.

So who was it who made that phone call? The ANC, perhaps? Mandela was still in jail on Saturday morning and probably had other things on his mind. We will have to wait for an answer on that one because Bacher's lips are sealed.

Mike Gatting, in comparison to his earlier efforts at press conferences, was positively eloquent. 'It is very heartening that the NSC and SACU will be able to get together, to sit down and talk, which they haven't done for a long time, and get around to normalizing sport here in South Africa. Hopefully this new spirit of compromise will take both parties a long way down the road towards complete understanding.'

Later, Gatt brought Johnny Woodcock of *The Times* up to date as Johnny had only flown in the previous evening from Australia where he had been covering the Pakistan tour.

'Good timing, Wooders!' Gatting smiled as he spotted the game's senior cricket writer on his way out of the clubhouse. 'It's been an interesting experience, to say the least. Some sections of the Press have been really awful which has made it doubly difficult and I'm disappointed that we won't get to play another Test. But I really hope some good can come of it now. I think just by being here we have forced people to face the issues and talk to each other.'

That was not an unreasonable point of view. The anti-apartheid movement will claim it as a total victory and that is all right. But no matter what simplistic slogans are shovelled out for the consumption of the Press, the issues here are always far too complex to fit into a few paragraphs. The only thing that matters is what happens from here. Even though the NSC's concession was smaller, it was nonetheless a concession and we will now have what, to all intents and purposes, will be four ANC-sanctioned matches before a veil is drawn over the whole unhappy business. That in itself is interesting because it is a first step down the road that Ali Bacher has foreseen but, to date, has been wary of. A great deal of careful diplomacy will be required to produce an acceptable solution, but these things have to start somewhere and the press conference at the Wanderers today had all the makings of the turning of a page and the beginnings of a new and more civilized chapter in the bloodied history of South African sport.

14 February

Even by the standards of the last couple of weeks this has been a hell of a day.

A tour of Soweto which included a close-up glimpse of Nelson Mandela, the man no one had set eyes on for twenty-seven years until three days ago, was followed by a one and a half hour talk with Dame Helen Suzman, one of the world's true political heroines. Valentines do not come much headier than this.

But let me start at the beginning. I was driven into Soweto by Ronnie Van't Hof, a financial consultant and former tennis player who has set up a trust fund to develop grass roots tennis in the townships. Although a teachers' strike was going to prevent any supervised on-court activity this afternoon, Ronnie normally conducts coaching sessions himself every Wednesday and wanted to see if any children had ventured on to some of the new courts that have been set up by local communities of their own accord. Happily they had.

I was also anxious to see what had happened to the courts that had been built as a result of Arthur Ashe's initiative here in 1973 and 1974. I had heard they had fallen into disrepair, partially because of the after-effects of the serious riots in Soweto in 1976 and partially because Ashe had decided it was politically unwise for him to return. Sadly this turned out to be correct.

As Van't Hof was not sure how to find the site of these courts, which are situated at Javabu in the heart of the sprawling Soweto ghetto, we picked up the full-time coach he had appointed for his programmes, Herman Takeba, so that he could direct us. Herman is a large, jolly man who benefited from some of the money Ashe had raised by making a trip to a tennis camp at Hilton Head Island, South Carolina, back in the seventies. Like all the aspiring black tennis players of that era, he had become the victim of politics, but was now obviously overjoyed to be back in business; able to make a contribution to a new start.

Soweto lies to the south of the high-rise towers of Johannesburg's downtown area and is less of a shanty town than I had remembered from my last visit seventeen years before. Garbage still litters the unpaved sidewalks and the golf course was eaten up a couple of years ago by tin roofed shacks built by newcomers drifting in from outlying areas. But there are signs of progress too. The YMCA and YWCA are housed in smart brick buildings and many of the one storey houses are neatly kept. Free enterprise in the form of fruit stalls and vehicle repair shops are springing up, creating an underground economy that is leaving government accounts perplexed as they try to balance their books. There is even a prosperous looking supermarket. Seventeen years ago, believe it or not, there were no shops in Soweto.

We turned down a bumpy side-street, edging past children and dogs playing in the road and wide-hipped women who made stately progress, some with large baskets of fruit balanced on their heads.

'It's OK, you're safe with me,' laughed Herman from the back seat. Ronnie played along with the joke, but actually he feels perfectly at ease in Soweto now, despite his blond hair which shines like a beacon amidst the sea of dark faces.

'Despite what the political activists might tell you, I have never run into opposition or unpleasantness here,' he tells me. 'If I see a demonstration or an excitable crowd, obviously I avoid it, but for the most part people welcome you. They seek your help.'

Directed by Herman, Ronnie suddenly veered off the uneven roadway and we began bumping over unkempt land towards a couple of single storey buildings that had been erected as administrative offices for the tennis complex. Before we got halfway there, four youths burst out of one of the buildings and sped away in the opposite direction, arms and legs flying as they hurdled a fence and disappeared out of sight. Heaven knows what they had been up to but it certainly wasn't tennis.

We got out of the car and there, lying disused in the hot Soweto sun, were the eight courts built in the name of Arthur Ashe sixteen years before. Long grass flopped over the edges of the concrete and pylons that were to have carried the floodlights stood like rusting sentinels over a half-forgotten dream.

It had been Ashe's dream to bring tennis to the children of Soweto and, because he was both a persuasive and caring man, he had cut through the bureaucracy of apartheid to set up a trust fund during his two visits here in 1973 and 1974. The trust was to be administered by Owen Williams, then South Africa's premier tennis promoter and now executive director of Lamar Hunt's World Championship Tennis organization in Dallas.

For a while it seemed that Ashe's vision would become reality. Apart from the eight courts that were built, programmes were set up and some of the best black players, including Herman Takeba, even got to visit the United States.

But then a whole series of ostensibly unrelated things occurred. Soweto was swept by riots in 1976; Williams left South Africa and Ashe decided not to return. The programme collapsed.

'It's tragic these courts are going to waste,' said Van't Hof as we surveyed the desolate scene. 'It wouldn't take much to put them back in working order. But we can't do anything until we are asked. We cannot impose ourselves on these people. I know they have other priorities and it is up to each local community in Soweto to invite us in.'

When would things change? Sooner, perhaps, than one dared hope and part of the reason for that hope was not so very far away.

'Hey, Nelson lives up that street,' said Herman as we began making our way back towards the centre of Soweto.

'Then let's go and see what's happening,' I said, my reporter's instincts getting the better of me.

When we turned the corner into the unpaved road where the Mandela house stood, there were two oil cans blocking cars from proceeding further so we got out and walked over to the group of some forty reporters and television camera crews who were milling around. Ronnie knew one of the photographers who promptly offered his steel camera case as a stool to stand on.

'He's in the garden right now,' said the photographer. 'If you stand on that you'll be able to look over the fence.'

So I clambered up and peered through the single strand of loosely coiled barbed wire that sat on top of the fence and gazed down upon the face of the man no one had seen for twenty-seven years until three days before. Mandela was no more than twenty yards away, sitting in a chair being interviewed by Ted Koppel of ABC News, whose *Nightline* programme, which is received throughout America five nights a week, is the best of its kind in the world. Koppel does not fly around the world to visit everyone in their back garden. Given the realities of the television age in which we live, Koppel's presence was the ultimate confirmation of Mandela as an international figure of lasting importance.

I was carrying a little automatic camera and as I raised to take a shot of the historic scene, I realized that I could perfectly easily have been taking another kind of shot; a shot with a gun. No-one had challenged either Ronnie or myself. Two white men had just walked up to that house and one had climbed and pointed something over the wall at Nelson Mandela. There had been no request for press credentials, not even a cursory question. The fact that no one shooting Mandela would have got out of Soweto alive was not the point. The martyr instinct is very strong in assassins.

After dropping Herman off at his office we drove over to Diep Kloof, a more affluent part of Soweto where the community *had* invited Van't Hof in to mastermind his mini-tennis programme. As I mentioned, the teachers' strike had prevented any organized activity on this particular Wednesday afternoon but when we got to the brand new complex of four well-laid cement courts, all were occupied with youngsters of varying ages and standards of expertise hitting balls about between themselves with others waiting their turn to go on. It was an encouraging sight.

'By making contact directly at the school level, I tried to keep out of the politics of the whole thing,' said Ronnie. 'And no matter what you might have heard from other sources I have not had one person come to me and suggest we were not wanted or that it would be better if we stayed away. We have had nothing but total co-operation from the local community here and look at the result. When Christo Van Rensberg and Kevin Curren came in last year to play an exhibition match, the response was incredible.'

Yet a few months later, when Van Rensberg who, unlike Curren, is still a South African national, played in the Australian Open he and other South African players found themselves the target of anti-apartheid demonstrators throwing black balloons on to the court. I know that was the only way they felt they could make a protest but, as usual, they were latching on to the most available instead of the most culpable target. How many of those demonstrators at Flinders Park had coached aboriginal children at anything? Protest has its place but positive action is better.

Before driving me back to the Forbes' house, Ronnie made a final stop at what they call Soccer City, the magnificent FNB Stadium that sits on the edge of the township and, although not completed, already seats 72,000 people. It was here that well over 100,000 crammed into every aisle to welcome Mandela home from jail two days ago. Incredible as it may seem, there is not a football stadium in Britain that can compare with this. If Soweto has better facilities, isn't it time British sport got its act together?

Gordon Forbes, who has known Helen Suzman for years, was kind enough to phone up and ask if we could go over to her house in nearby Sandton for a chat. It was clearly a bit of an imposition because Dame Helen was being besieged by every news organization in the world and had broken off a holiday on the coast to return to Johannesburg for a few days so that she could attend the Mandela homecoming. However, even though she is due to be up at 5 a.m. tomorrow to take part in a live satellite feed for Ted Koppel's *Nightline*, she graciously agreed to receive us.

'I was a bit tired when you called, but I've perked up a lot now,' she said, eyes twinkling, opening the door herself and then fetching drinks for us. Presumably there were servants around somewhere but they certainly do not wait on her hand and foot.

A beautiful lawn stretches away from the living-room windows at the back of the house which, in atmosphere and architectural design, could just as well be standing in Virginia Water. Dame Helen herself has an Englishness about her that one notices in so many non-Afrikaans South Africans. In her mid-seventies, she is a distinguished looking lady with greying hair and fine-boned features. And a wonderfully unpretentious charm.

We sat in her slightly cluttered study which was lined with books of every literary and political stripe, most of which would not have gained approval in the Parliament in which she served as the lone representative of the tiny Progressive Party for over thirty years. Looking at this small, refined figure sitting opposite, it was hard to imagine – until she started to talk – that she could have been capable of opposing, day after day, year after year, an entire assembly of bigoted male Afrikaners whose politics and policies were an affront to her innate sense of decency. More than the courage involved, I marvelled at the resilience and determination it must have required.

As a result of that heroic crusade in the teeth of hopeless odds, there is no white person on earth who has a greater right to speak out on what is correct or incorrect for South Africa and I was anxious to hear her views on how sport should be handled as far as boycotts were concerned.

'Sporting bodies that have moved away from apartheid and made a real effort in that direction need encouragement,' she said. 'Sport is an area where great progress can be made and the people running sports like cricket, tennis, athletics and soccer here should be helped to achieve it.'

It turned out that Dame Helen was not exactly in accord with the ANC over the question of sanctions in general.

'Did you see in the papers that the Labour leaders in London were saying to the prime minister, "How dare you think you know more than Mandela?" Well, I'm sorry but, much as I love Nelson, the fact is that she does know more about a lot of things concerning sanctions than he does. Margaret Thatcher has been running a country while he has been in prison for twenty-seven years. Nelson's a fine man, but there are a lot of things he can't possibly comprehend just yet.'

During those twenty-seven years, Dame Helen had visited Mandela in prison eight times and would have gone many more had she been allowed. On the last occasion, towards the end of P.W. Botha's term as president, she had made some comments that had angered the National Party leader.

'One of the problems with PW was that he was a bully,' she said. 'All this finger-wagging stuff. So unattractive. And, frankly, he was third rate. Not in de Klerk's league intellectually.'

One began to see how she had survived in the apartheid den; morally incorruptible, fearless, outspoken, always prepared to stand for what was humane and decent while her army of opponents tried to defend the indefensible. What an uncomfortable little pin she must have been, pricking away at the remnants of their conscience.

Gordon asked if she had ever been afraid, not needing to remind her that white liberals, as well as black activists, had been assassinated by the secret police.

'Oh, there was never time to be afraid, really,' she replied. 'Too much to do. You just put it out of your mind.'

Before we left, she showed us a book by Nathan Shcharansky, the Soviet Jew who had spent nine years in a KGB prison camp. She had taken it to Mandela on her last visit and he had sent it back to her soon after she retired from active political life with an inscription of which she was obviously, and justifiably, proud. It read: 'The countless tributes you have received on your retirement from Parliament show that you have acquitted yourself beyond words.' It was signed 'Nelson. 6.7.89.'

Now the man who had been a prisoner that day in July last year, the man I had seen only a few hours before, was receiving tributes of his own. What a pair they would have made had Helen Suzman and Nelson Mandela been allowed to serve in Pretoria's Parliament together.

15 February

Dame Helen was kind enough to lend me a book that I noticed lying in her study yesterday. It is Bruce Francis' account of the rebel Australian tours he organized with Ali Bacher that took place here in 1985/86 and again the following summer.

The first thing that struck me on picking it up was the total absence of a publisher's imprint. The title gives a hint of why. *Guilty: Bob Hawke or Kim Hughes?* it asks provocatively. For a lot of Australian publishers I should imagine that put it in the 'too hot to handle' category. It is an angry book.

'The players and I were charged, tried, convicted and sentenced by a series of kangaroo courts, with a viciousness that would have done credit to the Spanish Inquisition.'

Is that a little over the top? Probably not from where Francis sits and his book is an attempt to fight back by placing Prime Minister Hawke and a couple of members of his cabinet on trial for 'misrepresentation of the Gleneagles Declaration' and 'having acted in an intimidatory manner in an attempt to prevent the cricketers from playing in South Africa, which was tantamount to a denial of such fundamental rights as freedom of association.'

Francis' book is a detailed and slightly laborious attempt to show up the hypocrisies and inconsistencies of politicians who try to use sport for their own ends, a theme with which I heartily concur. I think I have stated clearly enough in the opening chapter why I believe South Africa is a special case and has only itself to blame for its isolation. But that does not extend to accepting contradictory arguments over whether sport should be allowed to act as a vehicle for good in some countries but not in others.

As Francis points out, the Gleneagles Declaration admitted, to quote from the text, that 'they were conscious that sport is an important means of developing and fostering understanding between people, especially the young people, of all countries.'

Fine. So why can't that be the case in South Africa? Because, according to our learned political friends, 'sporting contact between their nationals (i.e., nationals of the countries signing the Declaration) and nationals of countries practising apartheid in sport tend to encourage the belief, however unwarranted, that they were prepared to condone this abhorrent policy.'

While sympathizing with those anti-apartheid activists who say that they don't give a damn about the injustices imposed on athletes as long as the suffering of millions of black people is alleviated, I still cannot agree with the Gleneagles statement. Francis makes a perfectly valid point when he writes, 'Even in the case of the Moscow Olympics, the Western boycott was aimed not as a measure of disgust at the appalling restrictions of personal freedom under a Marxist totalitarian regime, but as a protest against the Soviet invasion of Afghanistan. I am not aware of a single instance in which a sportsman, sportswoman or athlete competing in the USSR or with Soviet nationals elsewhere has been accused of endorsing communism.'

And, just like the South African government, communist regimes all over the world have made capital out of the success of their athletes in international competition. Ever since the Second World War the Olympic battle for gold medals between the Soviets and the Americans has been based on little other than an attempt to prove whether communism or capitalism was the best system for nurturing a healthy young generation. So to justify a sporting boycott of South Africa on the grounds that it hands apartheid a propaganda tool is humbug.

When Arthur Ashe came here in 1973 he faced that question head on. Ashe, who was always far more politically aware than most cricketers, knew perfectly well that the Vorster government would use his presence for propaganda purposes. And, in his dealings with the influential minister of sport, Dr Piet Koornhof, he was quite frank about it. In return for being used, Ashe set out a list of concessions he wanted in return.

He told Dr Koornhof he wanted the Sugar Circuit (South Africa's annual tennis circuit) integrated immediately and it was.

He said he wanted a Trust Fund set up, to be administered by the liberal tournament director of the South African Open, Owen Williams, and it happened.

He said he wanted permission for South Africa's best young players to travel overseas and Dr Koornhof agreed.

Ashe got everything he asked for.

This raises two points. First of all, I don't think the cricketers, Australian, English or especially West Indian who have come here since, have extracted nearly enough from the government in return for their services. Instead of creeping in and out of the country looking sheepish, Lawrence Rowe and other West Indies stars, who were risking all manner of retribution back home, should have made the same kinds of demands as Ashe, including the right to speak out in condemnation of apartheid at every turn. They would have been amazed at how much freedom they would have been given to do so because there is one thing none of the cricketers have quite grasped. As much as they wanted the security which the money they were receiving would give them, the South African government wanted them more. Of course it was good propaganda for the white regime, but what price propaganda when cricket fields and tennis courts can be built so that thousands of black children can derive some purpose and joy out of life? I know the kids' own black leaders take the line that they will have to wait and suffer a little more so that cosmetic changes do not delay the fulfilment of the ultimate goal. But I do not accept that the very real progress that has been made in sport – far greater progress than has been achieved in any other sphere of society in South Africa over the past ten years – has interfered with the ultimate goal. On the contrary I think it has hastened it by showing highly dubious whites in this country that it is possible for the races to mix socially, competitively and amicably and that, in doing so, it has created a climate more conducive to the kind of bold reforms President de Klerk has set in motion these past few weeks.

I saw the results of the second point yesterday. Weeds growing up around Ashe's brave and sincere attempt to leave something substantial behind him. I totally respect Arthur's reasons for not coming back here after 1974. The arguments presented to him by friends such as Andrew Young and other, more militant, elements in the black community are very persuasive. I was there, too, when Ashe stoically accepted the barrage of criticism that was directed at him by a group of black journalists in Johannesburg in 1973. 'Go home!' they shouted. 'You're just giving encouragement to our enemies. Let us solve our problems our own way!'

After one more visit, Ashe took them at their word. But where is the tangible evidence that Ashe's absence these sixteen years has actually improved the lot of the black South African? Where is evidence as tangible as eight tennis courts, unused and decaying; money wasted, dreams unfulfilled? Of course they are a microcosm in the greater scheme of things. But the fact remains that when Ashe was here he created something, however small. What did he create by staying away?

Yannick Noah, Ashe's successor as the world's pre-eminent black tennis star, was asking the same question when we met in Jamaica at the end of last year. We were talking about what attitude black tennis players should take towards South Africa with Todd Nelson, a black Californian, Doug Burke, a Jamaican and Roger Smith from the Bahamas during a small tournament at the Half Moon Hotel in Montego Bay.

'I have stayed away from South Africa for eleven years now,' said Noah. 'And who has noticed? Who cares? I think that maybe it is time I got the biggest appearance guarantee possible out of the tournament down there and leave it all behind for black development programmes. At least that would be contributing something.'

Noah travelled the length and breadth of black Africa on behalf of the charity CARE until he started to become unhappy with the amounts of money he helped to raise that were actually getting through to their proper destination. He wasn't accusing anyone of anything dastardly. He was just fed up with the cost of bureaucratic bullshit. Yannick can't stand bullshit.

I am totally in accord with his desire to take an active rather than inactive stance against apartheid. I will not accept that it is a contradiction of my belief that South Africa deserves to be singled out as a pariah among nations because of its racist laws. I agree that every tool available should be used to uproot apartheid but, the more I see, the more I am certain that it is no longer constructive to use sport as such a tool. While every political means should be used to kill off the poisonous apartheid plant, sport should be allowed to sow the seeds of understanding and friendship between future generations. No other instrument of society is so well equipped for the task. Sport can heal. It must be allowed to do so.

Given the speed at which everything appears to be changing here, it is possible that the normalization of sport is not as far away as some may think. That, however, has not saved Gatting's men from another barrage of abuse in certain segments of the British Press. At breakfast this morning I was reading Ian Hobbs, *Business Day*'s London correspondent, who was quoting the latest *Daily Mirror* editorial.

'Mike Gatting and his jackals of cricket are coming home early with their bats between their legs,' it read. 'Having disgraced their country and their sport, it is only fitting that they should be abandoned by the South Africa to which they sold their reputations.'

Even allowing for a little tabloid hyperbole, it really is infantile stuff, quite apart from being marginally inaccurate. The SACU have not abandoned the English XI, not yet anyway, and even Peter Hain would have to admit that, albeit inadvertently, they have served the anti-apartheid cause in two important ways. Firstly by giving the movement a wonderfully evocative target and all the vital ensuing publicity at a time when they would have been hard pressed to find anything half as newsworthy and secondly by becoming the catalyst for the negotiations that will now take place between the SACU and the National Sports Congress. Obviously the demonstrators are claiming credit for that and so they should. But before you can achieve anything by demonstrating, it is necessary to have something to demonstrate against. It is one of those nasty, unpalatable and inconvenient little truths that all honest men have to swallow.

So by being here Gatting's team achieved something. Not with the foresight, political sophistication or even sense of morality with which Ashe integrated tennis in 1973 but, from whatever stance they approached it, they certainly achieved more than journalists writing vitriolic editorials in London.

Those who have been so harsh on Gatting can also be accused of inconsistency, not simply in their failure to treat all sports equally on the South African question – haven't there been a few British golfers playing down here recently? – but inconsistency within the confines of cricket. Looking at the back of Bruce Francis' book I see a picture of the side Kim Hughes captained here in 1985–6. In the middle of the back row stands Terry Alderman. Not only was Alderman reinstated in time to decimate England's batting last summer, but was lauded by the British Press for doing so. No one suggested that Terry was a disgrace to his country. Perhaps, being an Australian, the British Press thought it didn't matter. OK, so what about the fellow standing next to Alderman in that picture, Carl Rackemann? He was in South Africa, too, less than four years ago, but you would never have known it reading the Australian Press last month as the excellence of his seam bowling helped Australia gain the upper hand in the home series against Pakistan. The critics Francis went to such pains to expose seem to have short memories. Or double standards.

All of which makes me think that, providing this country continues to progress at the present speed, we may see Gatting and some of his younger team-mates back in England colours long before their five-year ban is over. In a couple of years even a *Daily Mirror* leader writer may be hard pressed to stand them up as villains. And if not a villain, then of course Gatt would have to be a hero. It's that black-and-white syndrome again. The only colours so much of my profession understands.

Nevertheless there is a great deal of work to be done before any such scenario can come to pass. It has been raining again this afternoon. For the past week the Johannesburg weather has been about as reliable as Bognor in April. Four times Ali Bacher's assistant, Francois Vedeman, has been trying to take me out to the townships to see some black cricket in progress on the fields set up by the development schemes. On each occasion there has been too much rain for the grounds to recover in time. Yet they were playing cricket at the Wanderers yesterday. Yes, there is still work to be done.

Verwoerdburg

16 February

The first ANC-approved cricket match took place today in a town named after the father of apartheid in front of a packed stadium of 15,000 without a black spectator in sight. This, surely, must be the final irony. But after all that has gone before, what else could one expect?

Verwoerdburg is a modern annex of Pretoria, made up of large office complexes housing high-tech companies. Centurion Park where the first of the re-scheduled one-day Internationals is being played is pretty high-tech itself and must rank as one of the most impressive cricket grounds in the world. The scoreboard, certainly, is the best I have ever seen. The use of colour helps one grasp the mass of information displayed, with the score of the current innings showing in red. Other unusual items include the run total of the partnership in progress, the over rate, bowlers' figures and runs taken from the current over. It must be wonderful for the statistically-minded spectator, but for reporters working against a deadline, it is an absolute delight.

With the threat of demonstrations removed, the crowd is by far the biggest of the tour so far. Those without tickets for the main stand which stretches across one end of the ground, spread themselves on the grass banking which surrounds the rest of the playing area, setting up family picnics amidst the knots of young supporters who grow noisier as day turns to night and the lights come on. Borrowing a pair of binoculars, I scan the entire ground and finally spot four Indians seated in one of the enclosures. They are the only non-white faces on view apart from the ice-cream and soft drink vendors.

Gatting won the toss and decided to bat which didn't prove to be the wisest decision of the day. Had no one told him how much dew settles on the field after dark? Skidding around with a wet ball did not turn out to be the best way to spend an evening.

That, however, did not prevent the English captain receiving a rapturous ovation from the grateful all-white crowd as he jogged on to the field at 55–2, arms twirling in familiar style and legs back-kicking to loosen those bulky muscles.

As always Gatting looked as if he meant business and proved it by driving Tim Shaw, the Eastern Province spinner back over his head for four off the second ball he received. Earlier, Shaw, who had been unlucky to be omitted from the 'Test' side, had trapped Broad, having him caught behind by Trevor Madsen. The Natal keeper needed to start proving himself pretty quickly because he had been brought into the team at the expense of Ray Jennings who had kept brilliantly at the Wanderers. So brilliantly, in fact, that he had equalled Denis Lindsay's twenty-three-year-old South African Test record of eight catches in a match. In addition he had scored 23 very valuable runs when South Africa had been struggling to get past the visitors' paltry first innings total. What else is a wicket-keeper supposed to do to safeguard his place in a side? Score faster seemed to be the hard-nosed answer from local experts I asked. Madsen, it seems, can nudge the score along very nicely.

So, of course, can Gatting, but he wasn't having it all his own way against some reasonably tight bowling and he was dropped at point on 27. But until French weighed in with some fine hitting, including a six-over long leg, the captain had provided the backbone of the innings, scoring 55 off 72 balls before Snell bowled him.

While all this had been going on I had taken the opportunity of brushing up on some of the history of the so-called rebel tours with Johnny Woodcock, who has edited *Wisden* as well as being one of the great *Times* cricket correspondents – a position he has now handed over to Alan Lee.

'First of all, one should remember this is not strictly speaking a rebel tour,' said Woodcock. 'No one has banned it. It may not be *approved* of, but that is different from being illegal. And neither the International Cricket Conference nor the TCCB have said it cannot take place. The TCCB has just told the players what will happen to them if they play here. But all the three- and five-day matches are designated as first-class fixtures and will be included in a player's career record.'

Woodcock had been at Newlands in 1982 when the side that had got itself together in such clandestine fashion in India in 1981–2 before turning up out of the blue under Gooch's captaincy in South Africa, heard that all its members had been banned from Test cricket for three years.

'They were stunned,' said Johnny. 'Although I'm not quite sure why. They must have realized something was going to happen to them, but I don't think many expected it to be as much as three years. I think they thought they would get away with a slap on the wrist and six months. Some of them were very sheepish about the whole thing although it was incredible how many big names nearly joined them. Ian Botham was only dissuaded when his agent at the time, Reg Hayter, flew out to India to talk him out of it and Bob Willis was damn nearly on the plane before a last-minute change of heart.'

Many people in the game think of Woodcock as a South African sympathizer, but he refutes that.

'Nothing annoys me more than when people say I am pro-South Africa,' he said. 'It's the hypocrisy I can't stand. On the way in, I read some of the articles that have been appearing in the tabloids back home and I am absolutely appalled at some of the things that have been written. Articles like that cause so much misery and unhappiness.'

By the time England had scraped past the two-hundred mark in their allotted overs Christopher Morris had arrived hot-foot from Soweto where his persistence had eventually been rewarded with an interview with Nelson Mandela for Sky Television.

'And do you know the first thing he asked me while we were waiting for the crew to set up?' Chris asked. 'Did I know Mike

Gatting! I said that I had met him professionally, hoping that admission wouldn't get me thrown out of the garden, but he just went on to comment that, in his view, the team shouldn't have come and that it was bad for South Africa and bad for South African sport.'

Mandela used to box in his youth and the fact that he was asking questions like that suggested sport was still a subject that concerned him. How much influence he will have in the talks that will inevitably develop between Bacher and the NSC remains to be seen. I just hope he realizes what kind of potential sport offers as a distraction from violence and other anti-social pastimes.

Apart from Madsen showing why he had been selected by darting up and down the pitch and hitting some lusty blows that carried South Africa to victory, there were one or two points of interest as the run chase continued under lights. Graham Dilley broke his duck by getting his very first wicket of the tour when he trapped Mark Rushmere lbw which was almost as much of a relief to the team as it was to him. It really was possible to get Rushmere out after all! But, of course, he seemed to have been chosen for the wrong match. Test cricket would be more his scene.

Then, as the light started to fade, the white clouds of smoke drifting across the ground from the numerous braais (portable barbecues) by which the spectators were cooking their burgers and sausages – a big custom in South Africa – threatened to create a new method of interrupting a cricket match, 'Smoke Stopped Play'. Happily the biggest cloud hung around long leg, but if the wind had not been so considerate, Jimmy Cook and Adrian Kuiper might have found themselves trying to handle Dilley and Cowdrey through a fog.

Then, at precisely 8.30 p.m. in the fifth match of the tour we had our first pitch invasion. Strange how these things work out. Demonstrators getting on to the playing area and possibly tampering with the wicket had been one of the recurring nightmares Bacher had had to endure during the early matches, but now, of course, the lone figure who ran on to the field waving a huge South African flag in celebration of Cook's fifty was not even black. He was just the type of faintly inebriated lager lout one finds at any ground in England. Three security men finally tackled him in a good-natured sort of way and there were some boos mingling with the cheers as he was led off. So much for pitch invasions.

Half an hour later Broad padded down towards the press-box to collect the ball from the boundary and his foot prints were clearly visible on the grass. Soon the dew was so heavy that the bowlers were having to dry it after every ball and it was hardly surprising that Jarvis dropped Cook just before Dilley finally ended the South African captain's fine knock of 72 by bowling him.

The crowd, boisterous, noisy, but generally good natured, enjoyed every minute of the thrills and spills and went home in high spirits when Madsen hit the winning run. But the mood in the English dressing-room was more sombre. Richard Ellison, who has played better than most on this tour, sat on the massage table staring into space, while Gatting bustled about making sure all the bags got taken down to the bus.

'Too many half-volleys,' he said in his usual blunt fashion. 'If we can't bowl better than that we don't deserve to win.'

The South Africans were happier, of course, although Tim Shaw, who is Marshall Lee's cousin and has played league cricket in the north of England for a couple of summers, put the victory celebrations into perspective. 'It is just very difficult to get motivated without proper international cricket,' he said. 'It's been great to play against these guys, but it would be stupid to suggest that this is the answer to our problems. With the political situation changing maybe we can look forward to something better in the near future.'

Once again one was hearing the frustration of the sportsman caught in the political web. No, sport cannot be totally divorced from politics, but the people who run sport must fight for a form of separation that would allow the games that we play to benefit society in a way nothing else can. 'Depoliticize sport,' Gerrit Viljoen had said. On that, at least, I can agree with the National Party.

19 February

The extent to which South Africa is a sports'-crazed nation is reflected to a large degree by the amount of sport one can watch on television. Over the past weekend I watched a day-long Saturday sports special that runs several hours longer than the BBC's *Grandstand*. It opened up with the new ATP Tour Highlights film of all the week's top tennis events and one was then able to settle down and watch England bludgeon Wales to defeat, live from Twickenham. Then, at 11 p.m. we had that day's soccer special featuring Sheffield Wednesday and Arsenal. Right match as far as I was concerned, but the wrong result. Arsenal lost 1–0.

On Sunday, the second of the one-day Internationals was given ball by ball coverage from Durban; live coverage, as it turned out, of yet another South African victory. Gatt must be really struggling to generate any morale among his troops by now, especially as the crowds have suddenly turned out in large numbers to inspire the home team.

The extent to which the demonstrations limited the attendance at earlier matches now seems clear. The idea of large groups of people – especially black people – being allowed to stage a public protest is still a very new concept to most white South Africans and it makes them very nervous.

These past few days have been spent trying to meet as many people and listen to as many different opinions as possible in a country that is now afire with talk of reform and change. The range of that opinion is quite extraordinary and I am always amazed at how many leftish white liberals manage to exist in this society and work assiduously and courageously for the kind of future that now, at last, seems possible.

A fascinating mix of opinion can always be found whenever Des and Dawn Lindberg give a dinner party or one of their musical evenings at their beautiful turn-of-the-century house with its wood panelling and minstrel's gallery. A couple of evenings ago, Gordon and I listened to a recital by a string quartet playing Dvořák. There were about fifty people there, white, black and coloured, all behaving as if this was the most civilized place on earth which it came very close to being – in that house on that particular evening. It was difficult to have to remind oneself that there were actually people not very far away like Eugene Terreblanche and his gang from the Afrikaner Resistance Movement who would have been offended to the point of violence at the sight of such an innocently congenial group of human beings enjoying some cultured entertainment in each other's company – just because their skin tones did not match.

The Lindbergs are both entertainers themselves, song-writers and singers who have donated a great deal of their time and talent in support of anti-apartheid causes. Obviously they have a wide range of contacts in the black community and earlier today Dawn drove me into the centre of Johannesburg to visit Anastasia Thule, an affluent black woman who runs a school and various other community-related projects in the downtown area which, incidentally, is now a totally black city. Virtually all the major white-run businesses have moved to the northern suburbs.

Mrs Thule and her husband have quite enough money to move out of Soweto now that restrictions on where blacks can buy a home are being relaxed, but have no immediate plans for doing so.

'Those of us who are better off have always said we will not move out of the townships until everyone is completely free to live where they want,' said Mrs Thule. 'We are not going to leave our people behind in poverty.'

After we had talked about the importance of building proper sports facilities – an importance which, I tried to stress, came behind only housing, health and education – Mrs Thule walked us down the street to the school which is run by a headmaster whose energy level is quite extraordinary. A tiny, wiry man with a huge smile, Seth Mazabuko spent five years on Robben Island before his release five years ago. Talking at ninety miles an hour with a clarity of diction that would put many schoolmasters in England to shame, Seth told us that he had earned himself three degrees while in prison.

'But it was not easy at first to take higher education,' he said. 'Until the Swiss Red Cross made heavy representations on our behalf we were not allowed to study for any degree that qualified you to teach. You see how they were? They wanted us to be educated, but not *too* educated! But in the last couple of years that I was there, things got better and now here I am with so much to do, so much to do!'

Just listening to him made the head spin, but it was obvious that any children being brought up under his supervision would learn two things above all else – how to speak beautiful English and an unbounded optimism that life's struggles can be overcome.

Ali Bacher is normally an optimistic man, but he will need every ounce of it now because things are obviously tense between him and the SACU President, Geoff Dakin, just at the moment. Bacher evidently upset Dakin when he included a clause in the compromise agreement he hammered out with the NSC to the effect that Gatting's team would not return for the second leg of their tour in November this year. Dakin has said publicly that Bacher, as the Union's paid executive director, did not have the authority to cancel the second segment of the tour. It would be better, at this delicate moment, if Dakin reverted to the kind of public statements he was making the last time the SACU and the NSC met back in November rather than try to sabotage the credibility of his most priceless asset, Dr Ali Bacher.

After meeting with Krish Naidoo on 9 November 1989, Dakin was quoted by John Perlman in the *Guardian* as saying, 'I have incredible empathy with the NSC's point of view. My guys were incredibly impressed by the quality of the debate and by the people we met and we have a massive desire to be in tandem with them.'

Not having had a proper conversation with Geoff Dakin, I have no way of telling if he usually speaks like that, but I do seem to recall Phil Edmonds telling me once that Dakin had been 'terribly impressed' that Edmonds had been at Cambridge. But that might just be Phil being mischievous.

What I do know is that Dakin's more recent statements have sounded a lot less conciliatory. Rather than indulge in a lot of presidential posturing, Dakin should leave the negotiations to Bacher and if the November tour has to be cancelled, so be it. Dakin is right to point out that things are changing too fast for anyone to make safe predictions about the future, but in the present climate, certainly, another Gatting tour would serve absolutely no useful purpose.

A great deal of money has been lost, of course, and both Dakin and Bacher have insisted that contracts will be honoured no matter what. Someone is going to have to do some hard bargaining.

A certain amount of mystery still surrounds the identity of the overseas caller who set in motion the whole compromise curtailment of the tour. At first it was thought that the call had come from the ANC headquarters in Lusaka. The *Star* reported last Wednesday that a high-ranking ANC official had contacted Bacher on the third day of the Wanderers 'Test' – a few hours before President de Klerk's announcement that Nelson Mandela would be released the following day – and urged that the SACU and the NSC 'not rock the boat' at this delicate time.

However, since then the plot has thickened. Although the ANC's hand has not been discounted, it appears that the call actually came from some South African businessmen in London. Like the ANC, who may well have urged them to act, they, too, would have been concerned that a further escalation in the demonstrations against the tour, which would almost certainly have come to pass in Cape Town, would have had serious consequences for anyone trying to improve the business climate between South Africa and its trading partners.

It can get serious, a little game of cricket, can't it?

Leaving South Africa

20 February

As I leave the house, Adrian Kuiper is carting the English
bowling all over Springbok Park. The ground in Bloemfontein is
full this time, aided perhaps by the attraction of one-day cricket
and the absence of demonstrators. At any rate, they are revelling
in this masterly display of power hitting against a ragged attack
that is obviously wilting in the sun.

Typically, Gatting brings himself on to bowl so as to save his
bowlers from further punishment. Gatting has always been a
selfless captain which is one reason why his team were so solidly
behind him during the Shakoor affair in Pakistan. Given the
circumstances few other captains would have been able to keep
the team spirit so high on this tour. There have been arguments,
of course, and a couple of blow-ups in the dressing-room over
team selection but, even though it has been difficult to translate
that spirit into effective performances on the field, at least there
has been some kind of willingness to try.

Every athlete needs some kind of motivation to perform at his
best and there has been little motivation on this tour other than
pride and a desire to support a captain who has been offering
himself up as punching bag on the team's behalf. Only die-hard
followers of the game will remember that Robinson, Maynard,

Athey, Ellison *et al.* were out here, but Gatting will have to live with the stigma for as long as South Africa remains a black-listed nation.

Given more match practice and better luck with injuries the results might have been marginally more respectable, but what could you expect from a team that had been guaranteed its money win, lose or draw? Knowing a large percentage of the game's followers back home would be quite happy to see them lose could hardly have added inspiration to their efforts, either, and if they were struggling to remain competitive now, let alone win matches, I cannot say I am surprised. It would have taken a combination of Mike Gatting, Mike Brearley and Jesus Christ to have avoided disaster in these circumstances.

Before I left, I had a word with Vince Van der Byl who, like two-thirds of the aforementioned trio, has played for Middlesex, and he readily admitted that the timing of the tour had been a mistake.

'Events ran ahead of it,' he said. 'One month before the tour began no one realized just how much disruption it would cause. But now, perhaps, some good can come of it. The two sides, SACU and NSC, must use their combined talking power to develop township cricket by coming up with specific projects that can be followed through.'

Van der Byl, who is heavily involved in community work in Alexandria and other townships, quickly reminded me of the pioneering work done in the field by John Passmore, an early liberal who put himself out on as long a limb as Helen Suzman, and then quoted four points made to him by a Mr Malumba, a black coach at Llanga near Cape Town.

'Mr Malumba said there were four major benefits which resulted from introducing cricket to black children,' said Van der Byl. 'Firstly, he said, it developed a working knowledge of English. Secondly, it had a paramount social benefit because studies in the US have proved a correlation between the number of sports fields available in underprivileged areas and the crime rate. Thirdly, there was the self-esteem the child derived from playing the game and the fourth factor was the value of proficiency at the game itself.'

Mr Malumba would appear to be a man after my own heart.

Sport, generally, rather than cricket in particular, must be recognized as a serious contributor to education, self-confidence and an alternate lifestyle to crime, all three of which are crucial to the development of healthy future generations. As I was saying to Anastasia Thule, what choice has a virile, unemployed teenager got in an underprivileged environment other than sport on one side or drugs, sex and rock and roll on the other?

Teachers too often overlook sport as an educational tool. Young people learn five times as fast if their imagination is stimulated. I well remember a conversation I had with a young waiter at a restaurant in Kuantan, a town on the east coast of Malaysia. He knew that Everton was in Liverpool and that Watford was just north of London and was owned by Elton John. But he wanted to know where Norwich was. Why? Because, at the time, Norwich City were top of the First Division. His knowledge of geography had been derived largely through his love of football and Brian Moore's programme which he watched every week on television. What is wrong with that? Dangle an attractive carrot and they'll learn far faster than trying to stuff turnips down their throat.

Van der Byl seems optimistic that progress can be made in the development of township cricket, despite the set-backs caused by the tour, but he is less encouraging in his estimate of how long it will take for the Springbok team to gain readmission to the international arena.

'I do not expect it to happen for five years,' Vince told me. 'The ICC is made up of too many countries who are not simply anti-apartheid, but anti-South Africa. It's not going to happen quickly.'

Everyone's opinions will be affected by the events which unfold in the coming months. Who can tell precisely what will happen to this beautiful, bedevilled country that is not even the same place it was when I arrived three short weeks ago? Will de Klerk and Mandela be able to keep the extremists at bay as they search for the final solution? How will the Conservative Party bigots react to the new reality – by cowering in their kraals or by attempting to block the unstoppable surge of history with the point of a gun? Will township violence be brought under control? The complexities may change, but they are unlikely to diminish.

But if one worries about the larger picture, I was left with an irritating reminder of the petty hypocrisies that such an abnormal society breeds. After Gordon Forbes bid me farewell at the airport, looking as fearful and as hopeful as any sane South African would over the future of his beloved land at this fateful moment in history, I found myself standing in line at passport control behind a Japanese businessman. He was asked whether he had been here on holiday or on business.

'Ah, business,' he replied.

He and thousands like him come to South Africa every month to add executive know-how to the giant Japanese corporations like Toyota, Toshiba and National Panasonic whose presence in the Republic is visible at every turn.

Fine. Maybe they are doing some good. National Panasonic, as we have seen, keep Ronnie Van't Hof's mini-tennis programme in Soweto alive to the tune of 600,000 rand a year. But if these companies are allowed to operate here, which they must do with the tacit approval of their Government, why is it that South African tennis players like Christo Van Rensberg and Danie Visser are not allowed to play tennis in Japan?

I suppose in a world that can somehow allow an argument to be put foward for a mass murderer like Pol Pot to be represented at the United Nations, it is of small consequence. But it still makes me mad. Businessmen are deemed important, so expedient measures must be taken to accommodate them. Athletes, meanwhile, are sacrificed so that countries like Japan and Sweden can score points with the Third World by seeming to be a great deal more self-righteous than they are. Athletes have no power base and are therefore expendable.

So happy the Japanese must be to make money out of South Africa and so happy to gain face in Black Africa by banning 'apartheid' athletes from entering their country. So happy to have hypocritical cake and eat it.

I watch my Japanese businessman throw his plastic around in the gift shop and remember instead the two little girls I had seen here on my arrival. The white one and the black one playing side by side until their parents whisked them off to different destinations. In the three weeks that had passed, their chances of a better, more united future had taken a quantum leap forward.

Although many of the hypocrisies, prejudices, illogicalities and just plain stupidities that the system of apartheid has wrought on this society remain in place for the time being, South Africa is a more hopeful nation than when I arrived. And, in retrospect, I am not sure Mike Gatting and his team did it too much of a disservice.

The presence of the cricketers not only proved that large, and mostly peaceful, demonstrations were possible, which was something very new for South Africa, but it forced both sides to confront the issue head on, focus on it and strive to find a solution through dialogue and compromise. As long as the SACU President Geoff Dakin does not try to muzzle Ali Bacher for reasons of pride or self-interest, the door that was so firmly shut may have been thrust ajar. Gatting's team may have been sporting mercenaries but they were a long way from being dogs of war.

'Over Africa'

21 February

The cancellation of the Cape Town Test meant that I had missed the opportunity of revisiting some of the loveliest parts of South Africa, the wine-growing country around Stellenbosch in the western Cape. I had wanted to go back, not simply to enjoy the magnificent countryside – although that would have been reason enough – but to see to what extent attitudes were changing at Stellenbosch University where, in 1973, Arthur Ashe and I had spent a memorable afternoon arguing with a couple of Afrikaans professors.

One, I remember, had tried to convice me he had more black friends than I did, as if it mattered.

'I have a regular correspondence with many good friends in African countries,' said the professor. 'An exchange of ideas and opinions is always stimulating.'

'Fine,' I replied. 'And if one of your African friends were to come here to see you, where would you take him out to dinner?'

I didn't get a straight answer to that straightforward question because there wasn't one that a supposedly intelligent human being could offer without sounding stupid, contradictory or dishonest. I don't have a very long fuse in situations like that and I needed a calming look across the table at Ashe to keep myself in check. Arthur felt it inside, of course, but you would never have known it from the immaculate front he presented to the world. His tennis teacher in Virginia, Dr Johnson, had taught him never to give the white man the opportunity to criticize his behaviour and Ashe had learnt his lesson well. No hypocritical academic with indefensible arguments was going to get through him. He just smiled a faintly superior smile and I bit my tongue.

But all that had been seventeen years before when apartheid was still in place. Stellenbosch students, and even many of their professors, have become determined to guide South Africa towards a more tolerable future. From what I heard, many were surprisingly liberal.

I would like to have found out for myself but, having raided the first-class section of our British Airways 747 for a copy of yesterday's *Times*, I discover that the paper's South Africa correspondent, Gavin Bell, has done some of the work for me.

In a long article on the Spectrum page, Bell has featured a farmer called Hempies du Toit. He writes:

'Seated behind an old wooden desk is the "baas", a stolid Afrikaner farmer, muscles bulging beneath a loose shirt, his feet bare. Before him is an open Bible, from which he reads in the guttural tones of his native language . . . A labourer rises and leads the little congregation in prayer. "Look upon our Government, Lord, and in our changing situation grant them wisdom." The farmer gravely nods his approval.'

But what does wisdom mean for du Toit, a thirty-six-year-old former Springbok prop-forward who is devoted to the farm his father handed down to him and which produces Alto Rouge, one of South Africa's oldest estate wines? Acknowledging change is one thing. But tolerating, or even welcoming it, is another. After all, as Bell points out, du Toit would 'resist fiercely any attempt to take the farm from him.'

'But,' the article continues, 'unlike others who cling defiantly to the illusion of separate development, du Toit is coming to terms with modern realities. In learning to live with Nelson Mandela, he has a start on many of his contemporaries, since he began questioning the old order long before P.W. Botha and F.W. de Klerk began dismantling it.

'The doubting process began when he was invited to add his

A view of the demonstrators from inside our cage at the Wanderers. The police found themselves in the unfamiliar position of having to stop whites attacking blacks.

Mike Gatting and John Emburey strike a surprisingly dainty ballet pose during a warm-up session at the Wanderers.

Chris Broad, a former rugby player, tries a drop kick to the party's
Welshman, Matthew Maynard, who still looks like a rugby player.

Chris Cowdrey offering slip catching practice to his colleagues.

David Graveney, just back from a business meeting, confers with his captain after the announcement that the tour had been curtailed.

This was a tour that attracted all manner of media. Here at Centurion Park in Verwoerdberg, Christopher Morris of Sky TV News chats with the doyen of the cricketing press, John Woodcock of *The Times*.

The barbed wire on Nelson Mandela's back fence, illuminated by my flash, frames the ANC leader and Ted Koppel of ABC News after an interview in the garden.

The Rocklands team that had to be disbanded for much of the summer because of the rebel tour. Henry Matthews, Orange Free State development officer, is seated third from right. Zebbie Makoena is standing behind Matthews' right shoulder and Brian Maloisane is seated front row extreme right. (Die Volksblad, Bloemfontein)

Another tense press conference for Mike Gatting, David Graveney and John Emburey, this time at the Landrost Hotel in Bloemfontein.

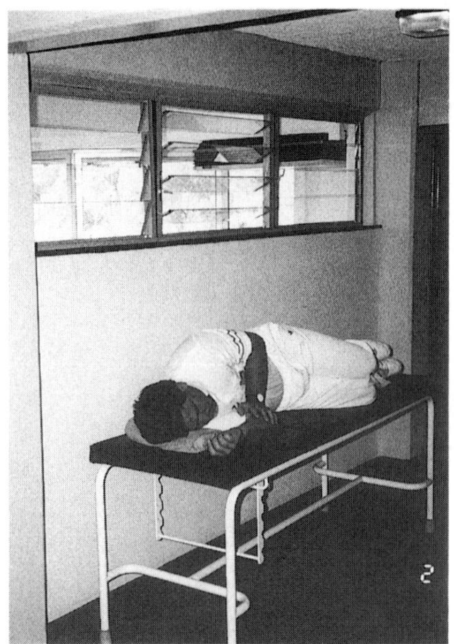

Amidst the furore, there was still time for the skipper to take a kip outside the locker room at Springbok Park in Bloemfontein.

Ali Bacher, Mike Gatting, David Graveney and John Emburey file out in to the unknown to accept the petition at the Jan Smuts Stadium in Pietermaritzburg.

Surrounded by 5,000 Zulus, Emburey and Graveney peer up anxiously at their captain as he receives the petition from Natal's anti-apartheid movement.

Devon Malcolm, the inspired choice. (Graham Morris)

Graham Gooch still has his eyes on it, but this was the ball that probably cost England the series – a lifter from Ezra Moseley at Port of Spain that broke the England captain's left hand in two places. (Graham Morris)

Gooch, forced to retire hurt for the first time in his career, cries out in agony as Laurie Brown tries to assess the extent of the damage. Clyde Best and Gus Logie look on. (Graham Morris)

Viv Richards on the rampage in Barbados as umpire Lloyd Barker finally decides to give Rob Bailey out caught behind. The stumps are obscured by Richards, showing how far Barker was on his way to square leg before stopping to give the decision. (Graham Morris)

Viv Richards in the press-box at the Recreation Ground, Antigua during his extraordinary confrontation with Jim Lawton of the *Daily Express* (seated). Matthew Engel of the *Guardian* is wearing his Augusta golfing hat and an expression to match. He had just arrived from the Masters where these sort of things don't happen. (Graham Morris)

Master Haynes is bowled while Master Greenidge keeps wicket during the lunch interval at Kensington Oval. But it didn't matter. Daddy got another hundred.

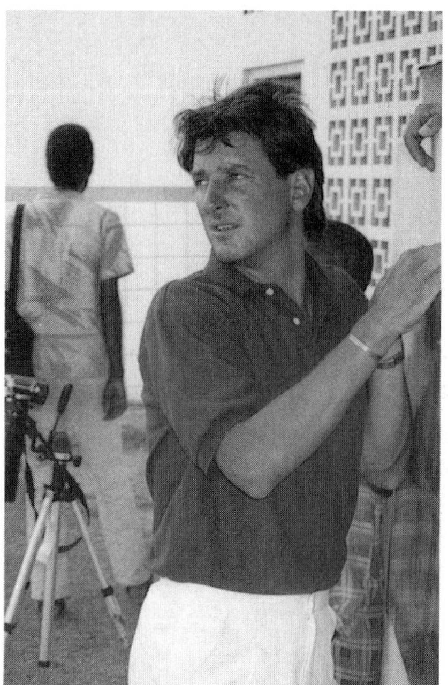

'No Admittance' says the sign. David Gower wondered just where he was supposed to be admitted during the latter part of the tour. Here at Kensington Oval he returns to visit his former colleagues in the press-box after being with the team that almost wanted him.

A slimmed-down, malaria-hit Mark Nicholas looking for friends at Kensington Oval after discharging himself from hospital.

Nasser Hussain, broken wrist bandaged, and Angus Fraser try to take their minds off what is happening in the middle as England slide to defeat in Antigua.

England's slip cordon in Barbados with Alec Stewart perched, as ever,
at forward short leg.

Alec Stewart and Philip DeFreitas indulge in a little soccer practice before catching
their late night flight out of Barbados for Antigua. In the background (left)
Graham Gooch and David Gower – two England captains who were to be confined,
for different reasons, to the role of spectator for the final Test in Antigua.

Casting a critical eye over the
net practice at Kensington Oval,
a Barbadian supporter from
another era.

A manager's work is never done.
When Micky Stewart wanted the strip
in the nets moved, he risked his own
fingers rather than Nasser Hussain's.

Part of England's black attack – Devon Malcolm waits his turn as Chris
Lewis runs in during net practice.

Graham Gooch sums up for
Christopher Martin-Jenkins in
Antigua.

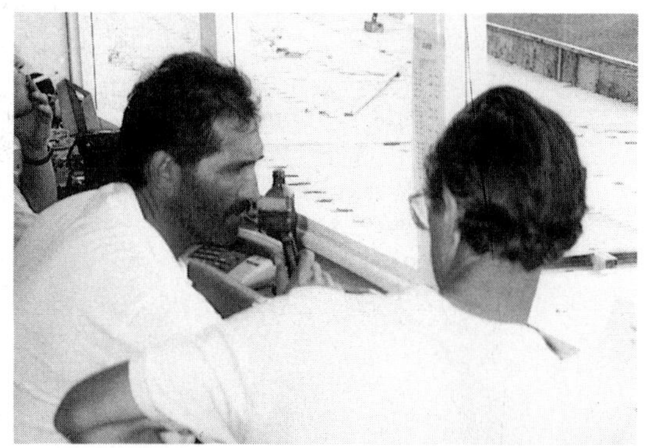

'So I made a nice hard, bouncy
pitch, man,' says Andy Roberts,
fast bowler turned curator at the
Recreation Ground. Chris Lewis
and Devon Malcolm, who would
settle for half his haul of
Test wickets, aren't arguing.

May Field, in one of his more
extravagant outfits, risks life and
skinny limb to celebrate the
West Indies' triumph in Antigua.

Left: Desmond Haynes, hungry for more runs, returns to the crease after lunch during his second century of the series in Antigua.

Above: The West Indies support group of 13th man Keith Arthurton, manager Clive Lloyd and physio Dennis Waight.

Opposite: Back to the fray, Robin Smith and acting captain Allan Lamb try to save England yet again in Antigua.

Cable & W
TETLEY BITTER TETLEY

Allan Lamb bats, Jeffrey Dujon watches.

Viv Richards, the master batsman.

considerable stature and skill to a national rugby team of young coloured players. As a child, farm labourers had called him "klein baas" (little boss) and, as he grew older, he became "meneer" (sir).

'"When I played for that team, the others called me by my first name. That was the first step. When you are in a team, everyone is equal and I realized I had no right to be called sir. That was a turning point in my life."'

If President de Klerk saw the light on his knees in church, du Toit's vision of a better future came on his knees in a rugby scrum. Sport, every bit as much as religion, has a part to play in a person's enlightenment and it should be allowed to do so by progressive politicians on both sides of the fence.

Du Toit's experience in literally rubbing shoulders with players of a different colour left an indelible mark on his psyche long after the physical bruises were gone. He is now able to take a perfectly pragmatic and open-minded view about the looming spectre of black power. Speaking of Mandela, du Toit told Gavin Bell, 'He came across as a person with a lot of dignity, and if he is the type of man who can unite the blacks, I think a lot of whites will follow him. If he looks after my interests, I'll go with him all the way.'

As we fly over the Limpopo and I leave South Africa after three extraordinary weeks, I could not have read a more encouraging statement than that. If an Afrikaans farmer and ex-Springbok forward can talk that way it is possible even some of the crazed and dangerous fascists of the right will listen.

But as if I need to be reminded that old habits die hard and that mistakes will still be made, the captain comes on and tells us we have just crossed into Rhodesia before hastily correcting himself. Nevertheless as the tittering dies down, I can't help feeling that with de Klerk and Mandela in leadership roles and men like du Toit helping to push the scrum in the right direction, victory for sanity, humanity and dear old democracy itself might be nearer than we think. Hope, suddenly there is hope.

WEST INDIES v ENGLAND (1st TEST)

Played at Kingston on February 24,25,26,28 (no play) March 1, 1990. England won by nine wickets. Toss: West Indies. Debuts: N. Hussain and A.J. Stewart.

WEST INDIES

Batsman		1st			2nd
C.G. Greenidge	run out	32	c Hussain b Malcolm		36
D.L. Haynes	c & b Small	36	b Malcolm		14
R.B. Richardson	c Small b Capel	10	lbw b Fraser		25
C.A. Best	c Russell b Capel	4	c Gooch b Small		64
C.L. Hooper	c Capel b Fraser	20	c Larkins b Small		8
I.V.A. Richards*	lbw b Malcolm	21	b Malcolm		37
P.J.L. Dujon†	not out	19	b Malcolm		15
M.D. Marshall	b Fraser	0	not out		8
I.R. Bishop	c Larkins b Fraser	0	c Larkins b Small		3
C.A. Walsh	b Fraser	6	b Small		2
B.P. Patterson	b Fraser	0	run out		2
Extras	(b 9, lb 3, nb 4)	16	(b 14, lb 10, nb 1, w 1)		26
TOTAL		164			240

ENGLAND

Batsman		1st			2nd
G.A. Gooch*	c Dujon b Patterson	18	c Greenidge b Bishop		8
W. Larkins	lbw b Walsh	46	not out		29
A.J. Stewart	c Best b Bishop	13	not out		0
A.J. Lamb	c Hooper b Walsh	132			
R.A. Smith	c Best b Bishop	57			
N. Hussain	c Dujon b Bishop	13			
D.J. Capel	c Richardson b Walsh	5			
R.C. Russell†	c Patterson b Walsh	26			
G.C. Small	lbw b Marshall	4			
A.R.C. Fraser	not out	2			
D.E. Malcolm	lbw b Walsh	0			
Extras	(b 23, lb 12, nb 12, w 1)	48	(lb 1, nb 3)		4
TOTAL		364	(1 wkt)		41

BOWLING

ENGLAND	O	M	R	W	O	M	R	W
Small	15	6	44	1	22	6	58	4
Malcolm	16	4	49	1	21.3	2	77	4
Fraser	20	8	28	5	14	5	31	1
Capel	13	4	31	2	15	1	50	0
WEST INDIES								
Patterson	18	2	74	1	3	1	11	0
Bishop	27	5	72	3	7.3	0	17	1
Marshall	18	3	46	1				
Walsh	27.2	4	68	5	6	0	12	0
Hooper	6	0	28	0				
Richards	9	1	22	0				
Best	4	0	19	0				

Umpires: L.H. Barker and S. Bucknor.

FALL OF WICKETS

	WI	E	WI	E
	1st	1st	2nd	2nd
1st	62	40	26	35
2nd	81	60	69	—
3rd	92	116	87	—
4th	92	288	112	—
5th	124	315	192	—
6th	144	315	222	—
7th	144	325	222	—
8th	150	339	227	—
9th	164	364	237	—
10th	164	364	240	—

En Route to Jamaica

'I know many of you will be interested in the Test score,' said the captain of the British Airways 747 'City of Peterborough' as we caught sight of the first string of Caribbean Islands after the Atlantic crossing. 'And I am happy to say we English have good news to report for a change. West Indies were bowled out in their first innings for 164 and England, in reply, are 80 for 2.'

Scattered all around me in the Club World section were Saturday's papers containing reports from the world's leading cricket experts on the likely outcome of the series that was about to start at Sabina Park, Kingston. England, they said collectively and unequivocally, didn't stand a chance. Most had even gone along with the defensive option favoured by the tour selectors of playing the young Essex batsman, Nasser Hussain, at No. 6 in place of a fifth bowler. Occupy the crease for as long as possible so as to give them less time to score their runs. This seemed to be the best advice anyone had to offer as a means of fending off the black onslaught. The pitch, it was true, had been turned over since the nightmare strip that destroyed David Gower's team, mentally and very nearly physically, in 1986. It was flatter now and considerably slower, too, if the track used for this week's match against an under-strength Jamaica XI was any guide-line.

Against modest bowling Graham Gooch had helped himself to a double ton.

But Courtney Walsh and Patrick Patterson, the Jamaican duo who were to make up 50 per cent of the pace quartet that Vivian Richards would have at his disposal in the Test, had been hidden from view. The Jamaica match was irrelevant. It was the Test that mattered and England had not won a Test against the West Indies since 1974 at Port of Spain, Trinidad. And nothing, according to the experts, was going to change.

It was the only sane and logical conclusion to come to. The West Indies were the champions of world cricket and England were sending one of the most inexperienced sides ever to leave Lords to face them in front of their own fervently partisan crowds on their own sun-baked wickets. It was a job for grizzled, battle-hardened veterans, not a fresh-faced bunch of newcomers who, apart from Gooch and his vice-captain, Allan Lamb, could muster a paltry 65 Test caps between them. Or was it?

As some writers had intimated, the team's inexperience could turn out to be its greatest asset. For the new boys, playing for England was still a thrill. Unlike the world-weary bunch I had just left in South Africa, this team carried no mental scars as far as playing in the Caribbean was concerned. Bedtime stories of what Marshall did to Gatting's nose would hardly have been on Micky Stewart's approved reading list as he tucked them up after a hard day's training at Lilleshall.

And that training itself was another factor in their favour. If this was one of the most inexperienced teams England had sent abroad, it was also, without question, the fittest. Ever since the last week of November Stewart and Gooch had been putting them through their paces, working on physical stamina and strength as well as the technical aspects of batting, bowling and fielding. True, the effects of all that were not immediately promising when Ricardo Elcock, the Barbados-born Middlesex paceman who had been a shock selection for the tour, broke down in the nets before the first match in St Kitts and had to go home. But, as Stewart admitted, Elcock, who had always suffered from a chronic back problem, had been a calculated risk; a not too unreasonable attempt to pair him with the Jamaica-born Devon Malcolm and fight fire with fire. It was rotten luck on Elcock that it didn't work, but when Chris Lewis of Leicestershire was called over from the 'A' team in Zimbabwe to replace him, England still had four black fast bowlers in the party with Philip DeFreitas and Gladstone Small making up a quartet that, hopefully, would be able to dish out a little of the West Indies' own medicine.

This, at any rate, was the theory and these were the straws at which the England faithful were clutching. But, of course, it was all a foregone conclusion. A couple of drawn Tests to prevent another 'blackwash' would be the most one could hope for. Avoiding outright defeat a minor triumph; winning a match? Ha, what a hope!

So what was the BA captain telling us? 164 all out? Greenidge, Haynes, Richardson, Richards . . . all of them for 164 on their own track at Sabina Park? Whatever else was going to happen from now on, England at least had enjoyed one good day!

It had not started out looking so good, apparently. Richards had won the toss and the world's most prolific opening partnership of Gordon Greenidge and Desmond Haynes had progressed in a leisurely fashion to 62–0 when Malcolm, who had so far failed to make them fumble at the crease, fumbled himself down on the fine leg boundary. The misfield induced Greenidge to go for a second run, but the Derbyshire bowler recovered swiftly and threw like an arrow to Jack Russell. Greenidge, run out, 32.

After that, incredibly, it was a procession. David Capel, with 2 for 31 off thirteen overs, accounted for Richie Richardson and Carlisle Best; Small caught and bowled Haynes for a barely believable top score of just 36 and Malcolm proved he could more than throw by trapping Richards himself lbw for 21 as the captain tried to avoid the densely populated off-side field with an injudicious pull.

That left Angus Fraser to mop up the tail which he did to the tune of five for 28 in twenty overs. During the previous summer's Test series against Australia Fraser had demonstrated that the big occasion did not prevent him from hitting the mark with the rhythmical regularity that had earnt him wickets by the bucket load for Middlesex. There had been little need for him to adapt to the new gospel according to Stewart and Gooch, St Line and St Length. He had been worshipping at that altar all his career. Basically it was the only way he knew how to bowl.

Small, once he had overcome a major stutter in his run-up some years before, had also settled down into one of the most accurate medium-pacers in England, but the accuracy achieved by Malcolm and Capel on this first day of the series had come as a major revelation. Everyone had been told to hit a length on or just outside off-stump and all had done it. To England's great discomfort, Terry Alderman had shown the value of bowling at the stumps during the Ashes series. Now Fraser had proved it all over again by clean bowling the last four West Indies batsmen, of whom Walsh, with 6, was the only one to score! Fraser's figures were the best by an England bowler at Sabina Park since John Snow claimed seven wickets in 1968, three years after Gus was born.

When England batted, Gooch was caught down the leg side off Patterson for 18 and Alec Stewart, making his Test début in the critical No. 3 spot, managed only 13 before he fended off a Bishop bouncer to Best at second slip. But Wayne Larkins, with two tour centuries behind him, was looking good again and Lamb stayed with him till sunset. Only 84 runs behind with eight wickets in hand. Was this possible?

Kingston

25 February

It is always a joy to return to Jamaica. Of all the islands I have visited around the globe none offers such a panorama of varied beauty or a people of such distinctive character, talent and humour. How many nations, this century, can claim to have produced a religion, Rastafarianism, and a music, reggae, all of its own? Social problems abound, to be sure, especially in the ghettos of Kingston, but try waking up to the sound of bird-song with the dew of dawn on the grass and sun rising over the Blue Mountains at some country inn and paradise does not seem so far away.

Normally I am billeted in some splendour at one of Richard Russell's villas near the Half Moon Hotel at Montego Bay where Richard is director of tennis, but the less lovely vista of Kingston will suffice this week.

'Goin' to da cricket, man?' asks my taxi driver. Where else?

Sabina Park is almost unrecognizable from the ground I last saw in 1968 when the England captain, Colin Cowdrey scored a century and then, along with his team, got tear-gassed for his trouble when the police misjudged the wind in trying to quell a riot on the other side of the field. Only the old pavilion, where we cowered as temporary guests in the West Indies dressing-room clutching handkerchiefs to our noses, remains. The old wooden press-box, perched so close to the boundary rope behind the wicket that you could almost shake hands with John Snow as he turned to run in, has been replaced with a functional concrete structure set a few yards back while opposite, at the southern end, the large 7,000-seat George Headley Stand, dominates the ground.

The place was filling up fast when I arrived with John Thicknesse of the *Evening Standard*, a survivor of the '68 tear-gas attack, and Jack Bannister, the only pressman, apart from myself and Graham Morris, to have made the long haul from that very different tour in South Africa. Even the press-box here has a different feel to it from those in Bloemfontein and Johannesburg. With no whiff of scandal in the wind – Ian Botham, remember, is not in the team – the tabloid newshounds are absent and ex-cricketers who have discovered they can write or talk as well as play, are here in force.

Mike Selvey of the *Guardian* whose writing is a lot more interesting than his bowling ever was; Tony Lewis of the *Sunday Telegraph*; and Vic Marks, newly appointed cricket correspondent of the *Observer* are supplemented by the likes of Phil Edmonds, who is here for a week to do some television commentary; Tony Greig, flown in from Australia to host Sky Television's inaugural satellite transmissions; Michael Holding, commentating for JBC and the most interesting press-box newcomer of all, David Gower.

Gower's exclusion from the touring party caused well justified outrage among followers of the game in England and, indeed, world-wide, but it is typical of the man that he has elected to come and cover the tour for *The Times*. No matter how badly he was hurt by the loss of the England captaincy for the second time in his career, coupled with the humiliation of total exclusion from the West Indies tour, sulking is not his style.

The Sunday crowd had packed Sabina Park to its 15,000 capacity and the buzz of expectancy that is unique to Test matches – as opposed to one-day hysteria – hung in the air. When I went out to have a look at the wicket before the 10 a.m. start, it looked flat, cracked and shiny. Old hands at studying cricket pitches didn't think the cracks were wide enough to cause trouble and the tendency it had shown to keep low seemed to offer the only real fear. Apart, of course, from Walsh, Bishop, Patterson and Marshall. Had they just been sleeping panthers the previous day, content to breakfast on a couple of English batsmen before pouncing to gobble up the whole meal? We were about to find out.

Larkins, 28 not out overnight, stroked a drive past cover for a couple in Marshall's first over and, apart from an edge past second slip and a hasty duck to avoid a bouncer, looked quite unphased by this demanding return to Test cricket. A cracking off drive for four by Lamb off Bishop signalled a further rise of confidence in the English camp and when Larkins took a single to mid-wicket to reach 35, the Northants opener had reached his highest score in Test cricket.

If Larkins turns out to be a success on this tour, Gooch will be happy to take the credit. He told his fellow selectors that there was no one he would rather open with than the man they call 'Ned' and that endorsement put Larkins on course for a remakable eleventh-hour reprieve from the county scrap-heap. He is thirty-six now and played the last of his six previous Tests eight years ago, having made his début in Melbourne in 1979. Perhaps only Gatting can savage average bowling with such ferocity as Ned, but whacking it around for Northants is not quite the same thing as dealing with the world's best quartet of fast bowlers. But, keeping our fingers crossed, he seems to be taking the transition in his stride.

Marshall, trying a different line, goes round the wicket to him, drops one short and Larkins helps himself to four more past square leg. That proved to be Marshall's last offering of the morning, but when Walsh replaced him at the press-box end, Larkins muscled an off-drive for another boundary. Then Lamb cut Patterson for four and I began to wonder if I was not still aboard that 747, dreaming impossible dreams.

But a warning sounded when I checked the scoreboard and then my watch. The score was 111 for two and the time was 11.11 a.m. If umpire David Shepherd was watching Sky Television back home, his feet would be firmly on the table right now. Spectators all over the country have seen him hopping about when the three ones come up, trying to adhere to the superstition that you must not have any contact with the ground when such a situation arises. To make matters worse we had a drinks break right then and, with the second delivery after the resumption Walsh had Larkins caught at first slip. But it was a no-ball. Shepherd's feet must have been pointing towards the ceiling!

Larkin's luck was shortlived, however. After he had reached 46 in a partnership of 56 with Lamb, a Walsh inswinger rapped low on the pads and he was adjudged lbw. Those studying television replays suggested it was missing leg stump.

But if that partnership had given England just the kind of start they needed to build a solid base for the innings, better was to follow. Robin Smith, who had been the only England batsman to go after Border's bowlers with any consistent success in the summer, had not reproduced that form in the early matches in the Caribbean and looked decidedly hyped-up about the prospect of batting in his first Test abroad. A push to leg got him off the mark for two on his first ball and then a loud appeal rent the air when he padded up to the second.

In between balls, Smith was into callisthenics in a big way; double knee bends, swaying this way and that and jumping about like a cat on hot bricks. This did not go unnoticed by the black cat at second slip and Richards soon called in more close catchers to circle Smith when Patterson, as lively as any of the pace quartet so far, steamed in from the George Headley end. Another wicket now, with England still forty runs short of the lead, could have put a fatal crack in the edifice of the England innings, no matter how assured Lamb was beginning to look. But suddenly Smith thumped Walsh one bounce down to the long leg boundary, did a little dance, and then helped Lamb take England to 132–3 by lunch.

Jeff Dujon, possibly too full of curried goat or some other Jamaican delicacy, dropped Lamb off Ian Bishop soon after lunch and then an over that cost Carl Hooper 13 runs gave England the lead when Lamb swept the spinner to fine leg for four for the second time in two balls. 167–3. Everything now is a bonus.

After the rain that ruined two one-day internationals in Trinidad, the weather is perfect. Clear blue Jamaican skies above and it is not even too hot. After a while I leave the press-box to join Peter Hayter of the *Mail on Sunday* and David Norrie of the

News of the World in some spare seats in the sun. Strangely they are the only vacant seats in the ground which now echoes with the perpetual hum and chatter of anticipation. No more than a ripple of applause greets English boundaries, the cheers are reserved for a ball that beats the bat or a hopeful appeal. South African crowds tended to be more generous in their appreciation of the visitors' efforts, but then every time Gatting was greeted as a hero walking out to bat over there, you had a feeling that it was a political statement. It is pleasant to be free of that.

Then, of course, the irony of the situation strikes me. Having been through all that palava in the great land of apartheid, where your complexion seems to matter more than your cover drive, here I am sitting amidst a crowd that is as overwhelmingly black as the one at the Wanderers was overwhelmingly white, watching two rather pink South Africans bat for England against the West Indies. Try explaining that to the extraterrestrials when they alight from their flying saucers. We human beings have a wonderful way of complicating our little lives.

The gate leading to the old pavilion opens and a familiar face covered in a day's growth of beard joins us. Nick Cook could not have been too far away from selection as one of the spinners for this tour, but he has decided to come anyway as the star turn for a supporters' group. At first acquaintance he does not seem like a man who would wish to complicate his life unduly. His expletive punctuated conversation reminds me of a serjeant major I once knew in the Army and he has some blunt things to say about Viv Richards' captaincy.

'He brought Hooper on at the wrong end,' he said. 'Bloody idiot took the pressure off completely. That George Headley Stand end is where the sight screen doesn't reach high enough, so why put a spinner on there when you have all these giant quicks who are so difficult to see when their arm comes over above the screen? Doesn't make sense.'

By the time Carlisle Best had been brought on with his off-spinners from that same end immediately after tea, Cook had returned to his supporters' group and presumably had plenty more to say on the subject. The batsmen were certainly looking more and more assured.

At 3.30 p.m. Smith reached a well-grafted 50 and ten minutes

later Lamb greeted Patterson and the new ball by banging it away
to mid-wicket for four to reach his first Test century abroad. At
least that was what the scoreboard said at the time. Two minutes
later it corrected itself. Lamb had 99. That sort of thing could
have completely unhinged a younger player. But scoring hundreds against the Windies was nothing new for this feisty little
character. Standing rock solid among the wreckage that had piled
up around him, Lamb had scored hundreds at Leeds, Lords and
Old Trafford during the 1984 series and another at Lords in 1988.
Given that proficiency against the world's most dangerous attack
it was strange that none of his nine Test centuries had been made
outside England. Surely he was not going to be denied again?

The answer came swiftly. After Smith had taken a single and
Lamb had cast a cocky glance at the dithering scoreboard, he
promptly cross-batted Bishop to long leg for a boundary that gave
him 103 unreversable runs. Shortly after he rose on his toes to cut
Patterson for another four and then, stealing a cheeky single to
Richards who dived to make a good stop, walked over to the
West Indies captain to congratulate him as Viv flicked the dust off
his red cap with those long, expressive fingers. Lamby was
enjoying himself.

How very different from 1986. Phil Edmonds, who is a close
friend of Allan's, had been telling me earlier about the scene in
the English dressing-room during the First Test here that year.

'Lamby came in at lunch having faced eighteen balls, ten of
which flew past his throat,' said Philip, grinning impishly. 'He was
white in the face and shaking. He looked like people do when
they have just been in a car crash.'

To be fair to Edmonds, he finds situations like that no less
amusing when he is on the receiving end and proudly showed off
his bruises, like Brian Close had done long ago, some time later
in the tour after he had taken a fearful battering from Marshall &
Co.

Lamb did not have a wonderful time in the West Indies in 1986,
but now it was suddenly a different world, or more pertinently
perhaps, a different pitch.

But maybe it was all starting to get a little too easy. Lamb took
three for a nice shot turned off his legs to mid-wicket, but off
Bishop's next ball Smith got a thick outside edge and Best took a

fine catch at second slip. The Hampshire batsman had made 56, exceeding his already impressive Test average of 49.85 and had shared in a stand of 172, some way short of the record for the fourth wicket in the West Indies – 249 between Andy Sandham and Les Ames here at Sabina Park in 1930 – but, under the circumstances, a partnership of considerable and possibly match-winning significance. At 288–4 England's lead was already well over a hundred and there were wickets in hand.

However, by the end of the day, the remainder had not produced quite as much as one might have hoped. Nasser Hussain, offered a head-high bouncer by Walsh as a welcome to Test cricket, hit three fours before departing for 13, caught by Dujon off Bishop and then, just before five o'clock, Lamb stuck out a tired-looking bat at a ball from Walsh that he might have left alone and Hooper took the catch at second slip. He had batted 364 minutes, faced 209 balls and hit 16 fours in a thoroughly responsible knock of 132 that was custom made to fit England needs.

Jack Russell, the wicket-keeper who was not supposed to be able to bat before he ended up as the third highest run getter of the summer against the Australians, again looked composed as he dabbed his way to 17 not out by the close, but by then David Capel and Gladstone Small had departed in single figures and England, 178 ahead, had two wickets in hand.

For the second consecutive day the West Indies had come out second best. Maybe this wasn't a dream!

26 February

Psychologically England need a 200 lead. Anyone who bought this book because it was £12.99 instead of £13 will understand why. It is the numbers game we play in our numerically dependant world. If the deutschmark is pegged at 3.01 to the pound business on the stock exchange can continue as normal. But how many times have you read about the pound being in crisis if it falls below an artificially set 'psychological' barrier. Let it drop two pfennigs to 2.99 and the City is in chaos. It's not the two pfennigs that matter. It's just that it *looks* bad.

A 199-run first innings lead for England against the West Indies at Sabina Park wouldn't look bad at all, but 200 would be worth a great deal more than one run to the morale. You can't argue about 200. It has that resoundingly emphatic ring about it which gives the opposition absolutely no chance of trying to make out that it is a trifle which can be overcome. A two-hundred deficit and the West Indies will be in deep shit and no argument, man. Not even in Jamaica.

If you have just two wickets left and 22 to make to reach that psychological goal there could hardly be a better character to have at the crease than Jack Russell. There is nothing frivolous about Russell. Like every brush stroke of his artwork, his every move on a cricket field speaks of serious intent. Like the drive he cracked straight past Walsh for four in the first over of the day, or the tip to third man to take a single off the last ball to protect Angus Fraser.

Carefully, studiously, Russell inched England towards that 200 lead and then, just when it had been attained, he tried to pull Walsh, got the ball on the splice and dollied an easy catch. Unkindly, one could say there was nothing else to come. In fact there was Devon Malcolm who looked totally bewildered by the first ball he received and, having got every imaginable piece of leg, pad and ankle in front of all three stumps, became one of the plumbest lbw victims in the history of Test cricket. No matter, England, thanks to Allan Lamb, had made 364 and that precious lead was precisely 200.

It was just after 11 a.m. – or an hour after the start of play – on the third day when Greenidge and Haynes reappeared. This is their 79th Test together as the most prolific opening partnership in history, but seldom can they have started a second innings in such an unfavourable position. As they prepared to face Malcolm and Small, they must have been asking the question on everyone's lips – can England bowl as well a second time?

In Small's first over, one kept low; the third delivery rapped Greenidge on the pads and the fourth was straight driven for four. Honours even. Then Malcolm, eschewing the short stuff, over-did pitching it up with a full toss that went unpunished, but the pace was there and Haynes did not look comfortable.

Small got one to rear up in the next over but, after two encouraging boundaries from Haynes, Malcolm yorked the Middlesex opener with a deadly ball that hit his leg stump. Two balls later it might have been 22–2 when Richie Richardson edged one between Russell and Larkins.

So much for my theory that first slip often stands too close to the wicket-keeper. As the man wearing the gloves must be given the freedom to dive to his right, he is frequently poaching catches right in front of first slip. So why doesn't the fielder stand two paces further away? You never find out the answers to questions like this unless you ask, so I tried it out on Phil Edmonds who has hung around enough close catching positions in his time to know what's what.

'They do get too close, occasionally,' he said. 'But it depends a lot on whose bowling. Take someone like Colin Croft, who basically moved the ball off the seam from off. But he could straighten it, too, which would leave the keeper moving to the leg side and then finding it an awful long way back to take the fine edge right about where a close-in first slip would be.'

Well, in this instance it was more a question of 'Yours!' in that impossible, split millisecond that close catchers have in which to react and the chance was gone. Even so Malcolm had figures of 1–12 off five overs and was rewarded by having Hussain moved into the foreward short leg position midway through his next over. If this was offered as a compliment to his new-found accuracy, it was deserved.

I climb the stairs to the top storey of the press building where a gathering of local media people and staff are enjoying a fabulous view almost over the bowler's arm. It is an educated audience which evidently does not need to be reminded that West Indies have work to do. When Richardson, with a sudden flourish, pulls Fraser away for four, a lady in a Rasta skull cap is not wholly impressed. After the Antiguan with a reputation for aggressive stroke play presents a full blade to Fraser's next delivery to execute a text-book forward defensive, she calls out, 'Dat's de way, Richie! Show dem de face!' Don't talk to this lady about the one-day stuff. She's here for the long haul.

Richardson, however, wasn't. With the score on 69, he tries to pull Fraser into the pavilion and is lbw. Carlisle Best's first ball flies off the top edge and high over point and the West Indies batsmen are beginning to feel an unfamiliar kind of heat – not the heat blazing down out of their Caribbean skies, but the heat of an English attack breathing fire, backed by a captain who looks as if he knows how to work the bellows.

Gooch crowds Best. Three slips, a gully, a silly mid-off and a forward short leg is the field set for Fraser who now has six wickets in the match and is unrecognizable from the bowler who was having problems earlier in the tour. Unlike some other seamers tried during England's difficult summer series of late, Gus is a man who can reproduce for England what he produces week in week out for his county – quality bowling that forces a batsman to play, but gives them little to hit. The big occasion just makes it more interesting for him, that's all.

No one was sure what the big occasion would do for Malcolm before this match but, having trapped the great Viv Richards in the first innings, here he was looking even deadlier this time and, having accounted for Haynes, he soon took care of his partner as Greenidge lifted his head going for the drive and holed out to Hussain at cover. 87–3 and still 113 runs away from making England bat again.

Just before tea Carl Hooper got an edge as he tried to play forward to one that cut away from Small and Gooch palmed the ball up at second slip for Larkins to complete the catch.

A strong cup of tea, boiled to suitable strength by the lady downstairs, was required after all this and I sipped mine in the company of Tony Lewis who had captained Glamorgan and England and P.H. Edmonds who wished he had captained Middlesex and England.

'You've got to hand it to them, the track-suit brigade work well together,' said Lewis. 'Stewart and Gooch understand each other and the fitness training has made all the difference.'

The Welshman allowed himself a little chuckle. 'Mind you, it wouldn't have suited me. Not my style at all. And there have been some famous examples of manager and captain not seeing eye to eye on tour. Look at David Clark and Ray Illingworth, talk about cultures clashing!'

'Yes, Micky's done a good job,' admitted Edmonds. 'I've never been his greatest supporter, but he's attending to business in a big way now and the results are beginning to show.'

Praise from Philip tends to resemble a hurricane warning on a clear blue summer's day. You batten down the hatches and wait for what's coming next.

'But, of course, Micky, Gatt and Peter Lush should all have been fired for what happened in Pakistan. I'm an old colonial boy, remember. In Zambia it was the BBC World Service we listened to. Not Voice of America or Radio Moscow or anything else that pumped out propaganda. We listened to the BBC, like the vast majority of other people in the Third World because it represented fair play. I like Gatt, but I'm sorry, by poking a Pakistani umpire in the chest he dented the image. You can laugh, but it's serious, man, I tell you. You can't lower the standards and expect to get away with it.'

Like John McEnroe and one or two other sporting eccentrics, one need never worry about being bored in the company of Phil Edmonds. If you want an opinion, he's got one, quite apart from what Frances has got to say about it.

By the time I had digested tea and Edmonds, another potent combination of Viv Richards and Carlisle Best were starting to give the West Indies the air of solidity it had lacked in the first innings. Both had something to prove although they were looking at Test cricket through different ends of the telescope. Richards, now thirty-seven, was conscious of his waning powers and was determined to show that he could still master a top-class attack and make it bend to his will. Best, no spring chicken at thirty, had made his Test début against England in 1984, but had been selected only four times since then despite being recognized as one of the most talented batsmen in the Caribbean. There were not going to be many more opportunities for him to demonstrate that he could transfer that talent to the big arena, but the longer the evening session wore on, the more likely it seemed that he would seize this one. Driving and cutting with Bajan flair, Best moved towards his half-century even though this wicket was far from being what he was used to batting on at the Kensington Oval. At one stage Russell stood up to Capel which said less about the Northants all-rounder's pace than it did about the sluggishness of the track.

If English hopes rose at the sight of Best suddenly hobbling up to the non-striker's end to complete a run, they were soon dispelled. What had looked like a badly pulled muscle was in fact Best's kneecap slipping out. Nasty as that may sound, it does not apparently cause any great inconvenience once it is nudged back into place and Best was soon racing up and down the pitch again as if nothing had happened.

The ball was also coming off Richards' bat with the ominous ring of a man in form and the crowd, shell-shocked by the events of the first two days, were beginning to enjoy themselves. On the little hill by the press-box, where the Red Stripe was flowing and the voices rising, an independent soul had positioned himself comfortably against the wire fencing. His racing bicycle was leaning against the fence; his feet were propped up on the bicycle and his head was shielded from the blazing sun by a large black umbrella.

White teeth flashed at me from underneath the umbrella. 'We not goin' to bat stupid like de first time,' he announced. 'These two goin' to bat for two days and set you 350. Richards, him get century.'

The umbrella gave a little twirl and the smile receded underneath it. Such is the backlog of confidence on which West Indies cricket now rides that defeat is not accepted as a rational possibility. Why should it? Pakistan beat them out here once in 1976–7 and once in 1987–8 as did Australia in 1977–8 but otherwise you have to go back to England's victory at Port of Spain in 1974 to find another occasion when this mighty cricketing machine was dismantled in one of its own workshops. If they mess it up in the first innings, then they put it right in the second. What else?

Well, Devon Malcolm was what else. As the Red Stripe began to have its effect, the Jamaican who bowls for Derbyshire started to take a bit of stick from a very small section of the crowd just down to our right. There were no more than about twenty of them and after a few jocular jibes, it began to get a little nasty. 'Hey, you Malcolm, which team you play for, man? You white man now, Malcolm!'

The chanting got shriller and, after turning to offer a little bow earlier on when he had been sent to field in front of them at long leg, Malcolm wisely ignored his tormentors and decided to offer a different kind of answer. He clean bowled Viv Richards. The effect was exactly as if a loudspeaker plug had been pulled out of its socket. One had to lean out of the press-box and make sure that someone had not come along with a giant sledge-hammer and poleaxed the lot of them. The silence was total.

Richards turned to survey his leg stump which was leaning at the sort of angle parking metres adopt when they have been hit by a car. Malcolm's yorker had hit it near the base after it had rocketed under the bat that Richards had been swinging through an arc which usually results in a six over mid-on. The expression on Viv's face as he inspected the damage suggested that this outcome had not featured in his list of possibilities when he selected the shot from his impressive repertoire. Having got rid of both openers, England's new boy had now got rid of the captain. Malcolm was becoming a menace.

He was also becoming a very good story and there was a frenzied air in the press-box as new leads were typed into Tandy's for immediate transmission to London in time for the last edition of the night. Even amidst all this high-tech communication it was comforting to note, however, that Ian Todd, cricket correspondent of Rupert Murdoch's great money-spinner, the *Sun*, was not only still phoning over his copy to an actual human being in Wapping, but was using a clothes peg to stop his notes flying away. Who needs a computer when you have a clothes peg?

Richards, who had hit five fours in his 37, had added 79 with Best. That left Best nine short of making England bat again, but Jeffrey Dujon, having survived a loud appeal for lbw from Malcolm off his first ball, soon took care of that by unleashing one of those beautiful cover drives that makes him the batting prince among wicket keepers.

Gooch, however, was smelling blood and, ignoring the fact that Best was moving into the sixties, brought up Hussain to pressure him in a catching position in front of the bat when Small was bowling. Best's initial reply was a drive straight through Hussain for four, but the ploy may have had the desired effect because two overs later, with his score on a Test best of 64, the man with the demanding name touched an outswinger from the ever-persistent Small to Gooch at second slip. Best's fine innings had lasted 136 balls and had included nine fours. England were very relieved to see the back of him.

Ditto Dujon who can be very dangerous once he gets going. But the West Indies are obviously short of practice against fast bowlers who bowl straight and, with the score on a Shepherd-hopping 222, Malcolm relieved him of his middle stump. Devon Malcolm, the wild man who could be relied on to bowl up a storm in the general, but not too specific, area of the pitch; Malcolm, the man who could make them leap and bounce for edges and snicks; this same Malcolm who had been the selection committee's great hold-your-breath-and-pray choice for the tour, was now in the process of clean bowling some of the West Indies leading batsmen on a none-too-fast track at Sabina Park. With sheer pace.

In the first innings, it had been Richards lbw and now in the second Haynes, Richards and Dujon had all been clean bowled while only Greenidge's ill-judged drive off a half-volley could have been considered fortuitous amongst his match haul of five crucial wickets. Malcolm was not only fast, but he was accurate. What a revelation!

Before the wind blew more clouds across the ground and a sniff of rain in the air, Ian Bishop gave the deserving Small another wicket, his third to date, by getting a thin edge to Larkins at first slip. That left West Indies on 229–8, just thirty runs ahead with only Malcolm Marshall, Courtney Walsh and Patrick Patterson left to make England's task anything more than a formality. I looked down to try and find my friend under the umbrella. But he was already on his bike.

Kingston

28 February

A day of total frustration. Water had seeped in under the cover at the northern end of the ground leaving a soggy quagmire six feet square right behind the stumps, precisely in line with the bowler's run up. There were also a couple of small areas in the outfield that still had surface water on them, too, but it was the patch near the wicket that created the real problem.

The umpires set a deadline of four o'clock for their final inspection and I spent much of the afternoon wandering around the ground with David Gower, chatting occasionally to Graham Gooch and Allan Lamb who came out of the dressing-room to do some stretching exercises near the bone-hard pitch. Gooch then sat, in a typically morose pose, on the roller which gave Graham Morris and the other photographers just the shot they needed to wire back to London to fill up some of the space that should have been occupied by headlines of an England triumph.

I had never met Gooch before. Despite what I may have said about him in the context of South Africa in the earlier chapters, I was determined to come here and take him at face value. With Gower to introduce us, I found him perfectly pleasant and rather more forthcoming than I had been led to expect. But then Alan Lee of *The Times* and others who have known him over the years

109

tell me that he has blossomed in recent months and actually started to look as if he was enjoying life during the Nehru Cup in India in October. Certainly he has little cause for unhappiness so far and is obviously champing at the bit to get on with this game.

'I'll play for half an hour if that's all the time they'll give us,' he said between sit ups. 'If we could just get them all out today it would be a bonus because you never know what this weather will do.'

I asked Gower what he thought of the state of the run-up at the press-box end.

'Not good,' he replied. 'But I've played on worse than this. I'd give my bowlers the option of ploughing through it or bowling round the wicket. But I'll be surprised if the umpires consider it fit.'

By bowling around the wicket, the worst of the soggy patches could have been avoided but all that became immaterial when play was duly called off for the day at 4 p.m. Surely the gods were not going to be so cruel as to steal the victory for which England were so deservedly and tantalizingly poised? One more downpour and it could be all over.

Although the poignancy of this situation was exceptional, cricketers are used to rained-out days and while the youngsters may fret at the lack of action, days such as this offer the older generation a chance to reminisce and there has been no lack of opportunity for that here this week. Many of the participants of the Test series of 1950, who were invited here for a fortieth anniversary dinner to celebrate the first West Indies victory in England, have stayed on. Faces that loomed at me out of the papers at the school breakfast table, larger than life to an eleven year old but greying now, faces belonging to Sir Len Hutton, Everton Weekes, Alec Bedser, Gilbert Parkhouse, and a bewhiskered Godfrey Evans. They have all been spending a suitable amount of time at the Pegasus Hotel bar by the swimming-pool, swopping tales with some other welcome guests like Reg Hayter, my mentor in journalism who covered the 1953–4 tour out here for the Press Association before starting the freelance agency that he still runs at the age of seventy-six.

Before heading out to check the state of the ground, I had found Robin Marlar of *The Sunday Times,* himself an off-spin bowler for Sussex and Cambridge University in his youth, chatting to Bedser in the lobby. Alec told me he had looked in on the Australian Open at Flinders Park when he had been in Melbourne in January and commented on the heat of the court that was making life uncomfortable for the tennis players. And speaking of Australian summers set him off on a train of thought . . .

'Mind you, it can't have been much worse than the heat we had to contend with in Adelaide in 1947,' said Bedser referring to the Test played during Wally Hammond's tour. 'Hot? You wouldn't have believed it. It must have been 130°F out there in the middle. Bill Edrich was so knackered at the end of the day he couldn't run in to bowl. Just took two steps and let go of the thing. Doug Wright was throwing up – or trying to. He'd only had orange juice and had nothing in his stomach. He needed more fuel than that with his run up. Longer than mine, it was.'

Bedser himself was evidently as strong as an ox. He'd walk to the ground in the morning, by which time the heavy flannel clothes they wore in those immediate post-war years were soaked through. Then he'd bowl all day, or the better part of it, thumping in off that economical but strangely rhythmical run – a run that seemed almost too beautifully co-ordinated for a man with such big ears, hands and feet – and hit the mark, line and length, ball after ball.

'Later, when he was captain, Len Hutton wanted me to bowl short on occasion. I think he wanted to give them back some of their own medicine. But I said, "Why? If I stop them scoring, they'll get themselves out." And that's what I set out to do. Before each ball, I'd say, "You're not going to score off this one, yer old bugger."'

And there were plenty they couldn't score off. What a one-day bowler he would have been!

Young Gus Fraser is a bowler after Bedser's own heart. Reg Hayter is probably prouder of the Middlesex youngster right now because, as Reg has been quick to point out, Fraser started his serious cricket at Stanmore, a cricket club that used to benefit from a few Hayter outswingers in days gone by. But Bedser has been favourably impressed by Fraser, with a couple of reservations.

'He's got to learn to swing it,' said Bedser. 'Once that high seam on the ball is reduced next year, he'll need another weapon. It's all a question of finding the right way to hold the ball; a way that is comfortable for him and fits in with his natural rhythm. And he should relax the wrist, too. Too many bowlers today bowl with a stiff wrist. It's restricting.'

Too few of the younger players are ready to listen to advice from those who have achieved great things in other eras. But I have a feeling Fraser is too intelligent to pass up the opportunity of benefiting from the advice of the master. With 236 Test wickets to his name at a time when the opportunities for playing Test cricket were so much rarer than they are today, Alec Bedser will remain as one of the great medium-pace bowlers of all time.

When play was finally called off, David Gower and I went looking for a tennis court, but the team had been too quick for us to grab one of the Pegasus courts. Graham Gooch, reckoned to be the best tennis player in the side, was playing singles against Gladstone Small on one court while Robin Smith and Alec Stewart were playing a batters against bowlers match against Gus Fraser and Philip DeFreitas on the other.

So we picked up a racket for David at the Liguanea Club across the street and, finding all the courts full there as well, headed up to the Wyndham where I am staying, along with Tony Cozier and many of the broadcasting media. The general manager, Bill Ezell, used to play a good game of tennis himself when he was in charge of the Wyndham at Rose Hall near Montego Bay, but I am not sure he has much time now. Life in Kingston moves at a faster pace.

The rain was almost too fast for us as well. David plays tennis right handed and moves like a gazelle, but I was just about to make a serious examination of his backhand when the heavens opened up once more and we had to repair to the bar. The tennis can wait but not the cricket. Let us pray it is not raining as heavily over at Sabina Park.

1 March

Graham Gooch pulled the curtains at five past six and peeked out at the sun rising over the Blue Mountains. Micky Stewart had been up at 5.30 a.m., but hadn't dared look out for half an hour. They needn't have worried. The rains had gone; the ground was fit and at just six minutes past midday, Wayne Larkins pushed a ball on to the off side and England had beaten the West Indies for the first time in sixteen years. Not the least pleasing feature of this historic moment was the way Viv Richards made a point of running after Larkins to offer congratulations and shake him by the hand. I hope the spirit which exists between the two camps can survive the next six weeks.

The only minor disappointment was the fact that Gooch was not still at the wicket to savour the moment right there in the middle. Not only would it have given England their first ten-wicket win since Ian Botham destroyed India in Bombay in 1980, but it would have offered the Essex captain that extra little bit of glory he deserved. There is no question that he must take an enormous amount of the credit for this stunning victory. While undergoing a personal transformation of quite extraordinary proportions, he has, with Stewart's help, also managed to transform English cricket.

Back in August, Jack Bannister and anyone else who knows anything about the proper odds on sporting contests would have given you a very attractive bet against England beating West Indies by nine wickets at Sabina Park. It was, frankly, unthinkable. This was not, after all, a victory stolen on a dark evening by the odd run. This was slaughter at High Noon, a totally commanding finishing flourish to four days of cricket that had seen England dominate *every day*. How big does a sporting upset have to be?

Apart from Gooch's dismissal, the morning went precisely to plan. Gladstone Small, leaping high into the air, took Walsh's off-stump after only four had been added to the overnight total of 229–8 and then Marshall looked somewhat uninterested at the sight of poor Patterson stranded in mid-pitch after he had called for a run. England's target was 41.

Larkins, who never likes hanging about, lofted a two through the covers in the first over but, to their credit, the West Indies bowlers kept it tight and Gooch had been at the crease for one hour and thirteen minutes when he turned Bishop to backward

short leg and saw Greenidge pull off a brilliant diving catch. But
Alec Stewart got his head down and let Larkins do the rest. Just
six runs more and it was all over.

Before the champagne started to drench everything and
everyone in the English dressing-room, a few of the heroes
appeared on the little balcony outside to try to put their emotions
into words. It wasn't easy. Micky Stewart, looking slightly
stunned, attempted to explain it all and then added, 'Things have
gone almost too well.'

Gooch refused to be drawn on whether this was the greatest
moment of his career ('One of them, certainly') and could not
resist taking a swipe at the British Press for having written off the
team before the start. He was also 'more than a little disappointed not to have been out there at the end.' That's Gooch
for you, the consummate, down-to-earth professional who must
look on in wonderment when his opposite number goes into one
of those Viv Richards victory jigs.

Gooch did, of course, lavish praise on his team. 'They all
played magnificently and I just hope we can go on from here,' he
said. 'With an inexperienced side you could go up or you could go
down. It's difficult to know how they will react.'

Not far away, Richards was managing to look as lordly as ever
in defeat. The pride of the man manifests itself with every
gesture, every pose, every utterance. Some call it arrogance and
there is some of that, too, but the true character of a champion is
only properly tested in defeat and Viv was coming through the
experience with his dignity intact.

'Although we played hard, we probably needed something like
this to wake us up,' he told a group of Jamaican reporters who
crowded round him. 'What is important, however, is that they
beat us in our own back yard and we have taken our beating. We
are not complaining about slow overrates, bouncers or what
have you. All that we are going to do is come back and win the
series.'

With that he turned the great aquiline profile to the world and
walked back into the West Indies dressing-room. The swagger did
not seem in any way diminished.

*

It is all taking a little while to sink in. The margin of the victory, as much as the victory itself, is what is so staggering. Basically England stuffed them out of sight. It is this, I think, that is making people pause before they write it off as a fluke. Obviously it is very difficult for writers and commentators who have been feeding off a steady diet of West Indies dominance for the better part of two decades to believe that anything fundamental is about to change.

But I am not so sure. If you forget the halcyon years and analyse what has been happening to this West Indies side in the last couple of series they have played, the image of invincibility is not quite as watertight as one might imagine. The batting, in particular, has sprung more than the occasional leak, never more so than in England in 1988.

Looking back on that tour, one finds that the three Texaco one-day internationals were all lost to an England team captained by Mike Gatting and again the margins were wide – six wickets; 47 runs and seven wickets. England, at the time, were one-day specialists and, in any case, I am not one to suggest that limited overs cricket is a fair yardstick for judging a Test side's true ability. Nevertheless World Champions should not lose three consecutive matches quite so easily.

After that, of course, Peter May did West Indies the favour of sacking Gatting and destroying the spirit in the England team. Even so, a look at the West Indies batting averages for that Test series makes alarming reading. Gus Logie, with 364 runs, an average of 72.80 and a top score of 95 not out, was easily their most successful batsman. And it was no use looking to the top order for the second leading run scorer. Wicket-keeper Jeff Dujon comfortably took that place with 305 runs at an average of 50.83 with 67 as his top score.

Gordon Greenidge was the only West Indies century maker in the five Tests, but his aggregate of 282 runs was far below what a top batsman would hope to score, even on English wickets. Desmond Haynes (235) and Viv Richards (223) were even more disappointing. Given this obvious batting frailty, it was amazing that Malcolm Marshall and his fast-bowling cohorts were able to dominate the series in the way that they did.

And now look what happened here in Kingston with no Logie to pick up the pieces. Dujon, whose stands with the little batsman – currently injured – propped up innings after innings in 1988, was left high and dry on the first day with 19 not out and was bowled by Malcolm, producing pace the West Indies are quite unused to facing, for 15 in the second knock. And the main batsmen? Incredibly only Carlisle Best, who has been struggling to convince the selectors for years that he is good enough, passed 50. The next highest score in either innings was Richards' 37 in the second.

In the context of what had gone on in England, this does not look like a one-off aberration to me. It suggests that some of the older stars are beginning to find the concentration required to bat for long periods at Test level very difficult to maintain. Even allowing for the presence of young lions like Richie Richardson – another disappointment in this particular match – and Ian Bishop who will form the backbone of the team for many years to come, the side seems to be dominated by great players whose appetite for the fight is no longer as voracious as it used to be. Who can blame them? This was Richards' 108th Test match. Greenidge is also nearing the most difficult century a cricketer can attain with 97 and Haynes is not too far away on 86. Nobody can go on forever.

Richards, for his own part, recognizes this and, in answering questions as to why he did not bat higher than six, said, 'Viv Richards is not what he used to be. We have some good young players and they deserve to play a leading role. I see my role now as trying to put things together if anything goes wrong.'

Those young players may need to be blooded at a faster rate than was thought appropriate a week ago. No one is suggesting wholesale changes, of course, but there is no question that the aura of invincibility has been broken and, providing Gooch's team believe that, all things are possible from now on. If the rain that everyone is predicting for Guyana prevents a result in Georgetown, West Indies will be feeling the heat when they go into the Third Test in Trinidad still 1–0 down.

I think England have a serious chance of winning this series now and, more importantly, so does Alec Bedser. I found him standing like a pillar of wisdom in the lobby of the hotel yesterday afternoon, waiting to be picked up for a game of golf.

'If England can continue to bowl on or just outside off-stump they could win the series,' said Bedser. 'They've got to keep their enthusiasm up, too, mind you which is not easy over two months of hard slog. The batsmen worry me a bit, too, but if everyone stays positive they've definitely got a chance.'

With extra hours to spare yesterday, I had seized the opportunity offered by a Jamaican friend called Tobi Phillips to get out of Kingston and visit Johnny Black at his house in the mountains. Johnny used to be a business man in Kingston, driving around in a company car with a coat and tie. Now his greying hair hangs in dreadlocks and he has become a fine photographer – a profession that allows him to lead his life according to his own rhythms.

He has been covering the Test at Sabina Park which is only thirty-five minutes drive away – if you know the way and can negotiate a few hairpin bends. It has been raining a lot recently and Johnny's world is encased in a glistening shroud of green vegetation, so thick and lush and spotted with bursts of colour that the concrete you have left behind no longer seems to belong to the same planet.

He lives alone with his dogs and his dark room, visited frequently by a girl-friend for company. His house is hidden up a path that lies alongside the Langley coffee plantation which was built by a Scotsman at the turn of the century and which still produces some of the world's best coffee beans. Johnny walks across the estate each morning to the ten-feet-high waterfall that drops down over the rocks. There is a little ledge where he leaves his soap and that, every morning, is where Johnny Black takes his shower. One thinks of Jamaicans shivering in the ghettos of New York and Philadelphia and wonders how they can ever leave this island.

A peace of mind and soul is required, I suppose, to live this kind of life and I envy those who can manage it.

After telling me something I did not know – that Sabina Park is named after a beautiful runaway slave – Johnny talked a little about the cricket and dismissed some of the rumours that had been flying around when water had got underneath the covers.

'No, I know those groundkeepers pretty well and they didn't

tip no water off the covers on to the run-ups,' Johnny laughed. 'But I tell you, they weren't hurryin' too much to mop it up, either! But England deserve their win. That West Indies team need to start payin' attention to business now.'

Before we left, Johnny led Tobi and I out on to the mountain road to a point he called 'Lover's Leap' where you could gaze down into the valley below and up into the Blue Mountain peaks where a giant waterfall, the source of Johnny's morning shower, cascaded down the sheer face of rock, a frothy white scar set against the tumbling riot of green.

'You ever seen anything so beautiful?' Johnny asked.

'No, I don't think so,' I replied before we descended out of this man's heaven into the other world, the world the tourists see.

3 March

After the two rain-ruined one-day internationals in Trinidad, all was sunlight and sensation in this third encounter as a finish that 50-over cricket is contrived to give West Indies victory by three wickets with Ian Bishop needing to score three runs off the very last ball from Angus Fraser. With a near hysterical crowd holding its breath for the instant it took Fraser to run in and bowl a slightly over-pitched delivery on off-stump, Bishop swung the bat and connected with a do-or-die drive to the extra cover boundary.

Bedlam ensued and one had to feel happy for the Jamaican crowd who had suffered so unexpectedly through so much disappointment during the Test. Although the one-day series will become a mere footnote to this tour as it fades from the memory bank (apart from the World Cup who can remember who won what in this form of cricket?), it did serve as a salutory reminder to this England team of just how quickly the West Indies can rebound from apparent humiliation.

England had brought in Philip DeFreitas for Nasser Hussain and spinner Eddie Hemmings for Devon Malcolm while the West Indies were forced into two changes through injury. Gordon Greenidge, who had strained his back, was replaced by Keith

Arthurton with Carlisle Best moving up to open and Ezra Moseley was preferred to Patrick Patterson on the basis of superior batting and greater control with the ball.

Graham Gooch won the toss which turned out to be a better decision for the team than it did for him personally. With only three to his name out of a total of 20, the England captain was bowled by Bishop. Unhappily, the 239 he had plundered off Jamaica seemed to have used up his run quota at Sabina Park.

Larkins, however, was again in good form, hitting seven fours in an innings of 33 before snicking an inside edge on to his stumps facing Walsh. Robin Smith and Allan Lamb kept the score ticking at more than four an over until the Hampshire batsman hooked Carl Hooper's off spinner down Malcolm Marshall's throat at long leg to end a good knock of 43. Alec Stewart, however, was out first ball, playing forward to Hooper and being caught behind by Jeffrey Dujon. If it touched, it was the thinnest of edges.

With David Capel in support, Lamb then took charge and was nearing his 50 when he lost his partner who gave Dujon another catch, this time off Bishop after scoring a valuable 28. Lamb was not at his most flamboyant. When his half-century came up in 84 balls it had contained only two fours and a six, thumped over long on off a full toss from Viv Richards who, initially, had been hard to get away. By the time Bishop bowled him, Lamb's 66 had guided England towards a final total of 214–8 – maybe a dozen runs short of par on a slow pitch that never offered stroke-makers much encouragement.

It started to look considerably better by the time Gladstone Small bowled Best round his legs for four and DeFreitas, getting one to rise just short of a length, forced Desmond Haynes into giving Smith an easy catch at backward point for 8.

With a Test failure behind him, it was now Richie Richardson's chance to show the Jamaican crowd that he was a worthy Antiguan heir to Viv Richards. But at first they were far from convinced. Realizing that it was up to him to repair the innings, Richardson started slowly and with Carl Hooper also showing little inclination to get after the England bowlers, West Indies fell behind on the run rate. When Capel kept Hooper tied down with a maiden over, sections of the crowd started to grow restless and

the batsmen were told in no uncertain terms at just what pace
they were expected to proceed.

But Richardson knew exactly what he was doing. Having
settled in, he was just starting to press the accelerator when
Hooper took the signal to heart and advanced down the pitch,
missed Eddie Hemmings' off break and was bowled for 20.

Viv Richards announced his presence by hooking Small for six
with imperious ease over square leg and, as the tempo picked up,
Richardson offered his one chance, smashing Small straight at
Hemmings who couldn't hold on. Chris Lewis came on while
Eddie retired for repairs but he was soon back, wheeling away
with that economical off-spin that was soon restricting two of the
world's most fluent stroke-makers to little more than two an over.
But Richards and Richardson were enjoying each other's company as two Antiguans might and in one over from Capel, Richie
helped himself to 16 runs – a six that Stewart, reaching up, could
only help over the square leg boundary; a drive for four that
Small might have made a better effort at stopping and then a
glorious drive over long on for his second six in three balls. The
crowd were now singing a very different tune. For the first time
West Indies had edged ahead of England, having scored 158–3
at the end of that thirty-eighth over as compared to England's
156–4.

But Hemmings immediately cut short any premature West
Indies optimism by having Richards caught low down at point by
Small for 25 and having Keith Arthurton caught behind by
Russell with the very next ball. Hemmings, who is going to have
to struggle for every scrap of recognition on this tour, had
suddenly taken care of Nos. 4, 5 & 6 in the West Indies batting
order. At 158–5, the balance had tipped back the tourists' way.

But in Jeffrey Dujon, battle-hardened and elegant as ever,
Richardson found the perfect partner and between them they
added 46 priceless runs, cutting and driving and scampering the
kind of singles that win one-day matches. Richardson's brilliantly-
worked hundred came up in the forty-seventh over and
immediately afterwards Russell dropped him off DeFreitas' last
ball of the over.

A skied two into the covers by the Antiguan took the score to
204–5 and the match was on the brink of its final drama. Fifteen

runs off the last ten balls, then a classic straight drive for four by Dujon, made it 11 off 9. The next ball saw the end of the Jamaican keeper, caught by Smith off Small for a vital 27 off 37 balls.

Inch by inch the West Indies crept nearer, 7 runs off 7 balls, then 5 off 5. Fraser swung it England's way by having Ezra Moseley caught by Gooch in the covers off the first delivery he faced. 5 off 4. Ian Bishop missed down the leg side; 5 off 3; then took two to backward point and failed to make contact with one outside his off-stump.

And so, for that instant, the noise died away and everyone held their breath. One ball and no one wanted to be in either Fraser or Bishop's shoes. One of them was going to lose the match for their team and who would wish that on an honest cricketer? Fraser, desperate not to drop one short, erred the other way and the powerfully built young man from Trinidad let the full flow of his bat despatch the ball first bounce into the charging crowd.

It was, above everything, a match for the spectators; great for the local fans and another boost for Sky Television back in England whose ball-by-ball coverage had been given the sort of start executive director Dave Hill could barely have dared dream about.

But for the players, the match will be consigned to the dustbin of all those other one days they have sweated through, especially in Australia where limited-overs cricket is milked for every dollar it can raise. Exciting though it may be, a last ball win is nothing more than a lottery and proper cricket is carefully constructed to be a great deal more than that.

So back to the serious stuff and on to Guyana. Even though I won't be there, I hope it doesn't rain.

Trinidad

22 March

Having negotiated the famous upside down Trinidad Hilton – all the rooms are on floors below lobby level – I find myself back amongst a team that has played frustratingly little cricket in the last two and a half weeks. It not only rained in Guyana, it rained so long and so hard that the Second Test was abandoned and a one day played in its place.

That, apparently, was not a universally popular decision because everything dried out in time for play to have begun on what would have been early afternoon on the fourth day allotted to the Test. There were those who thought that a day and a half's proper cricket would have been better than a one-day knockabout that did not seem to inspire much enthusiasm among the participants.

The result of this unscheduled one day was almost precisely the same as the official match played at Bourda eight days before. On March 7 England batted first, scored 188 and lost by six wickets. On March 15, England batted first, scored 166 and lost by seven wickets. In both cases West Indies won the toss.

At least it gave the cricket-starved audiences in Georgetown something to cheer and enabled England to arrive here still 1–0 up. But from a playing point of view it has hardly helped because boredom and lack of match play are insiduous poisons that can sap a touring team's moral.

There did not, however, appear to be anything wrong with England's moral when they fought back from the most unlikely position to win the four-day match against the President's XI at Guaracara Park on their arrival here in Trinidad. After being sent in, England could not capitalize on the absence of Patrick Patterson with a severe migrain after just six overs and Winston Benjamin with a back strain after 15 and were struggling at 225–7 at the end of the first day. Only Gooch with a dour 66 and Bailey, following up a 42 at Bourda with a good looking 52, made any real headway against the Presidents' attack.

All out for 252, England restricted their opponents to 294 after Brian Lara, Trinidad's twenty-year-old left-handed captain had underlined his claims for a Test place with a beautifully struck 134 in 180 balls with a six and 19 fours. It was only his fourth first-class century, but the experts are convinced England were merely being given an early glimpse of a future Test star.

Apart from Gooch, who again passed 60, England's top order were disappointing for the second time in the match on a pitch that started to keep low and they ended a rain-interrupted third day at 135–6, just 93 ahead.

However Robin Smith had been not out overnight and it was he, staunchly supported by Philip DeFreitas in a stand worth 53 and Chris Lewis who hung on for eighty-two minutes while making six, who turned the match around. Agonizingly, Smith was left on 99 not out, despite having added another 20 runs with Devon Malcolm at the other end. When the Derbyshire paceman did have to measure up to an entire over from Patterson, he got as far as the fifth ball, had a heave and was bowled. Normally that type of stroke might have been considered irresponsible, but as someone remarked, rather unkindly, 'He might as well take a whack at it because he's as likely to connect that way as he is giving it the defensive prod.'

Poor Malcolm. He probably felt worse about it than Smith.

At any rate, England, having set the President's XI 236 to win, quickly got in among the wickets and snatched a memorable victory by bowling them out for 123 with DeFreitas taking 4–54 and Malcolm 3–29.

From what I have heard, two spin bowlers had particular reason to look back on Guaracara Park with frustration bordering on despair. One was Robert Haynes, the young leg-spinning all-rounder from Jamaica, who took 6–90 in England's second innings and was promptly excluded from the West Indies Test squad for the Third Test that begins here in Port of Spain tomorrow. The other was Keith Medlycott, the tourist's un-capped left-arm spinner who was deprived of a last opportunity to stake a Test claim by not even being selected for the match against the President's XI.

From the West Indies point of view Haynes' omission seemed to make very little sense. He had not only taken three wickets playing for Jamaica in England's first innings at Sabina Park earlier in the tour, but had struck an impressive 98 – the top score in Jamaica's first innings total of 311. So quite apart from his credentials as a legitimate all-rounder, he had proved that his rare style of bowling posed a definite threat to the English batsmen who rarely get an opportunity to test their skills against quality leg spin. Apparently Haynes was told of his omission from the squad just as he was about to join Gus Logie at the wicket during the home team's second innings at Guaracara Park. His reaction was somewhat understandable for a very disappointed young cricketer. With his startled captain looking on from the other end, Haynes launched into a furious bloody-minded assault on the English attack, striking five fours in an innings of 30 that lasted just twenty minutes. He should be forgiven for that and quickly offered the opportunity his talent deserves.

The decision not to give Medlycott a game was cruel and reflects poorly on the England selection committee for this tour which comprises Graham Gooch, Allan Lamb and Micky Stewart. His hopes had been raised in Georgetown when he was encouraged to spend hours wheeling away on a tennis court at willing batting colleagues so that his spinning finger could get the work it needed. If there was to be one Test on this tour where his type of attacking spin bowling could pay dividends, it was here at the Queen's Park Oval where the pitch traditionally offers assistance to any bowler with the ability to make the ball turn.

How many times has it been said that spin bowling is a dying art? And how many times have Test selection committees, often abetted at the county and State level, helped to stick another knife into those bodies that are still twitching, by denying them the chance to prove otherwise? Will they never understand that, in doing so, they are also helping to kill cricket? Of course crowds love to see great fast bowlers in action and no one is denying that fast bowlers will continue to win the majority of matches. But that does not mean that they have to be played to the total exclusion of a player who can add variety, skill, interest and, in the case of an Abdul Qadir, real magic to the game. And even among all those assets, I have still not mentioned the most important one when one considers what is driving people away from Test and regular first-class matches – the tempo at which proper cricket is played. Contradictory as it may sound, by bowling slow, spinners also bowl quickly. Only they seem capable of doing something about the over rate which dropped to the absurd level of twelve overs an hour – and sometimes less – at Sabina Park.

I know the plan was for England to come here and match fire with fire on what were expected to be lightning-fast Caribbean wickets and that, even on a surprisingly dead track in Kingston, four quicks won the match for Gooch's team. I understand, too, that Gooch himself was in favour of bringing only one spinner, but was out voted by Ted Dexter's selection panel. But even though Hemmings and Medlycott showed what they could do by almost saving England from defeat against the Windward Islands with eight wickets between them in the second innings, neither is going to be given a chance on the one pitch here in Port of Spain that traditionally justifies the inclusion of their type of bowler. Hemmings and Medlycott are going to have to be very good team men to keep smiling for the rest of this tour.

23 March

The Third Test was nine minutes old and in its third over when Gordon Greenidge turned a fast delivery from Devon Malcolm neatly into Alex Stewart's hands at foreward short leg. It was still less than half an hour old when Desmond Haynes, captaining the West Indies for the first time, drove wildly at a ball outside his

WEST INDIES v ENGLAND (3rd TEST)

Played at Port of Spain on March 23,24,25,27,28 1990. Match drawn. Toss: England. Debut: E.A. Moseley.

WEST INDIES

C.G. Greenidge	c Stewart b Malcolm	5	lbw b Fraser	42
D.I. Haynes*	c Lamb b Small	0	c Lamb b Malcolm	45
R.B. Richardson	c Russell b Fraser	8	c Gooch b Small	34
C.A. Best	c Lamb b Fraser	10	lbw b Malcolm	0
P.J.L. Dujon†	lbw b Small	4	b Malcolm	0
A.L. Logie	c Lamb b Fraser	98	c Larkins b Malcolm	20
C.L. Hooper	c Russell b Capel	32	run out	10
E.A. Moseley	c Russell b Malcolm	0	c Lamb b Malcolm	26
C.E.L. Ambrose	c Russell b Malcolm	7	c Russell b Fraser	18
I.R. Bishop	b Malcolm	16	not out	15
C.A. Walsh	not out	8	lbw b Malcolm	1
Extras	(lb 4, nb 7)	11	(b 2, lb 13, nb 12, w 1)	28
TOTAL		199		239

ENGLAND

G.A. Gooch*	c Dujon b Bishop	84	retired hurt	18
W. Larkins	c Dujon b Ambrose	54	c Dujon b Moseley	7
A.J. Stewart	c Dujon b Ambrose	9	c Bishop b Walsh	31
A.J. Lamb	b Bishop	32	lbw b Bishop	25
R.A. Smith	c Dujon b Moseley	5	lbw b Walsh	2
R.J. Bailey	c Logie b Moseley	0	b Walsh	0
D.J. Capel	c Moseley b Ambrose	40	not out	17
R.C. Russell†	c Best b Walsh	15	not out	5
G.C. Small	lbw b Bishop	0		
A.R.C. Fraser	c Hooper b Ambrose	11		
D.E. Malcolm	not out	0		
Extras	(b 10, lb 9, nb 16, w 3)	38	(b 2, lb 7, nb 6)	15
TOTAL		288	(5 wkts)	120

BOWLING

ENGLAND	O	M	R	W	O	M	R	W
Small	17	4	41	2	21	8	56	1
Malcolm	20	2	60	4	26.2	4	77	6
Fraser	13.1	2	41	3	24	4	61	2
Capel	15	2	53	1	13	3	30	0
WEST INDIES								
Ambrose	36.2	8	59	4	6	0	20	0
I. Bishop	31	6	69	3	10	1	31	1
Walsh	22	5	45	1	7	0	27	3
Hooper	18	5	26	0				
Moseley	30	5	70	2	10	2	33	1

FALL OF WICKETS

	WI 1st	E 1st	WI 2nd	E 2nd
1st	5	112	96	27
2nd	5	125	100	74
3rd	22	195	100	79
4th	27	214	100	85
5th	29	214	142	106
6th	92	214	167	—
7th	93	243	200	—
8th	103	244	200	—
9th	177	284	234	—
10th	199	285	239	—

Umpires: C. Cumberbatch and L. Barker.

off-stump from Gladstone Small and was caught at third slip by Allan Lamb for a duck.

By 11.26 a.m. West Indies, put in to bat by Graham Gooch, were 29–5 and the cramped little press-box was full of English reporters furiously taking notes and still not really believing what they were jotting down. Kingston had been incredible enough but 29–5? Was the England bowling really this good or the West Indies batting really that bad? It was still too soon for coherent analysis because things were happening too fast.

Angus Fraser, relieving the menacing Malcolm after the eleventh over, had Richie Richardson caught behind by Jack Russell as the Antiguan played forward looking for the one that cut back. It didn't. Four overs later Fraser rapped Carlisle Best on the fingers and Stewart's commiserations were of little use because two balls later the only West Indian to get past 50 at Sabina Park guided a shorter ball from the Middlesex seamer at a nice, high catchable height to Lamb. That made it 27–4 and when Jeffrey Dujon was lbw padding up to one from Small that cut back on him in the next over, half the West Indies side were out for 29.

By this time there was pandemonium in the Learie Constantine Stand where large numbers of English supporters were getting pink from the excitement as well as the sun. Signs draped over the balcony advertised the presence of Crook Town CC and Evenwood CC, County Durham. What stories they would have to tell when they got home. If it wasn't all being beamed back on Sky TV, no one would have believed them!

Seeking to press home his advantage, Gooch brought back Malcolm in place of Small in the twenty-first over and England's new strike weapon soon had little Gus Logie hopping as he played balls down off his chest. Unlike Viv Richards, who was suffering from haemorrhoids once again, Logie was fit in time to return to the West Indies side and it was amazing to think that, yet again, everything depended on this pint-sized Trinidadian's ability to start filling up the West Indies barrel with a few much-needed runs. An uppish drive through vacant mid-off enabled Logie to bring up the 50 as he and Carl Hooper tried to repair some of the damage. But smack on High Noon, Malcolm fired the bullet that would have effectively destroyed the West Indies innings. Logie, beaten by sheer speed, got an edge and Russell, diving in front of first slip, dropped the catch. It was 58–5 and Logie was on 17. Before long it would prove to be England's worst mistake of the day.

After returning from lunch at 66–5 in a positive frame of mind, Logie and Hooper played the kind of shots that were needed to get the England bowlers off their back and they had added 63 for the sixth wicket when Hooper, once again promising more than he produced, edged a ball from David Capel to the wicket-keeper. 92–6. Hooper had made 29.

With Malcolm Marshall suffering from a damaged finger, the West Indies had brought in the thirty-two-year-old Barbadian, Ezra Moseley, for his Test début, a controversial choice in the more militant areas of the Caribbean as he had been a member of the rebel team that had gone to South Africa six years before. If that had left a bitter taste in people's mouths, Moseley's introduction into Test cricket no doubt left an equally bitter one in his because he was out for nought in the first over he faced against that Jamaican who had chosen a different and rather more acceptable kind of exile. Hanging out his bat at a wide delivery from Malcolm, Moseley gave Russell another chance to atone for his earlier slip-up by leaping high to his right to seize the ball as it flew off the edge.

Russell's fourth catch of the innings was not long in coming; Curtly Ambrose giving Malcolm his third wicket as he failed to middle another quick one. At 108–8 that really should have been it, bar the odd whoop from a Logie supporter, but the hometown boy had other ideas and, with Ian Bishop playing sensibly at the other end, he started to build something worthwhile out of the rubble his colleagues had left him. It was, after all, a role to which he had become quite accustomed.

A typical flashing cut for four earnt Logie his 50 and a standing ovation from the Queen's Park Oval crowd who were just beginning to recover from the stupefied silence that had enveloped them in the morning.

At tea, West Indies had advanced to 139–8 and the momentum continued afterwards with Logie cutting beautifully whenever the bowlers failed to pitch it up. Finally, after 74 precious runs had been added, Bishop, who had looked a very well-ordered No. 10, was bowled by Malcolm for 16 scored off 63 balls. Courtney Walsh's twin responsibilities were clear, to get Logie to his hundred and West Indies past two hundred. It was no fault of his that neither target was reached. After Logie had taken a single off a mistimed drive, Walsh was left to fend for himself for the remainder of Malcolm's over with Logie on 98 and West Indies on 199. The crowd were poised for a mighty celebration and few batsmen in the long history of Test cricket at the Queen's Park Oval would have deserved it more than Gus Logie.

But in the next over from Fraser, Logie flashed extravagantly outside the off-stump, going for his favourite cut, and Lamb took the catch at deep gully. You had to feel for the man. He had single-handedly saved his side from total humiliation and yet had been denied the satisfaction of scoring what would have been his fourth test hundred. Centuries are particularly elusive for Logie. On this same ground in 1984, he had made 97 against Australia; he had been left 95 not out against England at Lords in 1988 and later the same year made 93 against Australia at Perth.

After this kind of performance, the decision to stick with a four-man pace attack had been wholly justified. Hopefully that view will still hold after West Indies have batted a second time. Malcolm, rapidly becoming the inspired choice out of many daring selections for this tour, was the pick of the bowlers with four for 60 off twenty overs. Fraser, once again the perfect foil with his nagging line and length, had three for 41 off 30.1; Small two for 41 off 17 and Capel, more expensive than the others, one for 53 off 15.

Once again Malcolm's startling pace, backed up by the relentless accuracy of his colleagues, had exposed the weakness in the West Indies batting line-up. But the continued failure of the world's most experienced opening partnership is beginning to look ominous. Battle weary they may be, but Greenidge and Haynes are both still too good to go on getting scores like 5 and 0.

Just to compound Haynes' miserable first day as Test captain, the Middlesex opener dropped a routine catch at first slip – off Wayne Larkins off the last over of the day when Hooper had been brought on to see how the wicket was responding to spin. By then Larkins and Gooch had added 44 with no apparent discomfort and England returned to their upside-down world at the Hilton very much the right way up.

The same cannot be said for the atmosphere surrounding this Test in Trinidad. From all accounts it is a good thing Viv Richards is not playing after the remarks he made in Guyana about the West Indies being an African team. Quite apart from the reaction amongst the non-African population of that South American country, the reaction here in Trinidad, where the black population is actually outnumbered by those of Indian or Chinese descent, has been extremely indignant.

When Robin Marlar and I caught a taxi back to the hotel we got an earful from a somewhat wild-eyed driver with his cap pulled around to the side of his head.

'That Richards has no business talking that way,' he said in an accent still embedded in the sub-continent. 'Indian people here very upset, I tell you. Very upset. Frankly, I am not racist at all, you see. But if he feels like that, then I am happy to see England win. Many Indians, we would be happy to see England win.'

I think I remember meeting a taxi driver in Pietermaritzburg who would get along very well with this fellow. Like their cousins in South Africa, Indians in Trinidad seem to have the same kind of antipathy towards black power. Indian cricketers I had been speaking to at the Oval had voiced much the same opinions on the subject of Richards' less than tactful remarks and had complained bitterly about the lack of opportunity given to Indian players – with spinners the main victims, of course – in West Indies' sides over the past decade. The days of Ramadhin are long ago.

So race is an issue here, too. Despite the very different circumstances, the problems are similar, a clash of cultures creating suspicion and ultimately fear. From what I am told, the situation in Trinidad is not getting any better and once again the lovely innocent game of cricket is providing the perfect excuse to bring all these emotions out into the open. Can no one just get on with the game?

24 March

England, crawling to 189–2, didn't get on with anything much today and even allowing for the technical and psychological excuses, the spectators had a right to feel aggrieved. Fazeer Mohammed, writing in the *Sunday Guardian*, called it 'one of the least memorable days in the history of cricket at the Oval.'

There were three main factors that contributed to it – the sluggishness of the pitch which did not encourage stroke play, the normal dawdle at which West Indies bowled their overs (although, by the standards of this tour, thirteen an hour was not too bad), and the fact that Gooch's men had got their heads so far down in an admirable 'thou shall not pass' mode that no-one remembered to peep over the parapet and reassess the situation. Had they done so, they might have noticed that West Indies much feared pace attack was not only looking a bit listless, but was being supplemented by some very ordinary off-spin bowling from Hooper.

Although Moseley was consistently lively and Ambrose seemed to galvanize himself into action after tea, the extent of England's caution was really not justified. To have allowed Hooper, who does not spin the ball that much, to have got away with thirteen overs for just 23 runs was absurd. If Gooch had been served that kind of fare while playing for Essex, he would have helped himself to about 12 an over. Obviously Test cricket imposes its own restrictions on a batsman's willingness and even on his ability to play strokes, but even allowing for the circumstances, this was a wasted opportunity of major proportions and I just hope England are not left regretting it if things get tight at the end.

To alleviate the boredom, I walked around the ground to take a look at things from a different viewpoint with Peter Baxter and his *Test Match Special* team. As so many people have discovered the ultimate satisfaction for a cricket fanatic is to sit watching the game with a radio and listen to the expert commentary pouring in through his ear-piece. Sitting behind Christopher Martin-Jenkins, Tony Cozier, Trevor Bailey and the two guest summarizers for this Test, Gerry Gomez and Derrick Murray, offers the same opportunity with a little extra insight. The pros make it look, as well as sound, easy, but if you are not used to talking into a live microphone the tension level is pretty high.

Gomez, who is a practised and one might say voluble public

speaker, betrayed a certain amount of nervous tension through the fluttering of his hands which were never still when he spoke. There is nothing unusual about that. Even as practised a politician as the late Robert Kennedy tried to keep his hands out of view when he gave a speech because, quite literally, they shook.

Gomez' deep voice, however, betrayed little as he made the inevitable comparisons between what he was seeing and cricket as it was played in his day. When a snick from Larkins dropped four-feet short of Hooper at third slip just after lunch, Carl clutched at it, missed, and let it go through for four.

'You must get everything behind the ball,' said Gomez and, plucking names from the past, added, 'Richie Benaud and Graeme Hole never let anything through when they were in the slips for Australia.'

It was fun listening to Gerry. Along with Jeffrey Stollmeyer, Worrell, Weekes and Walcott and the spin twins, Ramadhin and Valentine, he played in the first Test match I ever saw, during my school holidays at the Oval in 1950. England didn't make very many, I seem to remember.

There was more nostalgia on view in the pavilion which is really a double-tiered stand with a bar and offices at the back. At lunchtime a very large lady with the kind of grandmotherly bosom that children like to sink into sits behind a trestle-table dispensing sandwiches which are cut at her side by a young, doe-eyed assistant. The pepper sauce is hot; almost as hot as some of the looks Grandmama's assistant is getting from the friskier members.

All around us are the kind of team photographs that adorn pavilion walls all over the world. Young Stollmeyer and Gomez are to be found in a Trinidad team playing in the 'Inter-Colonial Tournament' of 1939, but even as late as 1970 the echoes of a bygone age are still strong for there is the Duke of Norfolk's XI, captained by Colin Cowdrey with E.W. Swanton as treasurer and team members as diverse as Chris Old, Mike Denness and the Earl of Cotterham.

By the looks of things, the bridge game going on just at the top of the stairs might have been in progress since 1970, too, for as John Thicknesse, who is a bit of a player himself, and I noticed yesterday it has a certain air of permanence about it that the crash of wickets or the thunder of sixes does nothing to dispel. An event of great moment on the field of play is recognized with a cursory glance over the shoulder by one of the elderly gentlemen seemingly engrossed in their hand. But somehow I suspect they have a better idea of what is happening out there than is apparent.

Not that today's proceedings required undue attention. Larkins, having scored marginally faster than his captain, reached his first Test 50 in 203 minutes and 146 balls, but did not last much longer, hanging out his bat to Ambrose and offering Dujon the catch. The stand had been worth 112 and therein lay the justification for the slow-scoring rate. West Indies had lost eight wickets by the time they had scored 112 which still takes a bit of digesting. The chasm between the two teams can't be this big, surely.

It certainly didn't look that way when Alec Stewart, with all of one Test and 13 runs behind him, arrived at the wicket as England's No. 3 and departed after an hour and a half's batting for 9. Having played Ambrose quite confidently early on, he finally got a nasty lifter and touched it to Dujon as it passed his nose.

A wildly exciting over by today's standards followed with Curtly, all uncurled and alert now, opening Lamb's eyes with a rearing bouncer and then getting cut majestically for four. Typical response, that, but even so Allan didn't know much about the next two deliveries.

At 5 p.m. the umpires brought the whole thing to a merciful end by offering England's captain and his deputy the light and it didn't take much of an executive decision out there for them to accept. Gooch, having started on 19 not out, had managed to score 64 runs in the entire day which was barely believable. But he was still there and, from that all important point of view, the ploy had been a success. Another day to England – the sixth in a row. The miracle continues.

Gooch stopped at my table on the way out of the coffee shop tonight. He had watched Ivan Lendl's defeat by Emilio Sanchez in the Lipton Championships that I had been covering in Key Biscayne and had heard Lendl's remarks when Mary Carillo interviewed him at courtside for ESPN, the American sports network that is beamed via satellite all over the Caribbean.

'I thought that was a bit off, Lendl saying he didn't really want to be there,' said Gooch. 'That didn't sound too good, did it? He doesn't have to play those tournaments, does he?'

I explained about the contractual bind Lendl had got himself into with Adidas, the company that had clothed him for most of his career until he signed with a Japanese manufacturer for more money than Gooch or any other cricketer will ever earn from their game. Under the terms of the old contract Lendl had agreed to play at the Lipton for a certain number of years because it was an Association of Tennis Professionals endorsed event and Adidas was the official sportswear company of the ATP. Millions of dollars are involved in all these deals, sums of money that would leave the TCCB gasping if they found themselves dealing with such high finance.

The TCCB, quite rightly, would also be horrified at the thought of a batsman having a microphone shoved under his nose as he climbed the pavilion steps just after being given out to be interviewed on live television. But that is routine procedure at big tennis tournaments and Lendl, moments after an embarrassing defeat, could be excused for being rather typically tactless.

But there were two things I found quite interesting about Gooch's little visit to my table. Firstly that he would bother to come over and talk to a journalist he barely knew which suggested that his phobia about the Press was evaporating somewhat and secondly that he had picked up on what Lendl had said. Was he subconsciously seeing the Gooch of 1986 in the West Indies mirrored in Lendl's unhappiness at having to play where he didn't want to play? If so, he was showing no sympathy for Ivan's feelings just as many people had shown none for his when the anti-apartheid movement was hounding him from island to island four years ago.

It was too brief and too pleasant a conversation to get into questions like that, but the England captain continues to surprise me. He is a far more relaxed and approachable figure than I had been led to believe. But then the responsibilities of leadership coupled with a little success can change a man, even those who seem most set in their ways. Ask F.W. de Klerk.

All Gooch's hopes of building on Saturday's hard graft were dashed in the first over today – a first over delayed almost two hours by persistent drizzle – when Bishop got one to lift and swing away and Dujon took the catch. Gooch had added only one to his overnight score of 83 and the way that Bishop, probably the biggest and fastest bowler Trinidad has ever produced, was getting the ball to rise and move did not augur well for the remainder of England's batting line-up.

Lamb was soon ducking into a bouncer from the deceptively nippy Moseley, who was proving a very capable deputy for Marshall, and when Ambrose was brought into the attack after lunch he created just as many problems, surprising Lamb with a shooter and then producing a superb delivery which landed on middle and leg and cut away to the off. But England's perky vice-captain handled it deftly.

Robin Smith was soon getting the Ambrose treatment, too, on a pitch that was offering much more assistance to the bowlers than it had the previous day. But it was Moseley who made the next breakthrough, bringing Smith forward and then beating him with one that moved away. The resulting edge gave Dujon his fourth catch of the innings and England were 214–4.

But worse was to come. Rob Bailey, brought in at No. 6 in place of Nasser Hussain who had injured his wrist during a fall on the tennis court, was out first ball. Moseley contrived to produce as nasty a ball as could be imagined for a raw Test batsman with just one cap behind him. Leaping up just short of a length, it had Bailey trying to fend it away in front of his body and Logie was there at short leg to take the catch. It was noticeable that Bailey, a natural front-foot player, had moved forward and then back as he tried to negotiate the delivery whereas both Gooch and Larkins had been moving back and across to anything short of a length.

Without another run scored Bishop bowled Lamb when a bouncer caught the batsman's visor and ricocheted on to his leg stump. A tough way to go but this, suddenly, was the kind of tough cricket that England had been expecting from day one. Finally they were tasting the sort of medicine that West Indies fast bowlers had been able to prescribe at will for series after series. Now, at last, the battle was joined.

There was no doubting who would have emerged the victor from this particular session, either, had David Capel, having scored just one, not survived a routine, head-high slip catch off Moseley. Amazingly, for one of the world's safest close catchers, Greenidge put it down.

It was an expensive miss. In a partnership that stretched for almost two hours over the tea interval Capel and Jack Russell stopped the rot by adding 29 very valuable runs even though they allowed Hooper to bowl three maidens. But the circumstances were now very different from when Gooch had been prodding the spinner back down the pitch yesterday.

After Russell top edged Walsh to Best at second slip for 15 and Small was lbw to Bishop for a duck, Capel had to rely on the imperturbable Gus Fraser to help him prolong the innings. Guiding a straight bat with a cool head, Fraser kept the West Indies at bay in a stand of 40 before he gave Hooper a catch at third slip off Ambrose for 11. He had faced 57 balls and faced them well.

By then England had progressed to 284–9 and Capel was playing just the sort of innings he had been chosen for – a superbly gritty and well-constructed rear-guard action that was enabling England, after a major fright in the middle of the day, to add a little flesh to the bare bones of their achievements on Friday.

Devon Malcolm, greeted by an Ambrose bouncer, swayed out of the way of it and then danced about like a heavyweight relishing round two of a title fight. Relish may be too strong a word for Malcolm's attitude towards batting, but he certainly doesn't allow himself to look intimidated and he managed to survive three overs, in some form or fashion, before Capel, knowing it could not last, swung at Ambrose and gave the big man his fourth wicket by driving the ball straight at Moseley.

Ambrose, with 4–59, had been the most successful bowler, but Bishop had looked just as dangerous and Moseley, with 2–70, probably deserved better figures. The day ended with Greenidge and Haynes unbeaten as they set off in pursuit of England's 89 first innings lead and honours, for the first time in the series, were about even. In the face of some really hostile bowling, England had recovered from the precipice of total collapse and had shown that they had the character to stand firm.

The notice passed around the press-box yesterday had stated simply that there would be a cricket match between the West Indies media and the foreign press at the Carib Sports Ground. Great, everyone thought. Or at least some of us did and proceeded to do nothing about it.

The alarm bells only started ringing when an item appeared in today's *Trinidad Guardian* listing the teams. Gary Sobers, Derrick Murray, Tony Cozier and Tony Becca were supposed to be playing for 'them' and, get this line-up, Geoff Boycott, Tony Lewis, Mike Selvey, Tony Greig, Ted Dexter, Vic Marks and Chris Martin-Jenkins amongst a few others were supposed to be playing for 'us'.

At 11 a.m. Derrick Murray appeared in the lobby of the Hilton and asked Martin-Jenkins where our team was. Chris, less than totally articulate for once, mumbled something about not being too sure and hurried off in search of Peter Hayter. The problem was, of course, that no one had been put in charge and so, naturally, nothing had happened. The previous evening David Norrie, who is an old hand at corralling wayward pressmen and moving them in one direction, had toyed with the idea of getting a team together, but the interest seemed a bit half-hearted and anyway, the likes of Dexter and Lewis never had the slightest intention of playing. Golf had already been arranged.

'I think we ought to do what we can,' Martin-Jenkins told Hayter, John Etheridge and myself in the lobby. 'There's obviously been a cock-up, but we don't want to appear rude.'

It was 11.15 a.m. Muttering about a pulled muscle in his neck, a disability that would obviously have a dire effect on his ability to move the ball away from the bat, Peter sat down and proceeded to hit the lobby phone with feverish Hayter-like intent. People were then prised away from their tandys; I scooped Scyld Berry off the edge of the swimming-pool and Vic Marks was nabbed on the way back to his room. By 11.45 a.m. Hayter's neck muscle had not improved, but we had a team.

It turned out to be a very enjoyable afternoon, even for our inspiring captain Christopher Martin-Jenkins who flung himself at a ball skidding past him at mid-off in the very first over and got hit on the upper lip. But Christopher has always been pretty stiff in the upper lip department and, staunching the flow of blood, he adopted the new Goochian spirit of the proper team and announced, 'Take that as an example of the commitment I want from all of you!'

We were about to be duly impressed until some of us noticed a former England and Somerset off-spinner giving him an old soldier's look from mid-wicket.

Needless to say there was no sign of Sir Garfield or even Derrick Murray among the opposition, but they were captained by a former Trinidad batsman Alvin Corneal and were lethal enough to hit Mark Ottway in the jaw – a blow which, remarkably, did very little to alter his features. Under the circumstances we were delighted to win, thanks to our heroic captain, Man of the Match Martin-Jenkins who shrugged off his injury with true Corinthian spirit to bat and bowl in his customary style – a style embellished, it must be said, by a strategically placed strip of elastoplast. No lip mikes for him for a couple of days.

The afternoon was made all the more pleasant by the fact that we were playing on the Carib Brewery Ground where, naturally, the local product was in plentiful supply. God knows what will happen if they play this match against the Australian Press.

During the course of my negligible contribution to the proceedings, I was given a useful lesson in just how difficult it is to stop the ball on Caribbean fields. This was a pleasant ground with a well-laid matting wicket and a lovely vista of palm trees and sugar cane if you happened to be fielding at the right end. (From the other side, Tim de Lisle spent most of his stint at long on looking at the back end of a brewery but, as I have said, there were compensations.) What was common to all areas of the field was the uneven turf which is endemic to the majority of cricket grounds out here.

'We get very spoiled with our outfields in England,' said Vic Marks helpfully from cover as I tried to get something, anything, behind a ball that bobbled about in front of me. Considering Sabina Park and the Queen's Park Oval were not much better, I took my aching limbs back to the hotel with a healthier respect for the fielding standards that are being set by both England and the West Indies on this tour.

'Demon Devon!' The words were emblazoned in red across the back page of the *Trinidad Guardian* and the West Indies batsmen won't argue with the hyperbole. The West Indies batters really don't have much left to argue about after yet another day that saw Malcolm and his colleagues rip the heart out of their line-up with the kind of bowling that wins Test matches and which should definitely win this one. England 2–0 up? Well, I did suggest Kingston wasn't a fluke.

The fourth day left the situation like this: West Indies, at 234–9, are just 146 runs ahead and the pitch, with the occasional ball keeping low, is showing no real signs of breaking up, despite numerous cracks. England never found out whether it is taking spin or not, firstly because they didn't have to and secondly because they couldn't have done anyway unless Gooch had asked Rob Bailey to bowl. West Indies may want to find out very badly indeed but only Hooper will be able to tell them. If they end up yearning for Robert Haynes and his leg spin it will serve them right.

At lunch, with Greenidge and Haynes having taken the total to 76–0, there had hardly been a hint of what was to come. Both men had taken their time, batting almost as dourly as England had on Saturday and a big score loomed. But then, just over an hour after lunch, Greenidge stuck his leg a long way down the wicket to Fraser and was given out lbw by umpire, C. Cumberbatch. Greenidge was unimpressed and I must confess I can't remember seeing a batsman losing an lbw decision so far forward. He had batted 126 minutes for 42.

But if England had been a shade lucky they quickly capitalized on it. One over later, the thirty-fifth of the innings, Haynes, trying to turn a lifting ball from Malcolm to leg, deflected it off the back of his bat to Lamb in the gully.

Carlisle Best lasted two minutes. The lbw decision this time was indisputable as he went on to the back foot in trying to dig out a delivery that kept low. Suddenly three wickets had fallen in eight balls and it was not over. For the second time in three innings, Dujon was clean bowled by his fellow Jamaican. In Kingston the keeper had at least survived twenty-nine balls. Here

– none. From 96–0, West Indies had been split apart and were now tottering at 100–4. Four wickets in nine balls and three out of four for Malcolm who, at the rate of ten hugs a wicket, was having the breath pumped out of him by his ecstatic team mates. He still had enough left to bounce one high over Logie's head, however, in a none-too-sensible attempt to clinch his hat trick. But the damage had been done and, once again, little Gus was being asked to survey the shambles and repair the damage.

For an hour and twenty-three minutes, Logie did his best but, in the second over of Malcolm's new spell after tea, he went for his favourite cut shot and Larkins, grabbing the ball at the second attempt, completed the catch at first slip. 143–5. Richardson, realizing that neither the pitch nor the English bowling was going to yield runs unless a real attempt was made to put bat to ball, cover drove Small beautifully for four and then repeated the shot with equal panache off Malcolm. But when Gooch, in an inspired bowling change, replaced Small with Fraser and then Malcolm with Small, the ball no longer found the middle of Richie's bat. In the fifty-ninth over, an edge to slip just failed to carry off Small and then the Warwickshire seamer did him again, this time fatally, when a thicker edge was taken by Gooch at second slip. Richardson had scored 34 much needed runs, including five fours.

Moseley, on a king pair in his first Test, seemed quite unperturbed at the thought of a double duck and promptly straight drove a Fraser half-volley for four; flashed and missed outside the off-stump, berated himself and continued on his merry way with another straight driven boundary and a three to long on. Fraser, whose expressive body language manages to convey his feelings without the need for much gesticulation, looked extremely put out at being hit for 11 in an over by a No. 8. But Moseley can bat as well as bowl.

His partnership with the studious Hooper was just beginning to threaten England's momentum when Lamb hung on to a brilliant catch at third slip when Malcolm got one to lift and clip the edge of Moseley's bat. The ball was actually past Lamb when he grabbed it two handed reaching back. At 200–7, West Indies had doubled their score since the post-lunch blitz, but they were still a long way from being able to afford the kind of low comedy that claimed the next wicket.

Ambrose, playing the ball neatly to point, presumably made some sort of a call as he set off on a full-scale charge to the other end of the pitch. But if he did, Hooper either did not hear or did not believe it. Instead he just stood there, two yards out of his crease, as Ambrose galloped past, leaving Hooper, the last West Indian with any hope of making a big score, as the man who had to go. Poor Curtly. The other end of the pitch must look awfully close when you only need about three strides to get there.

When Greenidge and Haynes had gone in at lunch still looking so hungry for runs, Bannister's press-box odds on England taking the new ball at 200–8 would have been pretty generous had anyone bothered to ask. But now the task was almost done and Ambrose, having straight driven Small with some flair on his way to 18, flashed at Fraser and gave Russell the catch. England, with just one more wicket to take, were left to reflect on another astonishingly successful day.

28 March

If England had a soothsayer travelling with them, the warning would have been clear. Beware the Ides of March! Graham Gooch would have been told not to go to the sporting temple today but, like the Caesar he has almost become, he would have gone anyway and still been cut down by a man who, not so long ago, could have been classified as a co-conspirator. Gooch and Moseley were, after all, both South African 'rebels'.

Only time will tell whether the ball that broke Gooch's hand in two places will prove to be a much bigger disaster for England than the huge cloud which settled over the Queen's Park Oval and deprived them of a victory that at lunch, with 71 of the 151 required with only one wicket down, appeared to be a mere formality. Unhappily, I fear that it will. For the next Test in Barbados and possibly for Antigua, too, England have lost an inspiring captain, their best batsman and a useful change bowler for a side that is packed with specialist batsmen. There could be no unkinder cut than that.

Nor an unkinder deception than a morning of brilliant sunshine that greeted the crowds pouring into the ground. At ten o'clock there was hardly a cloud to be seen on any horizon, let alone England's. Nor was there much delay in getting rid of the last West Indies batsman; Walsh falling lbw to Malcolm in the third over with just five runs added. The wicket gave England's quiet new hero figures of 26.2–4–77–6 with match statistics of 10 for 137. Among post-war fast bowlers playing for England in the West Indies, only John Snow, with 10–142 in Georgetown in 1967–8, had done as well although, in the last Test England won prior to this tour, right here in Port of Spain in 1973–4, Tony Greig ended up with the startling analysis of 13 for 156.

All England's bowlers, coaxed and cajoled by an ever-attentive Gooch, had excelled, but for Malcolm it was a triumph. Not since Frank Tyson shocked Australia's batsmen in 1954–5, has a genuinely quick England bowler sprung from the shadows to dominate a tour as Malcolm has here and Len Hutton's team were, in any case, not nearly such underdogs in that series as Gooch's side when they arrived in the Caribbean. Tyson, with 10 for 130 in Sydney, took twenty-eight wickets in five Tests on that tour while Malcolm has now taken fifteen in two on wickets that have not been nearly as fast as anticipated. By any standards, it must rank as one of the most unexpected success stories for an untried fast bowler in the history of Test cricket.

And, of course, it should have won England the match. Despite Larkins early dismissal in the eighth over, there were no real alarms for England as they began their second innings soon after 10.30 a.m. with a whole day to make 151. Or so we thought.

It was Moseley, once again the pick of the bowlers, who removed Larkins in his first over as Ned flashed outside his off-stump and Dujon took his fifth catch of the match. The score was already 27–1 and Gooch was going nicely. But Moseley's first over proved to be but a pinprick compared to the crushing blow he delivered in his second when Gooch, brought down to the striker's end after Stewart had taken a single to long leg, dropped his bat in pain as he tried to fend off a rising ball on his leg stump.

Laurie Brown raced out to attend to him, but England's captain was obviously in agony and had to be led off. In 74 Tests, he had never retired hurt. There is never a good time but this was one of the worst. Just behind the pavilion the clouds were beginning to build.

Bishop started to get some bounce but once, when Stewart ducked, the ball kept low. A fifth–day wicket can be expected to behave like that. Nevertheless Stewart and Lamb negotiated everything safely until Stewart seemed to decide that, if he was going to make it in Test cricket, he might as well do so playing his natural game. So he proceeded to take 12 off Bishop in the fifteenth over, two of the three fours coming off calculated slashes over gully's head and the third from a magnificent pull to leg. When the rain, starting as little more than a drizzle, sent the players into lunch ten minutes early, it was 73–1. The sky looked bad. But there was still time. Or so we thought.

Then, as if feeling guilty for failing to heed the rain dances that had been going on outside pubs all over Jamaica at the end of the First Test, the weather gods really went to work on England's chances. An enormous black cloud appeared over the ground, deposited a tanker load of water in about ten minutes and moved off towards the Northern Range, a group of hills that form an attractive backdrop to the Queen's Park Oval for people sitting at the pavilion end. But that cloud was not finished. Incredibly, as if on signal, the wind changed and, as soon as it hit the hills, the same cloud came right back to unleash another downpour on the already sodden turf. After that, no one needed to tell England they were in trouble.

On the players' balcony just to the left of the pavilion, Alec Stewart, not out 31 and seemingly on his way to confirming his promise as Test batsman, stared out at the rain with just a towel over his bare shoulders. For all cricketers interruptions for rain are a part of everyday life but for England and Stewart, in particular, could there ever have been a more frustrating stoppage than this?

Gooch reappeared, having had his hand X-rayed at the local hospital and his bearded features gave nothing away. The hand was not bandaged but I noticed he was very reluctant to produce it for a TV close-up when Tony Greig interviewed him for Sky. 'Just badly bruised,' Gooch said.

That was the official line as the rain continued and little knots of spectators congregated below the players' dressing-room to discuss the situation with typical West Indian vigour. Soon the situation was increasingly dominated by Trinidad's answer to the entire Rastafarian movement. Dressed in a siren red track suit with fake crocodile trimmings, this was one 'dread' who was about to be *heard*, man, and no mistake. The dreadlocks framed handsome features and a huge smile that lit up the gloom. Having positioned himself at the bottom of the Jeffrey Stollmeyer stand which juts out a little to the side of the pavilion, our Rasta man had his audience banked up behind him and, having attracted their attention with a few amusing remarks, proceeded to go to work on the England team, some of whom were reading newspapers out on the balcony.

Inevitably Devon Malcolm was the focus, as he has been all tour, but with Philip DeFreitas and Chris Lewis also on view, the 'dread' was in his element.

Having recognized Malcolm's presence, the 'dread' then turned his attention to the man known as 'Daffy' to his team mates.

'Dat DeFreitas, him *spin* bowler, man,' he announced, effecting an effeminate leg-break. 'Nuttin' more than a *spin* bowler!'

Daffy gazed down at him with a suitably superior air while the little group of hangers-on surrounding the speaker fell about laughing.

'But there!' he exclaimed theatrically, pointing a long, expressive finger at the expressionless Malcolm. 'There is Devon Malcolm. Come *home*, Devon. West Indies need you. Come home and you could be great pace bowler 'cause you not so bad now, y'know!'

Malcolm smiled benignly from behind his spectacles while above him on the upper tier, Gus Fraser gazed down on this by-play between the crowd and his black team mates. It would not have been entirely new to him coming, as he does, from a dressing-room at Middlesex that is virtually half black.

Even if DeFreitas will be tempted to knock the head off the next batsman he gets in his sights, it was all light-hearted stuff and the crowd leaning over the railings from the adjoining stand were well entertained as the depressing afternoon wore on.

At 3.35 p.m., the sun put in a sheepish appearance and by then twenty groundstaff were hard at it, having resisted the temptation to – oops, sorry, man – dump the water that had been lying on the covers straight on to the pitch. Instead they were producing sacks of sawdust in wheelbarrows and were jumping up and down on strips of hessian which were being laid over the wetter patches. That's one of the enduring charms of cricket, modern technology is never allowed to interfere with man and his plough.

But once umpires Barker and Cumberbatch, managers Lloyd and Stewart and captains Haynes and Gooch had all traipsed out to the middle at 3.56 p.m. everything, by cricketing standards, happened with the speed of light. By 4.05 p.m. the teams were actually in the middle and, even if the West Indies looked as if they wished it wouldn't, the match resumed.

But for Alec Stewart the resumption was brief. Off Walsh's second ball, the Surrey player went for the same shot that had brought him two consecutive fours before the stoppage and cut the ball high to Bishop at third man.

Even that immediate success did little to alleviate West Indies unhappiness at having been called out to play in conditions that they obviously considered unsuitable. Walsh, bowling to the new batsman, Smith, stopped halfway through his run up and Haynes helped him spread some sawdust. English supporters started a slow handclap but that was nothing compared to the minutes that ticked by during the next over which Bishop attempted to start from the pavilion end. After a couple of trial runs through the sawdust this giant of a man understandably looked concerned about his foothold and, after a discussion with Haynes, the captain called up the smaller, lighter Moseley – hardly an improvement as far as the English batsmen were concerned.

But it was Walsh who removed Smith, snared on the back foot by a shooter and out lbw for 2. Two overs later the hapless Bailey shuffled to leg as Walsh made one cut back on him and was bowled. A pair. Bailey, one of the most elegant stroke-makers in county cricket, had waited years for his chance and now this. Cricket can be a cruel sport.

At 85–4 with little more than an hour's play left, England's thoughts were turning more to survival than victory in conditions that were as treacherous for the batsmen as the bowlers. But if Haynes harboured any thoughts of snatching an unlikely win, he showed precious little sign of it as the sawdust spreading and ball wiping routines continued to the fury of the English supporters away to our left in the Jeffrey Stollmeyer Stand.

No one is suggesting it is easy to take over as captain of a Test side, but Haynes had not distinguished himself in the role. The shot he got out to in the first innings was irresponsible; the dropped slip catch could, of course, have happened to anyone any time, but was particularly embarrassing for him in this match and, worst of all, he became embroiled in a slanging match with Alec Stewart that, amazingly, he continued as the players headed for the pavilion during one of the intervals.

There are those who say that Stewart is no angel himself when fielding at short leg so maybe there is some history here but the 'sledging', as the players call it, which goes on out in the field almost always stays there, out of earshot, and it is rare for the argument to reach the pavilion steps. But Haynes, a likeable, extrovert personality, is not one to hide his feelings and the nerve ends have certainly been showing during his first Test as captain.

Lamb and Capel tried to keep the scoreboard moving with well-judged singles and when the final twenty overs arrived the score was 106–5, but the time was 5.16 p.m. As play had never yet managed to continue past 5.55 p.m., the most England could hope for was another seven or eight overs. That meant scoring at more than seven an over which, in these conditions, was totally unrealistic. Lamb's marvellous last over slog against Bruce Reid in that one-day international in Sydney when he smashed the 18 runs required for victory all over the SCG was all very fine under brilliant lights with a white ball and a fast outfield. Here at the Queen's Park Oval, the red ball, dark and damp, was being lost in the gloom and the outfield was a swamp.

And, in any case, Lamb did not last long enough to even have a try. As soon as Bishop decided he could bowl, he replaced Walsh and had England's vice-captain lbw for 25.

It was now up to Capel and Russell. First of all they had to make sure England did not lose and then explored every remaining avenue that might lead to an improbable victory. The score had inched to 117–5, still 34 short of the target, when the umpires offered the light and, after frantic signals from the dressing-room, it was turned down. It was 5.45 p.m. and the sun had gone for good. Capel played and missed and then got one high on the bat that fell short of Walsh at square leg. He was having trouble sighting the ball and no wonder.

Hussain raced on, clutching the mandatory batting gloves, but it was advice from the captain that Hussain had to offer. The advice seemed to be 'grope on as best you can', but Russell had plenty to say about that and the batsmen had more to say to each other after Hussain departed. The sight of Ambrose being called up to bowl settled it. It was pointless to continue if Curtly was going to start bouncing them down out of the clouds and, after a series of confusing signals between Gooch, Stewart and the men in the middle, the whole sad affair was called off at one minute past six.

Only then was it revealed to the England team, let alone the public at large, that Gooch's hand was broken in two places. The policy had been to keep it from everyone deliberately so as not to give the West Indies a psychological advantage and equally not to depress a team that had come to rely on Gooch as a symbol of everything they were trying to achieve. The thought of losing him for the rest of the tour was as big a blow as could be imagined. How incredibly ironic it was that, four years before, Gooch would not have complained too much about a sore hand because he was hating every minute of the tour and actually asked to go home before the final Test in Antigua. Now, on a day that should have seen him leading his side to an impregnable 2–0 lead in the series, he was seriously hurt for the first time in his entire career. Beware the Ides of March.

Under the circumstances, Gooch was remarkably philosophical about the whole thing. 'It's just unfortunate that we got ourselves in a good position; played some good cricket throughout the match and yet did not get the result that I think we might possibly have deserved.'

There were mutterings in the press-box about being lied to by the England management over Gooch's injury but, in the circumstances, I think it was a legitimate piece of camouflage. England were, after all, on the brink of an historic victory that would have enabled them, at the very least, to draw a series they were supposed to have lost 5–0 and the considerations of reporters on deadlines has to come second to that.

Obviously another batsman would have to be called in. Before we left the ground, Peter Lush told me that Mark Nicholas' side in Zimbabwe had already been contacted and enquiries made. Mike Atherton, Lancashire's former Cambridge University captain, who has been scoring a hatful of runs on the 'A' team tour, is the obvious choice.

En Route to Barbados

29 March

Mike Atherton was the choice but apparently he is suffering from a groin strain and will not be fit. So two other names have been thrown into the ring, both almost as surprising as each other. Only a couple of days ago, Micky Stewart revealed in a matter of fact sort of way, that David Smith, who toured out here with Gower's team four years ago, had been on stand-by in England all winter in case an experienced player of pace bowling was required. That was news to everyone, but somewhat less surprising news than the second name which was David Gower himself.

From what David has been telling me, Gooch contacted him immediately on his return from hospital yesterday and asked him if he would make himself available to play against Barbados, if required. This was done even before Gooch told the rest of the team that his hand was broken so the decision to call up the most controversially discarded figure from the old regime was virtually a spontaneous one on the part of the new captain himself. It speaks well of both men that Gooch and Gower have maintained such an easy relationship on this tour. The happy coincidence that Essex were playing at Leicester last summer the day after it was announced that Gower had not been selected for the touring party enabled Graham to talk David through the decision and apply a little balm to the deep hurt that had been inflicted on one of the nicest men in the game. It could not have been easy but, judging by the way the two of them have been interacting out here, it seems to have been successful.

The proof of that lies in Gower's positive reaction to a plea for help. He had a net on arrival here today and will decide whether he feels in good enough nick to play tomorrow. One net as preparation for a three-day match after a shoulder operation and six months out of the game is hardly sufficient, but I bet David gives it a go. In his deceptively diffident sort of way, Gower is always excited by a challenge.

The tour selection committee's challenge at the moment is to find eleven men fit in body and soul to play at Kensington Oval. Micky Stewart is adamant that Jack Russell should be given a rest and that has complicated matters because Alec Stewart has joined the sore finger brigade. The manager tried to sort out the possible permutations for me as he ordered a round of drinks at the open-air bar of the Rockley Resort tonight.

'If David Gower plays, Rob Bailey will keep wicket. If David doesn't play, David Bairstow will keep wicket. Oh and David Smith is on his way and will arrive tomorrow night.'

David Bairstow? This touring party is growing by the minute. But, in fact, there is hardly any shortage of people to choose from now because the island is crawling with English cricketers of various vintages and as Yorkshire are playing some matches here, Bairstow is an obvious choice. That also means, of course, that Martin Moxon is here which throws a considerable question mark over the validity of calling in a replacement cold from England, who will not, in any case, arrive in time for the three-day game, when an opener of comparable standard is already here, warmed up, as it were, and ready to go.

But the nomadic Smith, who was discarded by Surrey for a second time in 1988 before moving on to Sussex, obviously still impresses Stewart as a player of fast bowling. I just hope he picks it up all right after indoor nets and a dose of jet lag.

After Micky had moved off to join his friends, I had a couple of beers with Eddie Hemmings who is proving that an over-forty can still pull his weight as a member of one of the fittest cricket teams ever assembled. Eddie strikes me as the sort of person who could have fitted into any era of the game's history. He is, in a sense, timeless. Although totally dedicated to the high-powered training routines that have made this team what it is, his values and love of the game and pride in performance are such that one could imagine him wheeling away, providing basic off spin to balance the offerings of a Tich Freeman or a Roley Jenkins or a Tony Lock at the other end.

Predictably, he is scornful of the 'rebels' who went to South Africa with Mike Gatting.

'All the guys who went to South Africa went for one thing, the money,' he said flatly. 'They put that before playing for England. I don't understand that. Money's never been the most important thing for me even though I am still playing now partially because I have earned so little during my career and I have a family to look after.

'But look what those guys have given up and for what? Not much more than I will be able to earn in the next three years if I manage to stay part of the England set-up. And there were some young guys in that side, too, with as much as ten years of Test cricket ahead of them if they hadn't gone. But I don't have any sympathy for them, I tell you that.'

Hemmings was obviously very disappointed not to be chosen for the last Test, but is stoically accepting his fate like an old pro for whom the illogicalities of the game no longer come as a surprise.

'I wouldn't have played myself at Sabina Park, but I would have done on that track at the Queen's Park Oval,' he said. 'And I tell you what, I'd have done Logie long before he got 98. I told him so, too, and he just laughed and said, "Glad you weren't playing." He knows he gets done by spin.'

But Hemmings is still taking pride in being part of a team that has amazed the cricketing world. 'We all feel part of it,' said Eddie. 'Just because you're not in the team doesn't mean you slack off. All the reserves were out training at eight in the morning at Port of Spain. Every member of this team has a lot of heart and a lot of spirit and that is what has made the difference so far. It's the West Indies who have looked as if they don't want to play. We want to get out there and get on with it. That much was proved right at the start in the First one day. Gooch wanted to get out there for ten overs after the rain but they didn't want to know.'

They think the world of Eddie Hemmings at Nottingham and no wonder after all the years of service he has given the county. Even his batting is treated with respect. I remember a lovely incident in a Test match at Trent Bridge recently when England wickets had been falling so fast that the pavilion steward had been virtually standing guard holding open the gate that leads on to the field, so rapidly had the batsmen been passing to and fro.

Eventually the comfortingly well-padded figure of the local hero appeared, moustache bristling under his helmet and, after he had passed the steward, the man turned to the members, and said, 'Ay, reckon I can close gate now. Eddie's in.'

1 April

April Fool jokes are supposed to be concluded by midday. Obviously Desmond Haynes was unaware of this because he allowed Barbados to bat on way past the lunch interval on the third day of this match against the tourists, eventually setting them the absurd target of 435 in a theoretical fifty-six overs and thereby killing such interest as was left.

When are cricketers going to wake up to the harsh realities of life, their life, no less? When are they going to get it into their heads that they are paid performers whose income is derived from public interest and that if they insist on kicking sand into the faces of that public, it will walk away. And not only will but is. There were more people watching Barbados score an unexpected Davis Cup victory over the Bahamas down the road at the Paradise Hotel than there were at Kensington Oval today and this, remember, is supposed to be the most cricket-mad island on earth.

Thankfully, I am not the only one disgusted by Haynes' decision. No one is better qualified to comment on the attitude of the Barbados captain than West Indies' foremost commentator, Tony Cozier, who is also cricket correspondent of the *Daily*

Nation and a Bajan himself. With his permission, I am happy to re-print here the article he has written for tomorrow's paper.

'The utter cynicism of modern cricketers dealt another telling blow to the image and well-being of the game at Kensington yesterday.

Desmond Haynes' decision to carry his innings well into the afternoon, deliberately killing a match with exciting possibilities, was made with a pointed and callous disregard for those few who had paid to watch it, the hundreds of thousands of others who were following it on radio and in the Press and for Barbados' proud cricketing reputation.

It was suggested that it was a tactical manoeuvre designed to keep the Englishmen in the hot sun for as long as possible under some strange illusion that that would grind them into the dust and shake their resolve for the Test match starting on Thursday.

It might have escaped Haynes' notice that hundreds of thousands of Englishmen actually pay a lot of money to stay in our sun for hours on end and that those English players it might just have affected for the Test, the fast bowlers Devon Malcolm, Gladstone Small and Angus Fraser, weren't even playing in the match.

It certainly should have occurred to him that England's resolve would have been far more shaken by a little more of what they had endured on Saturday, bowled out 158 and 209 behind on first innings, and the embarrassment of defeat. Surely, as Barbados captain and one with a proven and wholehearted commitment to the local game, he is not unaware of our history and our grand record against England teams at Kensington or, professional cricketer that he is, of his responsibility to those who support him and the game with the high prices they are charged to come through the gates.

Perhaps, as he gazed around the empty stands, he might have pondered on the future of the game and wondered to himself why spectactors now avoid such matches like the pox.

It may be pleaded in mitigation that he is far from alone in such bloody-minded folly. Indeed, he is not. Englishmen, even of this very tour, are as culpable as Australians and Indians and New Zealanders and all the other so-called professional cricketers these days who distort the intended spirit of this great game and then can't understand why young people are turning away from it in droves.

Barbadians stand second to none in our love of the game and we expect it to receive better treatment from those who have been entrusted with the responsibility to look after it, no matter whatever else others may do.'

Although, as Cozier intimates, it is particularly sad that this could happen on an island associated with everything that is good about the game, Haynes should not be singled out as a lone culprit. Cricketers, and especially captains, all over the world are putting their game and their livelihood in peril if this cynical disregard for the pleasure and satisfaction of the spectators who have actually paid at the gate, as well as those following it through the media, is allowed to continue.

In an age when alternative sporting attractions are multiplying by the minute, cricket simply cannot play fast and loose with the demands of that dwindling number who still value the unique rhythms and technicalities of a sporting contest spread over three, four or five days. One of the most pleasing aspects of this tour and, to a lesser extent the Australia-Pakistan series that has just been concluded, has been the re-emphasis on the importance of the Test series as opposed to the wham-bam and thank-you quick fix of the largely meaningless one-day Internationals. But Test cricket cannot survive in isolation. For the sake of the players themselves, the three- or four-day game has to be nurtured as a breeding ground for the ultimate test of a cricketer's ability – Test cricket itself.

There are those amongst my colleagues in the press-box – mostly of the tabloid persuasion, you will not be surprised to hear – who are talking in terms of Test cricket being dead and buried by the end of the century. I have yet to meet anyone remotely connected with the game who *wants* that to happen. So why, in heaven's name, is everything not being done to *prevent* it happening? Why are three-day matches killed off for pathetically

selfish and insular reasons? Why are over rates allowed to drop
to a level that slows down an already leisurely game to a pace
that would embarrass a snail? Why are spin bowlers so often
discarded on the flimsiest pretext? Why are pitches not produced
with both bounce and speed so that batsmen and bowlers of all
types can maximize their skills in the most entertaining manner
possible?

To an outsider, the only logical conclusion to draw is that the
game has a death wish. All the questions I have posed above have
been set down a thousand times by writers and commentators
over the past decade and the infuriating thing is that I can never
find a soul who will say that spinners are bad for the game or that
over rates should not be speeded up. But what I can rarely find is
the will to do something about it.

It is blazingly obvious that cricketers are being ground into the
lime by schedules that have them careering around England on
dangerous motorways all summer to fulfil hopelessly crowded
programmes and then jetted around the globe, if they are Test
players, to compete on a virtual year-round basis. If they become
weary, stale and bereft of flair for the game they once played so
well, who can blame them? When are the administrators going to
accept the fact that quantity kills quality?

It is easy to dress players up in coloured pyjamas and send
them out under the lights night after night, as they do in
Australia, to keep the turnstiles clicking. Quite apart from the
fact that the players themselves become numbed by it all, there
must be a limit to the public's interest as well. For everyone's
sake, it would be a far better investment for the future of the
game if greater emphasis was placed on improving the quality
and attractiveness of the product that really matters, i.e. Test
cricket.

The fact that the counties, peering into their navels once
again, have rejected a call for a championship of four-day
matches is another classic example of the game's administrators
failing to understand the overall problems that the game is facing.
Fewer games would mean fresher players. Fresher players –
players, in fact, who have been given time to recover from
niggling injuries – play fresher cricket. The public will respond to
that. Money that could be lost by a reduction in the number of

county games, could be made up with bigger crowds for those that are played, providing some imagination is used with dates and playing times.

I have always found it extraordinary that mid-week county cricket is played at precisely those hours that makes it impossible for the normal office worker to attend. For two months in summer, it is perfectly feasible to play cricket until 7.30 p.m. at the very earliest. So why finish at 6.30 p.m.? Don't let any county treasurer tell me that an extra 200 people paying 50 per cent of the regular admission price would not be a welcome addition to the season's budget. Yet is any attempt made to investigate the possibility of this?

Have Middlesex or Surrey ever thought of hiring a couple of double decker buses – a great advertising vehicle in themselves – and parking them outside the Mansion House at 5.30 p.m. on match days so as to offer free rides to Lords or the Oval? If the close of play was 7.30 p.m., they would get the better part of an hour and a half's cricket which, after all, is as long as a football match. What better way to wind down after a stressful day in the City?

Anything that can lure people back to county cricket has to benefit the entire game, but nothing will happen unless someone starts investigating a few radical ideas. Waiting for the multitudes to wander through the Grace Gates is about as fruitful an exercise as *Waiting for Godot*, even if the play's author, Samuel Beckett, did patronize the place himself. Undignified though it may be, it is necessary in this day and age to go out into the highways and byways and lure people in. The days when gentlemen in bowler hats used to scuttle away from their desks if Denis Compton was still in at tea time have long gone. If they won't come, go and get them. At least it's worth a try.

Barbados has an excellent bus service, but that did little to improve the crowd for the match that ended today. The generally disappointing attendances at the Test in Trinidad were thought to have been caused, to some extent, by the Indian reaction to Viv Richards' African remarks, but there is no such excuse here. Kensington Oval will, hopefully, be full for the one day on Tuesday and the Fourth Test that starts two days later, but cricket fans here seem to have turned their noses up at a three-day game and after Haynes' match-killing declaration today, they may never come back again.

But Allan Lamb, who now finds himself in the hot seat, has a few things to answer for too, if, in fact, he is making all the match decisions himself which is not clear at the moment. Obviously he must be taking advice from Gooch and Stewart but, however it was arrived at, it was difficult to understand the logic of winning the toss and deciding to send Barbados in on a good wicket when so many England batsmen were crying out for a long innings.

Having decided to risk it and play, no one, of course, needed time in the middle more than David Gower. So what did Lamb do for his friend? Send the opposition in and bat him at No. 6. Not surprisingly, Gower had to survive more than a day in the field and wait until 1.15 p.m. yesterday afternoon before making his way to the wicket. By then Gordon Greenidge had cracked a superb 183 and Carlisle Best 95 off an England attack that had to rely on its spinners to take wickets.

On Friday DeFreitas, Capel and Lewis had managed just one wicket between them – Daffy getting Haynes caught by Bailey for nine – as Barbados raced to 340–4. But Keith Medlycott had already taken two wickets by the close and on the resumption he wrecked any ideas Greenidge might have had of scoring a double century by lunging to his left to grab a magnificent caught and bowled.

Hemmings, meanwhile, was enjoying himself every bit as much. Malcolm Marshall, not out over night, soon holed out to Lewis at long off and Eddie wasted little time with wicket-keeper Ricky Hoyte, who, I understand, is Everton Weekes' grandson, Henderson Springer and Tony Johnson. By the time Barbados were all out for 367, Hemmings had enjoyed a morning session of 6–4–7–4 and an innings analysis of five for 77. Medlycott finished up with 4–114 and it was an absolute pleasure to see these two loyal and under-used tourists prove that they were capable of doing what they were there for – taking wickets.

England, making a far from impressive reply, were all out for 158 and Haynes did not enforce the follow on. Only Nasser Hussain took advantage of a good wicket to make runs – punching cuts and drives, open faced and bottom handed, to such good effect that he had made 70 when the last of his colleagues departed. They included, of course, the man who was making the headlines back home – our erstwhile press-box colleague, Mr Gower.

Arriving at the crease with the score of 56–4 starkly reflecting England's plight, Gower middled the first ball he received from Marshall who had just trapped Smith lbw and, in the next over from Marshall, took a single, turning the ball to the leg side with that familiar ease. It was his first run since September. Unhappily there were not to be many more. After being dropped by Marshall off Victor Walcott, Gower battled on doggedly, facing twenty balls in thirty-nine minutes before turning Johnson clean as a whistle straight into Roland Holder's hands at square leg. That looked familiar, too.

He had made four and was not given the opportunity to make any more when England's meaningless second innings started after Haynes had declared at 225–5. If the management are serious about wanting to call on Gower's services then why was he not sent in first with either Stewart or Capel so that he could have a chance of playing himself into some sort of form? What is the point of calling on a player of Gower's class as nothing more than a stand-in? Is it not an impertinence quite apart from a wasted opportunity?

Having seen how this team operate, I can understand now why Gower was not selected originally. More than anything the pre-tour training would have tested his patience quite apart from eliminating the opportunity to have his shoulder fixed. A laid-back ex-captain with a somewhat sardonic view of the world was not what Stewart and Gooch needed as they put a new and relatively unscarred squad through their paces. But the preparation is complete; the ideology a fixed and proven success and Gower's presence can hardly be considered a threat to team morale. On the contrary, I would have thought it might have acted as an inspiration. Only three players in history – Boycott, Cowdrey and Hammond – have scored more Test runs for England than Gower. There is nothing he has to prove.

The dismal day ended with Capel not out 51 after Bailey had done his best to brighten up the proceedings by measuring a six on to the roof of the Sir Garfield Sobers Stand off Springer and then, next ball, resetting his sights to smite the off spinner clean out of the ground, over the road and into someone's garden. That must have made Rob feel better.

2 April

Barbadians are a polite and charming people who are obviously well versed in dealing with the hordes of British tourists who descend on their little island each winter. They can be thankful it is the cricket rather than the football supporter Barbados attracts otherwise the smile might not be so ready or so welcoming.

I pity the poor American tourists at the moment because the place really is swarming with Brits lured out here for the cricket, many of them shepherded around by the likes of John Snow, Bob Taylor, Brian Rose and John Price. In the pubs and restaurants, cricket is quite often the sole topic of conversation and much of it reveals the breadth of knowledge of the committed cricket fan.

I have been dining frequently at a restaurant called L'Azure in St Lawrence which is owned by Nina Clarke and her family – Nina being a live-wire young woman whose passion for cricket is revealed by the way in which she recounts Michael Holding's famous over to Geoff Boycott in the Test here in 1981 as one of the most stirring and memorable moments of her life.

But some of the L'Azure clientele are no less informed. At a table near me the other night three men of varying generations and a middle-aged woman spent their entire meal discussing the game at large, and I mean at large. Western Australia, New South Wales, Allan Border, Imran Khan, Nottinghamshire, Middlesex, Mike Gatting, David Gower and, of course, every aspect of the current tour were chewed over with their excellent meal. It certainly lent some credence to my theory that cricket followers are far less parochial than the average sports fan and that sports editors of British newspapers are not wasting their time if they send correspondents to cover tours in which countries other than England are involved.

The politeness of the Bajans extends to the roads which is just as well because most of them wind narrowly through streets with very little pavement space between the road and the picturesque wood-frame houses that give Bridgetown and its suburbs such an attractive air.

Yesterday when I was driving to the ground, a taxi driver slowed down to turn left. In confirmation of a blinking light that signalled his intentions, the whole operation was reinforced by a long, black arm that came snaking out of the driver's window. The arm was then put through a sweeping, almost majestic manoeuvre of such elaborate detail, including the finishing touch of a cocked wrist and pointed finger that the last vestiges of doubt as to what the driver was about to do were cleared from the mind. It was the sort of signal that would have left a BSM instructor in raptures. As I drove past I wanted to applaud. Even Nina might have agreed that it was almost as beautiful as Holding's bowling. Almost but not quite.

Yesterday evening we were entertained at the home of Peter Lashley, who played two of his four Tests for West Indies in England in 1966. Peter is now in charge of our welfare as the Cable and Wireless Public Relations officer and travels with us on the tour. The barbecue was enjoyed by a wide selection of the island's cricketing hierarchy including Minister of Tourism, Wes Hall, and Everton Weekes, who told me that he is off to America soon to manage another cricket tour. After spending a great deal of time in New Jersey, Everton thinks that there is a future for cricket in the States and although I would have serious doubts about the Americans ever accepting the traditional game, limited overs matches played under lights with coloured clothing, helmets and a white ball hurled down by 6 feet 7 inch black men – or any other colour for that matter – would be a concept American sports fans would be able to relate to with ease. All it needs is money to spend on proper marketing. After all if the United States is to host the World Soccer Cup, as they call it, anything is possible.

Keith Medlycott was the only English player to turn up. 'They know I'm not going to play much more so the management are pretty good and give me a longer leash than the rest,' said the gregarious Surrey spinner who will keep smiling right to the end. However, he did point out how difficult it was to be thrown into a match after several weeks' inactivity and be expected to bowl up to standard.

'I was so nervous just trying to get the ball to land on the pitch the other day, let alone fixing a proper line and length,' he admitted. 'No amount of bowling in the nets can get you ready for the stuff in the middle.'

Would he, I wondered, have rather been with the 'A' team in Zimbabwe where he would have played in so many more matches?

'Oh, no thanks, not on your life,' he laughed. 'I'm sure they had a great tour, but this is the only team to be with if you can make it. You've got to be in at the top then at least you've got a chance of being selected even if you do spend most of the time carrying the drinks! It's just such a great experience being out here and getting on the field with a player like David Gower was a tremendous feeling.'

As I was saying . . .

3 April

Well, they said 'thank you' to David Gower, packed him off to Hampshire who are out here touring and sent David Smith out to open against West Indies in the one-day international. The second David did better than the first. He scored 5.

I suppose you can argue that the need was for an opener but on what other grounds can a selection committee seriously prefer Smith and his 80 Test runs to Gower and his 7,383? The first ball was glanced to long leg for a single, but after that things did not really get any better and one could only feel sorry for him. He was hit on the helmet, then on the thumb and, after hanging on grimly for twelve overs during which time Larkins had helped himself to 27, had two stumps removed, playing across the line at an inswinger from Ezra Moseley. If that thumb injury is as nasty as it looks, it will have been an awful long way to come for five runs.

The match did not provide quite as thrilling a finish as the one day in Kingston but, considering that the kind of drizzle and low cloud that one associates with Birmingham on a bad day was enveloping the ground at ten o'clock, the 10,000 crowd were lucky to see 431 runs scored off 75.3 overs – the contest having been reduced to thirty-eight overs each.

After David Smith's departure, Larkins unleashed three magnificent square cuts for four and was looking just like the player that makes Northamptonshire hearts beat faster until he trod on his stumps as he tried to deal with a low full toss from Walsh. Robin Smith, relishing a fast, true pitch took only 84 balls to blast an entertaining 69 which might have been terminated at 33, but for umpire Barker's eagle eye. Mistiming an extravagant drive off Walsh, Smith holed out to Richardson at extra cover only to hear Barker call no-ball from square leg. The explanation was that the West Indies did not have the four men that are required inside the fielding circle. Haynes had plenty to say about this, but Barker, a portly figure who barely rises above the level of Ambrose's hip, remained adamant and Smith was allowed to continue on his merry way until he misjudged the length of Ambrose's arm and the speed with which that beanstalk of a man could bend. Sweeping up the ball off his own bowling as Smith called for a quick single, Curtly broke the stumps with the batsman still well short of the crease.

Allan Lamb, in his captain's role, ended up with 55 not out and Nasser Hussain, still pained occasionally by his damaged wrist, unbeaten on 15. The total of 214 was a reasonable one for a thirty-eight over match but, after Gladstone Small had Gordon Greenidge caught behind off a lovely delivery that left him, there was never much doubt that the target lay within West Indies' capabilities.

Eddie Hemmings, allowing just nine runs in his first four overs, steadied the run rate, but basically Desmond Haynes and Richie Richardson were in full flow and, as the sun appeared, there was nothing else to do but sit back and enjoy the spectacle of two master batsmen at work. Hussain, leaping high to take a two hander above his head at mid-on, eventually gave Hemmings a deserving wicket by catching Haynes after the West Indies skipper had made 45, but Carlisle Best took over and the momentum was never checked.

In an eventful thirty-fourth over Capel was hit for 17 off five balls and then had Best, who had just reached his 50, brilliantly caught by Stewart on the square leg boundary. Stewart, incidentally, was on as substitute for David Smith which did not suggest that all was well with the state of Smithy's thumb.

The Richardson-Best partnership realized 112 runs in eighteen overs and even though Carl Hooper and Gus Logie went cheaply, Jeff Dujon with one of those elegant straight drives that make the purists swoon, hit the winning four with three balls to spare to give the West Indies a four wicket victory.

Afterwards Sir Garfield Sobers, one of the most swooned-over cricketers of all time, made Richie Richardson Man of the Match and even the large contingent of British supporters went back to their hotels satisfied that they had seen some real Caribbean cricket – a considerable contrast to two days before.

4 April

England were hard at it in the nets at the Kensington Oval again this morning. At least those who could hold a bat were hard at it and that did not include David Smith who has joined the ever-growing list of English batsmen whose hands are beginning to look as if they have been through a meat grinder. It was Moseley's twelfth ball that did David, crunching the thumb against the bat handle. An X-ray revealed no break but Micky Stewart told us that Smith could not hold a bat today and that everything would depend on how he felt in the morning. Obviously the chances are not good.

Happily, news of Angus Fraser's pulled chest muscle is better although he spent the first half-hour in the net bowling chest on and at half-pace under Stewart's watchful eye. Later, when Nasser Hussain was middling the ball nicely despite a wrist that is still giving him some pain, Fraser worked up a bit of steam and said he felt better. It will be a real blow if he is not fit. Gus has proved the perfect foil for Devon Malcolm on this tour. Just when the West Indies batsmen think they have seen the back of Devon's pace for an over or two, on comes Fraser to nag away at their off-stump, frustrating them even more than Malcolm frightens them. Gladstone Small can play that role, too, but neither Phil DeFreitas nor Chris Lewis, despite a good spell against Barbados, have looked sound enough to fill Fraser's large boots.

After lunch it was the West Indies turn to take over in the two nets that are laid out on the playing field itself, rather like that other Oval at Kennington. The Kensington nets are just to the left of the pavilion and the nearest is open sided on the off for a right-hander so that a cut backward of point goes flying towards the balcony a mere thirty yards away. It concentrates the minds of the people who might otherwise be wiling away a sunny afternoon watching their heroes practise.

Veteran spectators position themselves more judiciously like the venerable old gentleman who cuts a remarkable figure as he sits in the shadow in front of the Challenor Stand directly behind one of the nets. He is safe there which is just as well because he looks as fragile as the long, thin cane propped against his knee. He is dressed in a faded black suit, with high backed collar and tie similar to those one sees worn by the earliest cricketers pictured in the sepia photographs hanging on the pavilion wall. His hat is of an indeterminate epoch as well and the expression underneath it is severe and unchanging. One senses that the eyes hidden behind small dark glasses have seen many a ball bowled at the Kensington Oval and that the players he is watching now are being constantly compared to Headley or Hammond or Constantine.

What he will have made of the preliminary warm-up session orchestrated by the West Indies' physiotherapist, Dennis Waight, heaven knows. Stretching exercises followed by a jog around the field with players flopping down every fifty yards for half a dozen quick sit ups was not in the pre-war itinerary for Test match preparation. But Waight knows what he is doing. After thirteen years in charge of the deadliest strike force in cricket, hampered by remarkably few breakdowns, Waight's credentials speak for themselves.

Dennis is an Australian, and rather more than a token white in Viv Richards' African set-up. When he says jump, this lot jump, and high, too. He may only come up to Curtly Ambrose's waist, but his neck is almost as thick as Desmond Haynes' thigh and the story of what he did to some Yank in a bar in Miami who insulted his wife is not only vividly told but frighteningly believable.

Yet Dennis is not a violent man. His bulging muscles are controlled by a pair of beautifully sensitive hands that can free locked joints and restore suppleness to the most weary muscles. He has worked with boxers and rugby league players back home in Australia, but now wants to set up a practice to look after old-age pensioners.

'So many people live in pain unnecessarily,' he told me one evening over a beer at the Rockley Resort bar. 'If affordable therapy is made available they can continue to lead comfortable lives.'

By fast bowling standards Ezra Moseley, at thirty-two, is nudging the senior citizen category, but in Waight's care it will be some time yet before he is pensioned off. While the young whippets got stuck into the batsmen in the nets, Dennis gave Ezra a special work over on the field, leaning with just the right amount of pressure on each spread-eagled leg, bending the Bajan into shapes you would not have thought possible. But, having been given a little of the Waight treatment myself for a pulled thigh muscle, I bet Moseley felt ten years younger afterwards.

5 April

England went into the Fourth Test here at Kensington Oval without the substitute opener David Smith, their best bowler, Angus Fraser, and with Allan Lamb leading the team for the first time in the absence of the man they will miss most of all, Graham Gooch. It is to be hoped – and, indeed, it can be expected – that Lamb will treat the honour of captaining England with a little more respect and loyalty than the last South African to hold the job.

Given that West Indies batted first on a good track that was marginally slower than the one used for the Barbados match and that Lamb is not as good a tactician as Gooch in the field, England could hardly have expected to have got away with anything better than the home team rattling up a score of 311–5, especially as Carlisle Best chose this moment to make his first Test hundred and Viv Richards the very same moment to put Devon Malcolm in his place.

Richards, apparently, had heard that Malcolm had been

WEST INDIES v ENGLAND (4th TEST)

Played at Bridgetown on April 5,6,7,8,10 1990. West Indies won by 164 runs. Toss: England. Man of the match: C.E.L. Ambrose.

WEST INDIES

C.G. Greenidge	c Russell b DeFreitas	41	lbw b Small	3
D.I. Haynes	c Stewart b Small	0	c Malcolm b Small	109
R.B. Richardson	c Russell b Small	45	lbw b DeFreitas	39
C.A. Best	c Russell b Small	164		
I.V.A. Richards*	c Russell b Capel	70	(4) c Small b Capel	12
A.L. Logie	c Russell b Capel	31	(5) lbw b DeFreitas	48
P.J.L. Dujon†	b Capel	31	(8) not out	15
M.D. Marshall	c Lamb b Small	4	(7) c Smith b Small	7
C.E.L. Ambrose	not out	20	c Capel b DeFreitas	1
I.R. Bishop	run out	10	not out	11
E.A. Moseley	b DeFreitas	4	(6) b Small	5
Extras	(lb 8, nb 18)	26	(lb 12, nb 4, w 1)	17
TOTAL		446	(8 wkts dec)	267

ENGLAND

A.J. Stewart	c Richards b Moseley	45	c Richards b Ambrose	37
W. Larkins	c Richardson b Bishop	0	c Dujon b Bishop	0
R.J. Bailey	b Bishop	17	c Dujon b Ambrose	6
A.J. Lamb*	lbw b Ambrose	119	(6) c Dujon b Moseley	10
R.A. Smith	b Moseley	62	(7) not out	40
N. Hussain	lbw b Marshall	18	(8) lbw b Ambrose	0
D.J. Capel	c Greenidge b Marshall	2	(9) lbw b Ambrose	6
R.C. Russell†	lbw b Bishop	7	(5) b Ambrose	55
P.A.J. DeFreitas	c & b Ambrose	24	(10) lbw b Ambrose	0
G.C. Small	not out	1	(4) lbw b Ambrose	0
D.E. Malcolm	b Bishop	12	lbw b Ambrose	4
Extras	(b 14, lb 9, nb 25, w 3))	51	(b 8, lb 9, nb 15, w 1)	33
TOTAL		358		191

BOWLING

ENGLAND	O	M	R	W	O	M	R	W
Malcolm	33	6	142	0	10	0	46	0
Small	35	5	109	4	20	1	74	4
DeFreitas	29.5	6	99	2	22	2	69	3
Capel	24	5	88	3	16	1	66	1
WEST INDIES								
Bishop	24.3	9	70	4	20	8	40	1
Ambrose	25	3	82	2	22.4	10	45	8
Moseley	28	3	114	2	19	4	44	1
Marshall	23	6	55	2	18	8	31	0
Richards	9	4	14	0	10	5	11	0
Richardson					2	1	3	0

Umpires: D.M. Archer and L.H. Barker.

FALL OF WICKETS

	WI	E	WI	E
	1st	1st	2nd	2nd
1st	6	1	13	1
2nd	67	46	80	10
3rd	108	75	109	10
4th	227	268	223	71
5th	291	297	228	97
6th	395	301	238	166
7th	406	308	238	173
8th	411	340	239	181
9th	431	340	—	181
10th	446	358	—	191

quoted in the English papers to the effect that he had the great Viv's number. Whatever Devon had said, it probably wasn't wise. Viv Richards, to quote the man himself, is probably no longer the player he was, but anyone who doubts that he is still a player had better watch out.

The stage was set for Richards' entrance after Small had induced Haynes to turn a ball into Stewart's sure hands at short leg at the end of the second over of the morning. That was Haynes' second duck in two Tests. Greenidge, with all those runs under his belt from the previous weekend, looked set to collect another bucket load when DeFreitas, who had cut down his speed and upped his accuracy in a conscientious effort to bowl as Fraser would have bowled, found an edge and sent Russell tumbling in front of first slip to take the kind of catch he wished he had taken off Logie in Trinidad. Greenidge had made 41.

Richie Richardson also promised more than he delivered, cutting Malcolm viciously a few times before trying to hook Small after lunch and top edging a skier which Russell waited for down the leg side. Richardson's 45 had come out of a total of 108–3. It was a critical moment. Even without Fraser, the West Indies line up had absolutely no reason to have a superiority complex about facing this English attack although you would never have known it from the way I.V.A. Richards strode to the wicket.

It was more than a month since his last first-class innings; fractionally less than a month since his thirty-eighth birthday, yet here he was, still apparently oblivious to the fact that every Test batsman in the world apart from the young Antiguan who had just departed, now wears a helmet. Still the cocked head; still the majestic profile under the peaked cap; still the exaggerated swagger of a man who looks as if he has just bought the world and sold it at a profit. Pride and arrogance marching hand in hand all the way to the wicket.

Once there, a hint of frailty was evident as he searched for some timing against Capel, but it was soon dispelled two overs later with a sweet four past mid-on and another less well-timed drive past mid-off. It was as if, having measured the ground for size, he was now ready to deal with whatever Lamb threw at him, and that turned out to be Malcolm.

Best took a single to give Richards the strike and the first ball was hooked straight on to the face of the scoreboard for six. The next delivery was cut disdainfully for two and then, as the ground erupted, came a second six from a hook that just gained enough elevation to clear a fielder. Still intent on giving the young upstart a lesson, Richards flailed wildly at the fourth ball and was lucky that the top edge carried high over Larkins' head at first slip. Nineteen had come off the over, eighteen of them from the master's bat.

What a performer! What a sense of occasion! No wonder he and Ian Botham understand each other. They both know what a stage is for and how to use it. Maybe they should take up acting and then Both could play Iago to Viv's Othello even if, after this performance, it is clear that Richards is not ready to recite, 'For I am declined into the vale of years.'

Yet although this calculated assault on the man who had clean bowled him at Sabina Park and then dared talk about it, was pure theatre, sport's priceless asset is that no script is ever etched in stone no matter whose hand is wielding the hammer. Richards had ridden the luck of the brave – or the plain arrogant – and had got away with it, but Malcolm could just as easily have had him caught. As it was Lamb took Devon off three overs later by which time Best, with two consecutive drives for four, had left the hero of Trinidad with the soul-bruising figures of 0 for 80 off fourteen overs. Richards had effectively smashed England's strike bowler out of the attack.

After taking 24 off two consecutive overs Richards calmed down a little and glided past his 50 with wristy ones and twos while Best brought the 200 and his own 50 up after facing 90 balls. But the Richards' hundred that the crowd were thirsting for was not forthcoming. Soon after tea, with the score on 227 in the sixty-third over, he touched an outswinger from Capel and Russell took his third catch of the day. He had scored his memorable 70 off 110 balls with two sixes and seven fours, but it still left him 23 runs short of the next milestone in his career – 8,000 Test runs. Only Sunil Gavaskar, with 10,122; Gary Sobers, Allan Border and Geoff Boycott will have beaten him to it.

Best, content to bat in his captain's shadow, now came into his own. A glorious straight drive off Small took him past his previous highest Test score of 64 and by the time the shadow of the Sir Garfield Sobers Stand had reached the square Barbados was ready to acclaim a new cricketing hero. Not a young one, to be sure, because Best is thirty and has taken his time to convince the selectors and maybe himself of his worth. But when two more boundaries off the hapless Malcolm took him into the nineties, he did not falter. Even the arrival of the new ball did not phase him. When he had made 98, Malcolm dropped one short and the ball was through mid-wicket like a bullet. It was the last shot of the day and it left Malcolm bleeding with 0–105 and Best virtually carried off, wreathed in smiles, on 102 not out.

It had been England's worst day of the series so far and for Graham Gooch the frustration level must have been high. Not that he gives too much away, even now. He had dropped by the press-box early on to chat to Graham Morris. The pins are still in the hand and he has been given a ball of Plasticine to help him clench and unclench his fist.

'The doctor advised against putting it in a cast because the recovery time is so much longer,' Gooch explained. 'It gets a bit sore doing it this way, but at least it keeps everything moving.'

6 April

Carlisle Best completed a truly fine Test innings today as West Indies took their first innings total to 446. Freed of the need to play second fiddle to Richards; freed of the tension that builds up as a batsman approaches his maiden Test century, Best set about enjoying himself in the sunshine, knowing that if he did, the crowd would, too. Although very much a leg-side player, Best unleashed a vast array of strokes to the delight of the folks packing the Kensington Stand who were soon getting into their own rhythm of drums and song. The place nearly blew up when Best cross batted Malcolm with the kind of improvised forehand that Boris Becker might have admired and over in the three Ws Stand, where the majority of the British support was situated, true cricket lovers could only sit back and enjoy the spectacle.

Viewed from the pavilion, the press-box or either of the stands adjacent to them, Kensington Oval, basking under blue Caribbean skies with the palm trees bending in the breeze at the far end of the ground, provides any sort of cricket person with a glimpse of paradise. And when a batsman of Jeffrey Dujon's classic elegance unfurls a cover drive of fulsome beauty, one is reminded that cricket, almost alone among sports, is not just about winning and losing, but still very much about how one plays the game.

Soon after this piece of poetry, Dujon departed, chopping a ball from the persevering Capel on to his middle stump. The Jamaican had made 31 out of a stand of 104 which had given the West Indies innings the substance it might otherwise have lacked. For when Best was out for 164, caught by Russell off Small, the wickets continued to tumble and, in fact, the last five only added 51 – a tribute to the way the England bowlers stuck to their task.

Gladstone Small, with 4–109 had been the pick of them, but DeFreitas and Capel had also had good spells and it was left to poor Malcolm to remain wicketless. Fifteen wickets in two Tests and now 0–142. Perhaps he had been trying a little too hard on a track that was probably a fraction slower than he had expected. He must also have missed Gooch's reassuring presence. From a distance it seemed as if Lamb's high-pitched, staccato tones, accompanied by some less than accommodating field placings, were not quite the kind of leadership a troubled and still inexperienced fast bowler needed.

Before this match John Snow had written a piece for the *Sunday Correspondent* which pinpointed, very succinctly, the stages a fast bowler needs to go through to achieve the desired end result. Snow wrote: 'Rhythm gives you balance, balance gives you control, control gives you accuracy and the opportunity to concentrate all your weight and effort into delivery.'

Trying too hard or striving for that extra something that just isn't there can destroy the rhythm and then the rest of the complex fast bowling machinery collapses like a pack of cards. That, basically, is what has been happening to Malcolm in this match and it is yet another facet of the tragedy of Gooch's absence that the captain who has turned Malcolm from a quick, wild county player into a Test match winner was not out there to get him back on the rails.

Of all the Test cricketers watching from the stands, and there were literally scores of them, none would have understood

Malcolm's plight better than the 'Black Diamond', Wayne Daniel. If Daniel had opted for British residency like Malcolm, he would have played seventy-five times or more for England instead of just ten for the West Indies, but even so his exploits for Middlesex will mark him down as one of the finest fast bowlers of his era. There are flecks of grey in the hair now but, at thirty-four, Wayne insists he is as fit as ever and looks it. Having left Middlesex, he is searching for a county and thinks he still has it in him to win a trophy for someone. I wouldn't bet against it.

'What has been happening to Malcolm out there could have happened to any fast bowler,' he said sympathetically. 'There are days when nothing quite clicks and then you try too hard and get all worried about it. Lamby should have taken him off earlier when he saw what was happening and said, don't worry, just relax. I think Goochy would have understood.'

As one of the quickest of quicks, Daniel is not blinded to the advantages of having a spinner on hand, something neither side has got in this match unless you include Richards himself in that category.

'Somebody's going to wish they had one if the pitch starts breaking up on the fourth or fifth day as it usually does,' said Daniel who has been pounding up to the wicket at Kensington Oval since the mid-seventies. 'We even had that guy from Trinidad, Clyde Butts, come here once and turn it on the first morning.'

Before I left him at the bar with some of his Bajan friends, I mentioned that I had been on the rebel tour in South Africa.

'I was a bit disappointed Mike Gatting went out there,' he said. 'I couldn't understand it really. He had so much to offer England. But maybe something can be worked out with the sporting bodies now. It would be great if that happened because South Africa has got some good players.'

But all that seemed far away when England started their reply to the West Indies total of 446. Ominously I notice that the scoreboard operators, in switching the names of the teams from one side to the other, as they do at the end of each innings, have inadvertently – or could it be perceptively – left a '1' under the wicket column which is now lined up against the name of Bishop.

Unhappily for England they knew what they were doing. In

171

Bishop's very first over, after a single to Stewart had given Larkins the strike, the Northants opener did what comes naturally when he sees a ball pitched a fraction short outside his off-stump – on to the back foot and whack. An inch further up the bat and it would have a nice little four to get the blood flowing. But, at cover point, Richie Richardson was already on his toes and, flinging himself to his right, he somehow managed to get a hand to it to bring off a spectacular catch.

But if the risks involved in going for one's shots at the start of an innings against this sort of attack had been clearly signposted by Larkins' first-ball dismissal, his colleagues did not take a blind bit of notice. With no wise owl to orchestrate proceedings by setting the tempo, the Trinidadian tortoise suddenly turned into Bajan hare as Stewart, with Bailey in support, set off on a run chase that seemed better suited to the Benson & Hedges Cup.

Bailey, putting his Port of Spain pair behind him, was off the mark first ball with one off the gloves to long leg and then Stewart cover drove Bishop for four and took a single off the last ball. Seven runs and one wicket from the over. Was this Test cricket? More importantly, could it last?

Well, it lasted until tea, anyway, by which time Stewart had been dropped on his way to reaching 21; Bailey, gaining in confidence, had made 11 and England, at 33–1, had been scoring at the barely believable rate of more than 5 an over. The crowd was abuzz and although a few impromptu matches sprang up around the edge of the playing area during the interval – including one between Master Haynes and Master Greenidge whose combined ages appeared to fall short of double figures – no one touched the batsmen's helmets that were left lying out in front of the pavilion to dry in the sun. Is there still a ground in England where equipment can be left lying around unattended? It would be nice to think so.

In the ninth over it was Bailey's turn to get carried away. Having turned Bishop past Logie at forward short leg for two and then taken an uppish four just behind square leg, he tried to drive a ball of fuller length, misjudged everything and was bowled. Rob had scored 17 and he knew he had missed the opportunity of making a great many more.

Lamb's appearance did nothing to put a break on the galloping scoreboard. The fifty came up in forty-six minutes; 51 had been scored off fifty-six balls and the innings was ten overs old before Stewart allowed Bishop to bowl him a maiden. With Lamb playing and missing occasionally, Stewart continued to look as if he had been opening the innings for England in the West Indies all his life as he cracked Moseley through the covers for four and then jabbed down expertly on one that shot through at ankle height.

Heaven knows what the score would have been by now if that shot of Larkins had gone for four and Ned had stayed in. The pair of them might have gone berserk. As it was Stewart continued to take chances in a very classy sort of way and finally outdid Dujon for elegance, going down on one knee to cover drive Moseley for four. Even this ground has witnessed few sweeter shots than that.

It was, however, Alec's last boundary. After turning the next ball for two, he tried another drive, got an outside edge and Richards took the catch at first slip. It was the sixteenth over, Stewart had made 45 and England had arrived in too much of a hurry at 75–3.

Some of the bowling had not been as accurate as Richards would have liked and Moseley, in particular, had not looked as consistently dangerous as he had in Trinidad. Much to the disgust of cricket fans back in Kingston, West Indies had decided to leave out Courtney Walsh, with his 131 Test wickets at 23.70 a piece, from the available quintet of Marshall, Moseley, Bishop, Ambrose and himself. Even though Lamb continued to edge the occasional ball above, through and around the despairing slips, West Indies could have done with Walsh's renowned accuracy as the afternoon wore on.

Marshall, still some way short of full-match fitness, made one rear up at Robin Smith, but England were back to their South African-born formation again and the partnership prospered as Lamb, evidently unconcerned with the cares of captaincy as far as his batting is concerned, cut Ambrose to the boundary and then off drove him for four with a typical Lamb-like flourish to reach his fifty in 92 balls.

Interestingly it had been Viv Richards who had done as much as anyone to check the scoring rate. At one stage he had bowled six overs for seven runs and if he could manage that with gentle off spin, what might Eddie Hemmings have done for England?

The 150 had just been posted in 189 minutes when the umpires finally offered the light and Lamb, having just found a way of getting Richards away through the covers, decided that this was no time to get greedy and led Smith off. He had made 63, Smith was on 17 and England back on some sort of an even keel at 155–3.

No sooner had the players disappeared into the pavilion than Gooch came out with a padded-up Hussain and proceeded to hurl balls at his young Essex colleague, baseball style, until the light went for good. They don't miss a trick, this England team.

7 April

Despite Allan Lamb's 100 and Robin Smith's gutsy, if lucky, 62, England were still struggling to keep on level terms by the end of the third day's play. They would, almost certainly, have been in far worse shape had West Indies' close catchers remembered to take some glue with them on to the field. For the entire morning absolutely nothing stuck and Smith was the happy recipient of this unusual generosity on no less than four occasions. He was put down in turn by Logie, Best, Richards and Dujon when he had scored 21, 32, 41 and 45 respectively. Although Logie's chance, high above his head at short leg was difficult, all were catchable by the standards West Indies have set themselves over the years and the look that passed between Richards and Dujon when the veteran keeper emulated his captain by dropping Smith in the same over off Moseley was worth framing. Moseley's expression, meanwhile, was that of a man trying to conceal an irrepressible desire to kill. Of the four chances, three had come off his bowling. If anyone feels, as some local politicians still do, that Ezra has not served enough penance since returning from South Africa, then he was serving some more right here.

Lamb had been keeping the edges – far fewer than yesterday, in any case – away from grasping hands and, as the cloud cover cleared, the measured milestones of a well constructed partner-

174

ship began slipping by to the vocal satisfaction of the English supporters in the Three Ws Stand who were never afraid to compete with the trumpets and hilarity that echoed across the ground from the Kensington side.

Immediately after lunch Lamb hooked Ambrose for four to achieve the distinction of scoring a century in his first match as England captain. It was his eleventh Test hundred and his sixth against West Indies bowling. The only other Englishman to score as many against West Indies, Colin Cowdrey, was applauding from the pavilion.

Then Smith saved the follow on with a cover drive off the despairing Moseley and shortly afterwards reached his own half-century with a pleasant on drive for three off Marshall. It had taken him 177 balls and it will not be the most faultless or spectacular he has ever scored but, possibly, one of the most important.

Good bowlers usually have the final say, however, and Moseley and Ambrose, who had also had Smith dropped, began to get their just deserts as the afternoon wore on. First Lamb fell lbw half-forward to Ambrose and then, just after tea, Smith had his bails clipped by Moseley. His 62 had been a marathon innings lasting six hours ten minutes, facing 239 balls. The partnership when it had ended with Lamb's dismissal for 119 at 268–4 had produced 193 priceless runs and had easily outstripped their combined contribution of 158 at Sabina Park. Another of Cowdrey's records, however, had never been in much danger. The world record for a fourth-wicket partnership in Test cricket, let alone the record for England against the West Indies, was the 411 Cowdrey and Peter May put on together against John Goddard's touring side at Edgbaston in 1957.

All this search for historical data had to be put aside for a couple of minutes during tea, however, because Simon Barnes, a paid-up member of the bird watchers' club, had spotted an Osprey dallying high over the third palm tree from the left at the far end of the ground. Earlier in the day I had admired a rather larger but equally graceful bird as Concorde, which British Airways had diverted from New York to meet demand, came swooping down out of the azure skies to embellish an already perfect canvas.

Simon's Osprey, however, proved more difficult to spot. Even Christopher Martin-Jenkins, who, being equally adept at telling feather from fowl, was invited to share in Barnes' discovery, needed a pair of high-powered glasses to spot what *The Times* had already identified with the naked eye. Staring hopelessly into the far distance, I was eventually brought into line with the target by Simon's impatient directions and caught sight of a tiny black speck. You've got to be keen to be a bird watcher.

Once the Lamb-Smith partnership had been broken up, the Richards' pace attack, not to mention the Bajan crowd, became a great deal keener on the cricket and Marshall, steaming in with something like his old verve, forced Capel into error and Greenidge proved that the West Indies could still catch by hanging on to a brilliant effort at second slip. Then in the next over Hussain, who had hit three fours in his 18, fell lbw and Marshall greeted DeFreitas with one that rose past his nose.

DeFreitas, in fact, was the only lower order batsman to offer any further resistance and his six over square leg off Ambrose was one of the shots of the match. But, having scored 24 he gave Ambrose a simple return catch and England were 340–9.

In singling DeFreitas out for praise, I may have been a little unfair on Devon Malcolm who managed to bring down the curtain on the England innings with a surprising flourish. He was actually bowled first ball by Ambrose, but as the umpire had called no-ball, Devon calmly turned round and banged the spreadeagled pegs back into place with the handle of his bat. 'Bad luck, try again,' seemed to be his attitude and Ambrose did not appear amused. Down comes the bumper which Malcolm avoids and the boos ring out from the Three Ws. So Ambrose pitches the next one up and gets driven, handsomely, through mid-off for four. The cheers had barely subsided when Ambrose gave him another one outside off-stump and Malcolm blasted the ball straight back to the same mid-off boundary. Ambrose, standing transfixed in mid-pitch, had to be led away by his captain.

Malcolm actually survived another over from Ambrose, moving his score into double figures, a major landmark for this No. 11, before literally falling out of the way of another bouncer that earned Ambrose a word of warning from the umpire. But, of course, it could not last and Bishop discovered the way to prise out the man who was not supposed to be able to bat, by going round the wicket, changing the line and bowling him.

England, 358 all out, had only added 90 after Lamb's departure and Greenidge and Haynes reappeared with an 88 run lead in their pockets. But one of the greatest characteristics of this England team lies in its capacity to strike back and, just before the light faded, Small had Greenidge lbw for 3 playing back. West Indies finished at 19–1 and another fascinating Test match was heading for a fourth day, rich in possibilities.

8 April

On Sunday morning, all dressed up in their best attire with the ladies in splendid hats and the men in jackets and ties, the vast majority of the good people of Barbados go to church. By the time many of them reached Kensington Oval at around midday, most of their prayers had been answered. Desmond Haynes, the first innings duck cast far from his mind, had passed his 50 and was nearing another Test hundred. And although Richie Richardson had gone lbw for 39, beaten on the back foot by one that kept low from DeFreitas, and had been followed by Viv Richards, who hit a mistimed drive to Small off Capel for 12, West Indies were still looking secure at lunch with 115–3 on the board, a lead of 203. Anything over 300 and England can forget it.

However assured Haynes may have looked at the crease, accusations of slowing down the play to suit his side's needs in Port of Spain obviously still rankled him because he reacted to Lamb's equally blatant stalling tactics by waving his bat as he came off for lunch, first at the England captain and then, very pointedly, at the press-box where many of his accusers sat. Not a man to conceal his feelings, is Desmond Haynes.

The point Haynes was making was perfectly valid; namely that any captain is going to do anything he can get away with if it suits his team's purpose. And as long as the game's law makers are stupid enough to make toothless laws, Haynes, Lamb or any other captain is going to manipulate the over rate any way he wants.

Lamb was faced with two options at the start of play. The one he favoured, obviously, was to make a quick breakthrough and get the West Indies out for about 200. The alternative, which became the only viable option as Haynes worked his way into form, was to keep it tight and give the opposition as few balls to hit as possible so that any declaration would come as late as possible. Lamb went after the second option with a vengeance. England succeeded in bowling at a rate of 11.2 this morning with precisely nine overs bowled in the last hour. If you are talking about the spirit of the game, it was a disgrace. But if you accept the realities of modern-day professional sport where defeat is feared more than victory is prized and almost anything is acceptable in the avoidance of one and the pursuit of the other, then don't blame Lamb. Blame the wafflers and the procrastinators who won't lay down proper penalties to safeguard the one aspect of the game that can destroy it as a spectacle more than anything else – the speed at which cricket is played. It beggars belief that the game's governing bodies in all Test playing countries do not understand how important this problem is.

Haynes completed a superb innings for his side just after tea with an on-drive off Capel. By the time it beat DeFreitas to the boundary, Haynes was leaping into the air, high-fiving Logie, punching victory salutes towards the Kensington Stand, waving his bat about and generally looking quite pleased with himself. God knows what he'd do if he ever scored a goal for Barbados in the World Cup.

Richards, being the cautious captain he is, kept his batsmen out there longer than should prove necessary after Haynes was eventually out for 109, skying one to Malcolm off Small. DeFreitas, who has really matured as a bowler in this match, grabbed a couple of well-deserved wickets towards the end getting Logie lbw for 48 – a typical Logie sort of score – and then having Ambrose caught by Capel. Dujon and Bishop were called in at 267–8 with about fifty minutes of light left, a total that left England with the hopeless task of scoring 356 to win – a figure they have never, ever achieved when chasing victory in the fourth innings of a Test.

If England were to have any hoping of surviving, they would need to take at least nine wickets into the fifth day and even then the task would seem mountainous. But it was not to be. In the very first over, Larkins, brought on strike by Stewart's unfailing ability to get off the mark straight away, fenced nervously at Bishop's delivery outside the off-stump and then, off the second ball he received, took a rising ball on the glove and gave Dujon a catch. 1–1 and the original opening partnership on which so much had depended had evaporated. Gooch out injured and Larkins out for a pair.

Obviously someone was finding it hard to take because a spot of crowd trouble broke out underneath the scoreboard where beer and sunshine had been producing the inevitable results amongst some of the British contingent. But even when the police moved in, it still looked like a tea party compared to Stamford Bridge on a Saturday afternoon and, generally, the rivalry between the fans has been very good natured.

However, no sooner had the flare-up on the boundary died down than the focus of tension returned to the middle when a ball from Ambrose shot down the leg side missing everything, it seemed, except part of Bailey's anatomy, probably clipping the back of the hip area. Obviously Dujon heard something because he leapt into the air as he caught the ball, launching an appeal which sent Richards and the other close catches into a wardance of delight. A whole huddle of fielders were still immersed in the process of self-congratulation when they realized that umpire Lloyd Barker was beginning to move out to square leg – it having been the last ball of the over – and Bailey was standing his ground. The whole tableau froze for a split second as all faces turned towards Barker who stopped about four paces away from the stumps, turned and, after a brief hesitation, raised his finger. Bailey slammed his bat into the ground in disgust and walked off, a picture of fury and dejection.

After a long day, Small, the designated night-watchman, appeared and, in Ambrose's next over, missed the second ball he received and was given out lbw instantly by Barker. England were 10–3.

Russell who, I felt, would have made a far safer night-watchman in the fading light, survived and England ended in disarray at 15–3 with a whole day's batting ahead of them if the match was to be saved.

Yesterday, before the sun started sinking on England's chances of saving this match, I asked Micky Stewart if we could have a chat. Originally he had suggested I go over to see him on the England balcony during the morning session, but the timing proved less than perfect as I found the manager holding an ice-cube to his upper lip. On another tour, the sight might have given rise to all manner of conjecture about which member of the team had taken a swipe at him, but with no Botham-type super-stars to be 'shopped' by bed-bouncing blondes, even the tabloids have been writing about the cricket during the past couple of months which, in light of Stewart's opinion of certain segments of the Press, must have come as a major relief to him.

There was a fairly innocent explanation for the swollen lip. 'You could say I miscalculated the angle at which Medlycott was throwing the ball to me when I was having a little hit this morning,' Micky mumbled and then added, 'Actually I wasn't looking.'

That at least let Medlycott off the hook. The last thing a player needs when he has already been relegated to chief dog's body on a tour is to hit the manager in the mouth. Poor Keith. No one could make a better job of hiding the frustration he must feel at having been given so little chance to prove himself out here. A smile is never far from his face and no man has ever walked more miles around a boundary rope, water jug in hand, dispensing drinks to parched colleagues in between balls as 'Medders'. Once he suffered the indignity of being chased off by Umpire Barker because there was nowhere he could walk in front of the Kensington Stand without being on the actual playing area. But that did not deter him. Within minutes he was back on the other side of the ground, chatting to English supporters, signing autographs and quenching Capel's thirst after a long bowl. Never underestimate the importance of a willing support group on tour. In this respect as well, this team has been well blessed.

After lunch Stewart was able to talk. First of all I wanted to get his side of the Mike Gatting story; the talk they had at Uxbridge and the apparent lack of communication that followed.

'Mike and I have never ceased to communicate, that's got to be understood,' said Stewart. 'Our personal relationship has always been excellent. What happened was a story that appeared in one of the tabloids a few days after our talk at Uxbridge written by a free-lance journalist called Paul Martin which spilled the beans on the fact that Mike was asking certain members of the TCCB for assurances that they still wanted him to be part of the England set-up. That wrecked it. Martin obviously had good sources because three-quarters of the story was essentially correct. But the fact that it appeared in a popular newspaper at that moment was the very worst thing that could have happened as far as getting a couple of the Board members who were not particularly pro-Mike to send him the right signals.'

Stewart is a very quiet and thoughtful talker. In press conference, he plays the dead bat with such bland efficiency that he is barely worth quoting. But he is a man with strong feelings and plenty to say, as I was to learn. He watched Devon Malcolm lift a large arm to take the sort of shy at the stumps that had cost England three overthrows a little earlier and gave a sigh of relief when Devon thought better of it. Then, after a few seconds pause, he said deliberately, 'The Press cost England Mike Gatting. The business at Nottingham and then this. That sort of thing, what they call cheque-book journalism, is not merely immoral, it should be made illegal.'

It is no secret that Stewart and Gatting got on well, some said too well, during Gatt's captaincy and the manager reiterated the point to me. 'During all the time we worked together I never had the slightest doubt that Mike was 100 per cent committed to England's cause. He would have done anything for the team. That, coupled with the kind of player he was, made him such a valuable asset. Of course, he still had a lot to learn, but you could not fault him on the kind of qualities we looked for in selecting this side. In many respects I have found Graham to be very similar in his commitment and resolve.'

According to some statistics I saw in *The Cricketer*, no batsman in the world made more first-class runs during the eighties than Gooch and Gatting yet the odds on having them both in the West Indies were always going to be long because, had the captaincy job not been available, Gooch would almost certainly have taken up the contract offered him by Western Province and probably gone off to captain the rebel team. The only chance of having them both seems to have rested with Stewart's ability to persuade the anti-Gatting faction on the TCCB that his special qualities of courage, commitment and talent were vital to the kind of inexperienced team they were going to choose. But as soon as details of the negotiations were leaked, the last hope was gone.

Talking of former England captains, I raised the subject of David Gower and confessed that I was somewhat confused by the whole incident. Nothing that Stewart said led me to change the largely unsubstantiated feeling I had that it was Gooch who made the initial overture and that Micky, while readily accepting that Gower's presence could be a life saver in extremis, let it be known that he would prefer not to have such a laid-back representative of the old way of thinking hanging around the locker room.

'By the time Graham injured his hand in Trinidad, we were down to the bare minimum of batsmen because Nasser Hussain also had his wrist problem,' said Stewart. 'So even though we sent for David Smith, we knew we might need two batsmen so David was asked if he would like to help out. We knew we were setting him up to a certain extent because he had not played a competitive game of cricket since September and it was bound to be difficult to adjust. But he agreed to play against Barbados by which time Nasser had come right so it was less of an emergency.'

I asked him about the rumour that had been circulating in the press-box the previous evening to the effect that Gower had been contacted once again with a view to standing by for Test duty in Antigua.

'Yes, it was agreed that we could call on him again if we ran into trouble for the Antigua Test. As it stands today Smithy still can't hold a bat and David is still on stand-by. We shall just have to see what happens.'

Broadening the topic of conversation, I tried to draw him out on his inner feelings of how the tour had gone. Wasn't he just a little bit surprised? Again the answer did not come quickly.

'No,' he said, pausing, searching for words that would not make him sound boastful. 'Look, you know what odds the bookmakers were giving on us winning a match out here. But I knew the work that had been put in and, just as importantly, I knew what type of player we had selected. Very deliberately we had gone for the type of person who is highly competitive and wants to win at everything he does. In this team we have types who would want to beat you at table tennis if they played you in the lunch interval. They are motivated to do well and they have great pride. As a result I just felt that if everyone produced their own par for the course according to their own individual abilities, based on their track record to date, that we would be all right.'

Largely because of the timing of the tour, Stewart had been able to prepare at Lilleshall in a manner that would have been denied earlier teams even if the inclination to work that hard had been there. But the point he wanted to stress as we continued to talk through the afternoon session as Desmond Haynes advanced to his century, was that the cream of English cricket not only had to be allowed to rise to the top at an early age, but it had to be separated from the froth that slopped about in happy, ignorant bliss on cricket fields all over Britain every summer weekend.

'There's no disputing that our sport gives thousands of people hours of wonderful enjoyment every weekend. They play their cricket and all end up in the pub having a great old time. That's wonderful. That's as it should be for the casual player. But it has got absolutely nothing to do with what we are about at the England level. Broadly speaking we have got our priorities all wrong in comparison to the West Indies which I consider to be the home of cricket.

'In England we have lovely grounds, most of them with nice pavilions and all the modern facilities. And the fields themselves are even and well kept. Where we fall down is with the two things that matter – the 22 yards on the square and the standard of player batting and bowling on it. In the West Indies exactly the opposite is true. They have rutted outfields, grounds that are often too small and very meagre facilities in their pavilions. But out there in the middle is a raised 22 yard square that is perfect. And each island has a hard nucleus of players who can play. As a result the standards are high.

'In England too many of our talented youngsters are lost in a forest of mediocrity. There are 600 clubs in my county, Surrey. Yorkshire has 1,000 and they are the ones that are registered. If you can hold a bat, you can get a game of cricket and long may it continue. But somehow we have got to devise methods of getting hold of the real talent and consolidating it at a higher level. Let's take an example. Christopher Martin-Jenkins has a boy at a public school which will have a good first XI, but from what I understand the lad is talented and has above average potential. If that is true, 75 per cent of the cricket he plays during the summer will be below the level of his capabilities. As a result he will never improve as quickly as he should. It is no wonder Australia produces better players at a younger age than we do because each city has programmes whereby talented youngsters are taken out of the school system to play against each other. Each city has sixteen clubs which play two-day matches so that a young batsman can learn to bat all day instead of having to go in and slog. That's what we've got to start emulating. Otherwise all our best talent will end up getting pissed in the pub on a Saturday night with the rest of them.'

Micky Stewart would seek no apologies for sounding hard-nosed about it. Even in the old days, amateurs at the Oval had to be pros at heart and Stewart is the pro's pro who has no illusions about what it takes to succeed in today's game.

'Touring teams in the old days used to play up-country games, have days off and be expected to turn up to three social functions during a Test match. It was a lovely way to do it, but today's tours are run on a budget-conscious calendar that gets you in and out with the maximum amount of cricket played in the minimum amount of time. As a result, the social life has been reduced, too. One function over a period of a Test is all we are agreeing to. Anything more would be out of the question. We get to the ground at eight in the morning and it's seven by the time we get back to the hotel. That's an eleven-hour day. How can you expect players to stand around at cocktail parties after spending six of those eleven hours out in the field? It's a different world now. It's tougher but we are learning to handle it.'

A couple of days earlier it had been announced back in England that the computer company, Bull, were going to sponsor a programme called the Development of Excellence. It was, of course, largely Stewart's brainchild. After what has been achieved on this tour, the powers at Lords will have to listen with a little more care to what he says about the required restructuring of English cricket. There are no short cuts to success in professional sport today. It is a tough business, fit only for tough people. Stewart recognized this from the moment he was appointed England manager three years ago and the success of his original team when Gatting took over the captaincy quickly reflected it. It was easy to forget, during the shambles which followed, that Gatting's team had won all three competitions in Australia in 1986–87, a triumph by any standards even allowing for the fact that the Australians were still eighteen months away from maturing into the side we saw in England last summer. Then there was the not inconsiderable achievement of getting to the final of the World Cup in India which, of course, was followed by Gatting's three-minute loss of control in Pakistan – three minutes that changed the history of English cricket. This was the moment when the hard-nosed regime of Stewart and Gatting went one step too far. Disciplinary action was called for, but proper handling from the officers could have got the sergeant's mess back on track. The CO of any good regiment can recognize the moment when his senior non-commissioned officers are becoming over zealous; the moment when a dose of measured discipline is required.

But instead of firm control, the High Command at Lords veered off in all kinds of absurd directions, first of all handing out £1,000 bonuses for all the hardship suffered in the trenches of Lahore and Faisalabad and then firing the captain several months later when a tabloid newspaper caught Gatting doing something stupid – succumbing to the dubious charms of a predatory female at midnight. Would those international athletes who have not done something similar please stand up? Mmm . . . I thought so.

Of course Gatting should have known better, but had the right kind of riot act been read to him in Pakistan, he might have learnt something. As it was, Stewart's well-laid plans for toughening up English cricket were torn apart at the seams and he was lucky to survive amidst the debris. There were moments when many observers doubted that he should have done, but I think those doubts must have been erased now. There is absolutely no question that the type of approach he is advocating is the right one because there is no place in this world for perennial losers. But that does not mean winning at all costs. The right balance which was lost in Pakistan, has to be found. In the West Indies in 1990, there was every evidence that the Stewart-Gooch partnership had found that balance, largely because the right kind of foot soldier had been selected for the mission. It is just another irony that this would not have been the case had not Ali Bacher drawn off the world weary and disillusioned troops for his South Africa campaign. And if they, in turn, have helped to accelerate the process of acceptance that Bacher is trying to achieve with the National Sports Congress in South Africa, could it be that everything worked out for the best, even allowing for the vilification of Mike Gatting? Am I being too optimistic? We shall see.

Moving a couple of seats further down the England balcony at the Kensington Oval, I was able to catch up with someone I had been hoping to drop in on in Zimbabwe as I flew back from South Africa – Mark Nicholas, captain of the England 'A' team. A hopelessly tight schedule prevented me from doing that but now, little more than a week after leaving Harare, he was not only in Barbados but had survived the unpleasant experience of being taken ill on the plane and put into hospital with suspected malaria within hours of his arrival.

Unhappily, the malaria had been confirmed and he was looking very gaunt and yellow compared to the plumper and pinker young captain I had first met in Sri Lanka four years before. His side was called the 'B' team then and, strangely, he and Peter Lush had turned out to be the big survivors from that winter's touring, no promotion but no sacking either, which was more than could be said for Bob Willis and David Gower who were in charge of the disastrous expedition to the Caribbean.

Those who had seen Nicholas, by accent and attitude, as a modern day Colin Ingleby-MacKenzie, were putting too much emphasis on the lighter side of his personality and overlooking the ambitious streak that lay beneath. Unlike Gatting and Gooch, Nicholas has been bred to lead and in Colombo he had struck me as someone who was totally comfortable with the responsibility of captaincy. There had, apparently, been moments at Hampshire when his players had felt less than comfortable with his leadership. However, the crisis had passed and the England selectors had been happy to entrust him with the demanding job

186

of blooding an even less experienced group of players than were going to the West Indies on the trip to Kenya and Zimbabwe.

Despite complaints about the slow scoring rate on the fifth day of one of the 'Tests', the tour was adjudged a success by Charles Randall, Richard Streeton and other knowledgeable observers who covered it and, from speaking to him, it became quickly apparent that Nicholas' determination to teach young cricketers just how tough and demanding the international game can be matched that of Stewart's.

'My team was selected on the same basis as the squad that was sent out here,' Nicholas said. 'We wanted players of a certain character, players with a driving ambition to succeed and I was very proud of the way they measured up.'

Nicholas was less optimistic about the immediate future of cricket in Zimbabwe where it is still very much a white minority sport.

'They are obviously missing the two top-rate players they have produced, Graeme Hick and Peter Rawson, an opening bowler who has gone to Natal,' Nicholas explained. 'And their other good players are coming to the end of their careers. Clearly they need an injection of talent from the black community, but at the moment there is only one good black cricketer, Ethan Dube, a nineteen-year-old bowler. What they need is either some West Indians or our own black players to go down there and teach a few local coaches. Then they could start spreading the game in the black communities. From what I learnt, it would be difficult for a white person to inspire the right kind of interest in the game where it is needed most.'

Providing the cricket is played in the right spirit, this sort of tour can only benefit the tourists – if they are properly led – and the hosts. It seems that they will become a regular part of the winter schedule in future and that is as it should be. Even tours one stage lower down the scale like the brief visit Peter Roebuck's team made to Holland last summer or the side Paul Parker took to Argentina earlier this year should be encouraged. Cricket needs friends and supporters wherever it can find them and men like Nicholas are proving themselves to be excellent ambassadors.

I spent the rest of the day trying to get some words on paper. I have yet to set foot on a beach in Barbados – or anywhere else on this tour for that matter – which may offer some idea of how time consuming the business of covering a cricket tour can be. I have no complaints about that, but it is necessary just once in a while to do something more active than sitting at the cricket or sitting at the typewriter.

So this evening I played tennis at the Barbados Yacht Club with Andrew and Sue Bloomfield, Jamaican friends who have become very involved in the tennis scene since moving here, and Norman Marshall, who played one Test for the West Indies against Ian Johnson's Australian side in 1954. Norman is a very tall man in his mid-sixties, is unbelievably fit and is the brother of the great Hampshire opener, Roy Marshall.

Over drinks in the clubhouse after four energetic sets, I learned a little about Bajan society. There is an interesting story, for a start, about why the Yacht Club is no longer called 'Royal'. Apparently, sometime in the sixties, the committee rejected a black person's application. As there were no black members at the time, complaints were voiced in high places and the Colonial Office back in London ordered that the club be stripped of its 'Royal' title.

That was all very fine and good, but the problem is that, even today, there are still hardly any black members.

'There's no problem about them joining now, of course,' Norman Marshall told me. 'It's just that they don't apply!'

I was surprised to learn that there is very little mixing on a social level between the 8,000 white Barbadians and the remainder of the 250,000 population. Everyone gets along fine in the work place but, come dinner-party time, the races stick to their own. Coming from Jamaica, the Bloomfields were quick to notice the difference.

'In Jamaica, we are such a hotch-potch with black, Indian, Chinese and white all mixed up that there is really no racial divide,' said Andrew. 'Our divisions are strictly between rich and poor which is not the case here in Barbados.'

After the tennis, the Bloomfields hosted a small barbecue at their lovely old house near the former British Garrison. Apart from Norman Marshall, Steve Camacho, secretary of the West Indies Board of Control, was also invited so the conversation roamed freely between cricket and tennis as we supped under the stars on one of those balmy Caribbean evenings that one dreams about on a typical English winter's night.

Camacho, who was capped eleven times by the West Indies in the sixties, is a big follower of British football and generally seems to have a broader grasp of the problems facing world sport than many cricket administrators. Although he was talking off the record, he agreed that cricket could not afford the kind of slap in the face it received from the Barbados match and insisted that Haynes was not acting under any suggestion from the West Indies team management concerning his decision to deprive England batsmen of extra practice by refusing to declare at a reasonable time.

'We have to ensure that the cricket we offer the public is of the highest quality,' said Camacho, 'and that, for a variety of reasons, is not always the case at the moment.'

Talking of quality, Steve played his Test cricket under the captaincy of Gary Sobers, a player he rates as the greatest all-round athlete he has ever seen. 'He could bowl any way that was required as well as bat, field and captain the team,' said Steve, 'and the most remarkable thing was that he did it all on about four hours' sleep and more than the odd glass of brandy. He was phenomenal.'

Interestingly, too, Camacho rated the Imran Khan of the early eighties right up there as a fast bowler with the fearsome West Indies quartet of Andy Roberts, Michael Holding, Joel Garner and Colin Croft. 'When Pakistan were touring Australia at the same time as us one year, I thought Imran was probably as good, if not better, than any of our lot,' said Camacho.

10 April

Nearly! Half an hour more would have done it but at 5.16 p.m. this evening, Devon Malcolm was given out lbw to Curtly Ambrose and England had failed in a quite gallant attempt to bat all day and so leave for Antigua tonight still 1–0 up. The margin, which became an irrelevance as the day wore on, was 164 runs.

At the start of the day, it seemed that the cricket itself might become an irrelevance, so fierce was the indignation over a report put out on BBC World Service Radio by Christopher Martin-Jenkins concerning the nature of Rob Bailey's dismissal on Sunday night.

First of all, this is what Martin-Jenkins said at the beginning of his report: 'Sadly, this thrilling and, in many ways, intriguing, Fourth Test is going to be overshadowed by the shameless win-at-all-costs attitude of the players.

'Both sides have cheated each other on the overs bowled and yesterday a very good umpire cracked under the pressure and gave an England batsman out against his better judgement and because Viv Richards, the West Indies captain, led an orchestrated appeal and demonstrations of jubilation.'

The uproar those remarks caused could be heard right across the island. Nor was it confined to the less informed sections of the community. Norman Marshall was seething about Martin-Jenkins' comments when we played tennis the previous evening and the former Jamaican Test opener, Maurice Foster, was very derisive about the whole thing when he spoke at the start of the day's play on Barbados radio. I was surprised by his tone and even more surprised when he dredged up the old 'teacher not liking to be beaten by the pupil' nonsense. England has now been beaten so many times at so many sports by countries it taught to play that the original relationship is barely worth mentioning, except as a historical footnote.

But, of course, what the reaction to charges of cheating did show was the sensitivity of any kind of criticism from former colonial masters. I know I am guilty occasionally of forgetting just how recent the colonial experience has been for black people of my generation and consequently need to remind myself of the reasons for certain patterns of behaviour. Once again I was taken aback by the intensity of the reaction.

There were pages of comment in both the *Nation* and the *Advocate* this morning and, of course, the politicians had to get into the act. The opposition shadow minister for sport, Senator Vere Braithwaite, suggested, 'The journalist should apologize for his remarks' and went on to say, 'The cricketers should essay to continue in the true spirit of sportsmanship and should not allow the British "gutter press" to interfere in a game which has contributed significantly to the promotion of social dialogue and understanding . . .'

If the senator thinks the BBC is broadcast out of the gutter where does he imagine the *Sun* is published? The reader may have an appropriate answer, but all that these remarks achieved was to show how far we were getting from the issue at hand.

As I saw it the real issue was this. Under the laws, rather than the spirit, of the game, the onus is not on the batsman to walk, no matter how sporting that gesture may be, if the batsman knows he is out. Nevertheless the onus is on the umpire to raise his finger if he is answering an appeal in the affirmative. Some umpires take longer to do this than others and no one complains if an umpire stands there for five or six seconds before deciding whether or not he thinks a ball would have hit leg stump. But Lloyd Barker, as he proved again today by adjudging no less than four England bastmen out lbw, is a fast decision-maker. If he thinks an appeal should be upheld, up goes the finger without hesitation.

Very markedly, this was not the case when Dujon, having taken the ball down the leg side, led a riotous appeal which was instantaneously echoed by the leaping slips and the cavorting Richards. Obviously they thought they heard something. Barker's initial reaction may have been that the ball flicked the very top of Bailey's thigh pad or maybe even his hip pocket. What was very clear was the ten to fifteen seconds that passed before, seemingly as an afterthought, he put his finger up as Bailey stared at him in disbelief. Most significantly of all, it being the last ball of the over, Barker had already taken four paces to square leg before he stopped and signalled.

Sitting in the press-box or in the commentary position those of us who had been watching Barker all series were given a distinct impression that he had either changed his mind or gone totally out of character in making a very late decision. Given that the strength of the appeal was at peak decibel level even by West Indies standards, it was wholly reasonable to suggest that Barker had buckled under the pressure. It has happened in the past to umpires as good as Barker in situations less strenuous on the nerves than the one we found ourselves in on Sunday evening after the noisily orchestrated crowd in the Kensington Stand had woken from a drowsy afternoon to support its fast bowlers with bugle, drum and song.

Christopher Martin-Jenkins was not criticizing Barker so much as the players for adopting the modern habit of pressurizing officials into giving decisions favourable to their cause. This is what Martin-Jenkins finds abhorrent and, being the sincere, fair and unbiased commentator that he is, he would be as critical of England, Australia or any team employing those tactics as he would the West Indies. This, of course, was conveniently overlooked as everyone with grievances to air seized on his comments as an affront to the West Indies reputation for sportsmanship and let the issue get carried away on the winds of emotion.

Viv Richards managed to remain quite rational about the whole thing when he went on a radio programme yesterday morning. Referring to his appeal, the West Indies captain said, 'I heard a noise and we appealed. My little jig is very ceremonial and I was hoping to celebrate getting the batsman out. I was not trying to pressure the umpire and I believe he made the right decision.'

Well, Bailey, who is not a cheat, was absolutely certain he had not hit the ball and the television replays, without being 100 per cent conclusive, certainly appeared to bear him out.

Richards, however, went on to make a perfectly valid point when he said, 'All sorts of comments have been made about this series which don't bother me. But these people should remember that the feelings of a lot of other people are involved. They should remember that we are playing this series in the Caribbean and these things are being said on our airwaves.'

In so many words, Richards was spelling out just how important cricket and the performance of their cricketers is to the masses of ordinary folk on the English-speaking West Indian islands. Cricket is the lone unifying factor amongst the island states – a unity Richards himself did little to help solidify with his comments in Guyana – and, as a result, takes on a disproportionate level of importance. In South America soccer inspires similar levels of passion but greater regional division because nation plays against nation. One of Clive Lloyd's great triumphs was to eradicate most of the inter-island rivalries that used to exist in

West Indies' teams of the past and make Jamaicans, Guyanese, Trinidadians, Bajans and Antiguans socialize off the field as well as play as one self-supporting unit on it.

Nevertheless, Martin-Jenkins was not the only person to be surprised by the intensity of the reaction amongst Barbadians, in particular. 'It disappointed me,' Christopher admitted. 'I love this place and I have always found the people to be very broad minded. It was an honest opinion, honestly expressed, but it was not accepted as such.'

Martin-Jenkins also went on to say publicly that he was prepared to withdraw the word 'cheat', but stood his ground to the extent of asking if other words such as professionalism and gamesmanship were not merely euphemisms. It is a very fine dividing line between the kind of win-at-all-costs attitude that the BBC cricket correspondent objects to so strongly and the kind of winning mentality that Micky Stewart was talking to me about a couple of days ago; the very mentality that has made this team as successful as it has been, even allowing for today's defeat. Absurdly slow over rates when it suits the fielding side's purpose; raucous appealing on the basis of dubious evidence and close fielders verbally harassing batsmen constitute a pattern of behaviour that blurs the line between gamesmanship and cheating and the laws of cricket need to be tightened to ensure that it is kept on the acceptable side of the fence.

Barker, in the meantime, told Erskine King, sports director of the *Voice of Barbados*, that he had not changed his mind over his decision to give Bailey out and, on hearing that, Martin-Jenkins said, 'If that is so, I apologize for giving a false impression and for conveying it in good faith.'

Under the circumstances, Martin-Jenkins had little option to apologize but, frankly, I think Barker was lucky to get it. Not because he may have made a bad decision – if, in fact, Bailey was not out – because all umpires make mistakes. No, Barker's far less forgivable mistake was to *give the impression* that he had been influenced by the strength of the appeal by changing his pattern of behaviour, setting off for square leg, stopping and then raising his finger. That is the action of a bad umpire which Barker, on his performance throughout the series, is not.

If English supporters had been scanning the sky for rain, they soon realized it was a fruitless exercise. Barbados is too flat to create its own weather like most of the Caribbean islands and gets all its rainclouds from the Atlantic. But there was nothing out there today and England's remaining batsmen were left to sweat it out under the sort of skies they had been praying for in Port of Spain.

Not that Alec Stewart or Jack Russell showed any great concern at the prospect of repelling the mighty West Indies pace attack for as long as it took when they kept the score ticking over at a surprisingly steady pace in the first hour. There was no possibility of England getting the additional 340 runs they needed to win, of course, but absurd notions crossed one's mind when Stewart, looking as confident as ever despite a couple of snicks through the vacant third-slip position, pulled Ambrose to mid-wicket for four; guided the next ball through gully for three and then watched Russell collect two off the next delivery which, with the help of a no-ball, meant that 10 had come off the over. It had also brought up a very worthy 50 partnership.

Ambrose, needless to say, did not enjoy any of that and in his next over, his fifth of the morning from the pavilion end, he made one rear up past Stewart's nose. It was the first time the Surrey player had been discomforted all morning and when Ambrose produced the perfect one-two – a ball that kept low off the very next delivery – it was too much. It found the outside edge and Richards, taking the catch at first slip, immediately went into the most extraordinary Antiguan war dance. It was 11.40 a.m. and England were 71-4.

Ambrose rapped Allan Lamb's pads on his first ball to the England captain and from that moment Lamb was virtually unrecognizable from the man who had played with such fluent authority in the first innings. He did manage a drive off Bishop which resulted in an all-run four but at lunch, with England on 79–4, it was Russell, on 19, who was looking the more assured of the two.

The pattern continued after the interval with the Gloucester-shire keeper a picture of intense concentration and bristling determination while his captain looked like an America's Cup skipper who had suddenly been put in charge of a tug boat. Lamb, with or without the responsibility of leadership, is in his element when he is out there dancing on the ocean waves, attacking on every tack. But ask him to get a crippled vessel safely back to port and he barely knows which lever to pull. Lamb had won matches for England, but he has never saved one and just when his side needed him to stick he couldn't. At 1.17 p.m. after just fifty-five minutes at the crease, he was gone, caught behind by Dujon off Moseley for 10. At least Moseley deserved to have someone catch something off his bowling after the frustrations he had suffered on Saturday.

Robin Smith was soon off the mark and looked as ruggedly immovable as Lamb had seemed imminently capsizable and throughout a long, hot afternoon he and Russell edged England nearer to a harbour that was suddenly, unexpectedly hoving into view. Russell, playing his best innings of the tour, waited for a Richards' off spinner to arrive and then pushed it through gully to bring up a 50 that had taken him 260 minutes of near flawless batsmanship in the most demanding of circumstances, beginning, of course, in his night-watchman's role in Sunday's failing light. Russell's quick hands are an enormous asset on a pitch where the odd ball keeps low because he can jab down on the ball at the very last second as it shoots towards his ankle.

Smith, meanwhile, was tempering his natural aggression in impressive fashion. I had the glasses on him as he shaped up to face another over of Richards' varied spin. A deep intake of breath, a quick back flick for both legs to loosen the muscles, and then the widening of the eyes as they locked on to the object that appeared out of Richards' hand. Front foot forward and a straight bat smothering any sign of spin. Then back for another little hop about at the crease and the same procedure all over again, each ball safely played constituting another inch forward to England's goal, another tiny triumph in the battle of wills.

When Richie Richardson came on to bowl at the southern end at 3.47 p.m. with the score on 165–5 it was, of course, just a ploy to get in another quick over before the new ball was due. When Bishop took it, he made Russell come down sharply on one that shot through off the seam and then had him rocking out of the way of a bouncer. Drinks were taken but although Eddie Hemmings fussed over the batsman, rushing off to fetch extra water from the Cable & Wireless drinks trolley, it was only a momentary respite. The critical period had started. Could England's last remaining five wickets survive the new ball? I had barely had time to notice that Russell wears a pair of wicket-keeper's inners under his batting gloves when Ambrose bowled him with one that kept low off his first ball of a new session from the southern end. Their partnership had yielded 69 runs and had kept the West Indies at bay for 2 hours 28 minutes. Russell himself had batted 309 minutes and faced 235 balls for a 55 that included just three fours. It would be hard to ask more of a night-watchman in similar circumstances but, of course, Jack Russell is a great deal more than a mere plug for an innings that is threatening to drain away in fading light. Since his 94 against Sri Lanka at Lord's in 1988, this neat keeper whose Test career was delayed by supposed batting frailty, had scored considerably more runs than many of the established England batsmen who have been given a chance to establish themselves in the team for their batting alone.

Smith, aware that his responsibilities had just become even more onerus, took a four to long leg off Bishop but in Ambrose's next over Nasser Hussain seemed hypnotized by a beast of a ball that rocketed out of Curtly's bobbling hand and curved towards him in a deadly 90-m.p.h. arc before dipping into a vicious yorker that left him plumb lbw.

Ambrose, whose place in this team was under threat prior to this innings, did a bunch of high fives with those members of the team who can reach ten feet with an upstretched hand – Logie is usually excused – and suddenly there was a sniff of victory in the air. Stewart, Russell and Smith had delayed the celebrations long enough and even as cautious a captain as Richards dispensed with the pretence that runs needed to be saved and encircled David Capel with three slips, a gully, a point and silly mid-off with Logie forward and Moseley back on the leg side. Only Bishop at long leg was not in a catching position.

But Capel survived and, as the shadow of the pavilion crept towards the square, Smith fought on, berating himself for taking his eye off the ball during a good over from Bishop. Then Hooper caught Capel at second slip off Ambrose, but it was a no-ball – the third time in the match a catch had been taken off a no-ball.

But this time it didn't matter. Ambrose trapped Capel lbw off the last ball of the same over and up went Lloyd Barker's finger once again. 181–8.

An accurate over from Marshall kept Smith at the southern end and Philip DeFreitas, facing the first ball of Ambrose's next over, went the same way as the rest. Lbw. It's 4.45 p.m. and, just below the press-box, a group of young Bajans, wait like sprinters in their blocks, ready to race on to the field when victory comes.

But Devon Malcolm, such a disappointment with the ball, is not going to cave in with the bat and the tenth wicket partnership actually lasts thirty-one minutes with Malcolm frustrating Ambrose yet again with defensive prods that find the middle of the bat. As a last defiant gesture, Smith reaches 40 by punching Ambrose through the covers for four. Even Malcolm got a boundary, alhough less elegantly than his pair in the first innings, when a ball flew high over the slips off a glove but, at 5.16 p.m., with just about half an hour's play left if the umpires would have offered the light at the same time as on other evenings, Barker saved everyone the trouble by going through the familiar routine once again – Ambrose raps the pads, up goes the finger and Malcolm is out lbw. England were 191 all out, Smith undefeated on 40, a per-sonal triumph in that he, too, had faced numerous overs from Ambrose during that bowler's deadly, match-winning spell. It rightfully earnt Curtly the Man of the Match Award from Everton Weekes for keeping alive his team's chances of winning the series.

The scenes at the end were disappointing. One had expected jubilation on an uproarious scale, but the Martin-Jenkins controversy had offered a target for those people who feel the need to oppose rather than merely support. There were probably no more than a hundred of them but they held placards above their heads and jumped up and down with feverish intent in front of the pavilion for about fifteen minutes after the match.

Christopher's name was plastered all over one placard but on the other, someone had written, 'England team are cry babies. They must learn to take their licks like we take our licks.'

As I stood out on the field amongst them, feeling quite unthreatened because the mood was not really nasty, I had a terrible sense of *déjà vu*. For the past three months I seem to have been attending cricket matches that are constantly being accom-panied by groups of black people leaping about with signs that do not tell the truth. Although I sympathized wholeheartedly with the underlying cause of the demonstrations in South Africa, it was still distressing to see them attack the wrong targets with blatant untruths.

'Gatting is a racist.' He isn't. 'England team are cry babies.' They aren't.

The England team, in fact, had not opened its mouth, collectively or individually, over Rob Bailey's dismissal nor had there been complaints about any other aspect of the match. But when the front-page headline on today's *Advocate* cries out 'Biased Brits' why should those people with an axe to grind bother to stop and think who they should be whirling it at – especially when Geoffrey Boycott adds his own pennyworth by calling a fellow Barbadian commentator a bastard.

All of us in the media need to take a long, hard look at our role in this increasingly shrill and distorted reaction to relatively minor incidents that erupt in the competitive arena. Tony Greig's hysterical commentary on Sky Television is only adding fuel to the flames lit on the back pages of the more sensational British tabloids who like nothing better than to get words like 'Cheat' or 'Bastard' emblazoned over their stories. Is our society really so conditioned to hype that this is the only way to attract the attention of the masses and, if so, who is to blame? It is not a comfortable question for those of us who work in either the print or the electronic media.

England lost a cricket match here today because, for the first time in the series, the West Indies were the better team. It would have been nice to have left it at that.

Antigua

11 April

We arrived here in the early hours this morning, many of us
courtesy of the British Airways manager at the airport who
squeezed the overload into the middle seats on the upper deck of
the 747 – seats that are supposed to be vacant if you are Club
World passengers. Inevitably there were squeaks of disapproval,
voiced in a variety of Home Counties accents, from those poor
souls who were on the long haul back to Heathrow. But as the
flight from Barbados to Antigua is less than an hour, their
discomfort did not last long. Full marks to BA for some inspired
improvisation.

The West Indies were not on board when we departed at
around midnight. Jeff Dujon, Gordon Greenidge and some other
Barbados-based members of the team had been involved in
persuading one of the leading reggae bands, Third World, to fly
in and play a free concert for the West Indies Players Association.
So the entire team was at the Shallow Draught with Greenidge
and Curtly Ambrose apparently scheduled to sing one of
Sparrow's songs, Congo Man. That could end up as a rehearsal
for a change of routine next time they take a wicket.

So in all probability, West Indies will arrive here with about as
little sleep as England got by the time they reached Halcyon Cove

at about 2 a.m. They were all on our BA flight, including the 'now you see him, now you don't' figure of David Gower. Rumours of his return to the fold seemed to gain serious validity when I noticed someone handing over a bundle of the England team's passports during check in at the airport. The one on top quite clearly belonged to D.I. Gower.

Any lingering doubts were removed when the sunshine boy himself appeared at the top of the stairway in our cabin; blond hair, deep tan, yellow England sports shirt and big smile. All terribly relaxed and unmistakably David. I noticed that the large man on my left who had been muttering caustically about overcrowding because of 'those cricketers' didn't have much to say after that.

Gower himself wasn't very forthcoming on his chances of actually playing in the Fifth Test although there must be a limit to the number of times he can get invited without being properly utilized. The fact is that David Smith's thumb is still very sore and Nasser Hussain's wrist is taking an unconscionably long time to heal. So although David managed to strain a thigh muscle scoring a 50 for Hampshire the other day, he is probably fitter than some of the official party. Anyway he's back and it will be interesting to see under what pretext they manage to leave him out this time.

After two weeks in the family atmosphere of the Rostrevor Apartments in St Lawrence, I am now billeted in a little hotel in the centre of St Johns that rejoices in the name of Joe Mike's. I spent a couple of nights here when England were shooing the cows off their practice pitches four years ago and although this team's practice habits have changed, the hotel hasn't except for the communal, satellite-linked television outside my door which has allowed patrons to watch the cricket on Sky from the other islands.

Not the least of Sky's achievements has been its ability to beam the feed around the West Indies so that some sort of competition can be offered to the endless stream of basketball and other American sport that is piped down to the islands on a twenty-four-hour basis. If the slow decline in cricket's popularity is to be arrested, television will have to play an important role.

Antiguans will have to go to the Recreation Ground, however, if they want to see this match. With such a small population to draw from, the Antiguan cricket authorities seem to want to make sure they get enough people in the ground. Although it is marginally larger in size than Barbados, there are only 83,000 Antiguans compared to a quarter of a million Bajans which makes it tiny indeed when stacked up against 2.5 million inhabitants of Jamaica and Trinidad's 1.3 million.

All the more amazing then that four of the West Indies team that will play here tomorrow will be Antiguan, Viv Richards, Richie Richardson, Curtly Ambrose and Eldine Baptiste who has been brought in for Ezra Moseley. Another change sees Courtney Walsh reclaim his place because, like Moseley, Malcolm Marshall has a leg strain. Carlisle Best is in worse shape than that, having broken a finger trying to catch the uncatchable Smith, and so Carl Hooper gets another chance.

Moseley's injury is, apparently, genuine, although if it had not been, someone might have had to invent one for him. Antigua is the most militant of the islands in regards to South Africa and no one was really sure whether it would be safe for the former 'rebel' tourist to play here.

One thing that has always worried me about Antigua is the total lack of a daily newspaper. An attempt is made at producing a newsless weekly *Worker*, but it is full of political speeches from people who are obviously afraid of free speech. However I did notice from the copy lying around my hotel that one lady had been brave enough to write a letter in support of Ezra Moseley whose name has obviously been a major topic of conversation here. But I suspect she is the minority.

WEST INDIES v ENGLAND (5th TEST)

Played at St John's on April 12,14,15,16 1990. West Indies won by an innings and 32 runs. Toss: England. Man of the match: D.L. Haynes.

ENGLAND

W. Larkins	c Hooper b Ambrose	30	(2) b Ambrose		10
A.J. Stewart	c Richards b Walsh	27	(1) c Richardson		8
R.J. Bailey	c Dujon b Bishop	42	(4) c Dujon b Bishop		8
A.J. Lamb*	c Richards b Ambrose	37	(5) b Baptiste		35
R.A. Smith	lbw b Walsh	12	(6) retired hurt		8
N. Hussain	c Dujon b Bishop	35	(7) c Dujon b Bishop		34
D.J. Capel	c Haynes b Bishop	10	(8) not out		1
R.C. Russell†	c Dujon b Bishop	7	(9) c Richardson b Ambrose		24
P.A.J. DeFreitas	lbw b Bishop	21	(10) c Greenidge b Ambrose		0
G.C. Small	lbw b Walsh	8	(3) b Ambrose		4
D.E. Malcolm	not out	0	not out		1
Extras	(b 5, lb 11, nb 15,)	31	(b 1, lb 8, nb 11, w 1)		21
TOTAL		260			154

WEST INDIES

C.G. Greenidge	run out	149
D.L. Haynes	c Russell b Small	167
R.B. Richardson	c Russell b Malcolm	34
C.L. Hooper	b Capel	1
I.V.A. Richards*	c Smith b Malcolm	1
A.L. Logie	c Lamb b DeFreitas	15
P.J.L. Dujon†	run out	25
E.A.E. Baptiste	c Russell b Malcolm	9
C.E.L. Ambrose	c DeFreitas b Capel	5
I.R. Bishop	not out	14
C.A. Walsh	b Malcolm	8
Extras	(lb 5, nb 13)	18
TOTAL		446

BOWLING

WEST INDIES	O	M	R	W	O	M	R	W
Bishop	28.1	6	84	5	14	2	36	3
Ambrose	29	5	79	2	13	7	22	4
Walsh	21	4	51	3	10	1	40	0
Baptiste	13	4	30	0	10	1	47	1

ENGLAND	O	M	R	W
Small	31	3	123	1
Malcolm	34.5	3	126	4
Capel	28	1	118	2
DeFreitas	27	4	74	1

FALL OF WICKETS

	E 1st	WI 1st	E 2nd
1st	42	298	16
2nd	101	357	20
3rd	143	358	33
4th	167	359	47
5th	167	382	86
6th	195	384	94
7th	212	415	148
8th	242	417	148
9th	259	433	154
10th	260	446	—

Umpires: D.M. Archer and A.E. Weekes.

Antigua
Fifth Test – Day One

12 April

Having won the toss, chosen to bat and ended up at 203–6, England, with the benefit of hindsight, would probably have liked to have seen David Gower striding out for his 107th Test cap today. It is possible, of course, that he would not have made as many as Rob Bailey's 42 or Nasser Hussain's 16 not out, but it is equally possible that he would have done what none of the England top five managed to do which was pass 50.

The fact is that Gower was named last night in England's 13 and fully expected to play. The 'pretext' for not playing him appears to have been made on the basis that Hussain finally decided his wrist would stand up to another battering and pronounced himself fit this morning. That left Stewart, Gooch and Lamb with the happy task of walking over to where David was practising and telling England's third most prolific run scorer in history that he was being left out of a side whose batting, brittle at the start, was now as splintered as most of the batsmen's fingers.

Frankly, I don't know how they had the nerve. Surely the business about remaining loyal to the original party was cast aside, if not in Barbados, then certainly when they named Gower among the thirteen players selected for this Fifth Test match. If that doesn't make him part of the team, I don't know what does. And if he is part of the team, how, in heaven's name, can he be left out when he is, with the exception of Lamb in the context of current form, the very best player among that thirteen? And not just the best by a whisker but by a bloody great mile. Lamb apart, none of the other batters in this team are in the same league as Gower and, unhappily, most of them never will be. Nor is it possible, as it is with Gatting and Botham, to throw a question mark at his ability to score runs off the West Indies. The last time England played here at the Recreation Ground, Gower scored 94.

The fact that a certain team plan, allied to superb fitness and carefully nurtured team spirit, has kept England in the hunt right up to the last match seems to have blinded the selection committee to the proper utilization of the talent available. At the risk of stating the obvious, some players are better than others and, nine times out of ten, the better ones should get picked, irrespective of conditions or any other extraneous factor.

England had eighteen players on hand when they arrived in Antigua yesterday of whom three, Gooch, Fraser and David Smith, were not fit. Of the remaining fifteen, Lamb and Gower were the best batsmen in the party and Small and Hemmings were the best bowlers. Yet when England went out to bat, two of the four best players available were not in the line-up. On whatever grounds you care to mention, that is very hard to justify.

Having played through what was supposed to be a tricky first hour with considerable aplomb, Stewart (who now bats like Larkins) and Larkins (who now bats like Gooch) failed to capitalize on what they had built. It turned out to be the story of the day.

With 41 on the board in the first hour, Larkins, draped in responsibility, dropped anchor while Stewart went after the bowling in what has now become his customary style. A gorgeous cut off Walsh for four was followed by an audacious pull over vacant mid-wicket off Ambrose for three. But, once again, it was too good to last. Stewart tried to drive one from Walsh that left him and Richards, juggling, held on to the catch at first slip. Stewart had made 27 in fifty-nine minutes. He'll get a big score one day.

At least Bailey did not have Lloyd Barker to contend with as he came out to make one last stab at salvaging a Test career. Barker was never scheduled to stand here, so psychologically Bailey could clear his mind of the past and concentrate on the problems in hand which, basically, amounted to quick and frequently short-pitched bowling on a fast, true and bouncy pitch prepared just the way a fast bowler would like it. Which was hardly surprising because it was prepared by Andy Roberts.

Roberts has moved on from being the only fast bowler in the world to have a street named after him within walking distance of his home Test ground to the only head groundsman with a street named after him anywhere. 'This,' Roberts had told us yesterday, 'would be a good pitch for everybody.'

There was no evidence to the contrary as England came in at lunch with 71 on the board for the loss of Stewart; Larkins having moved cautiously to 22 and Bailey, not entirely without alarms, to 15. As both men have recorded pairs on this tour, I suppose that could be considered progress.

The progress continued through the early part of a hot afternoon with the tall guys bouncing it and Baptiste seaming it and the batsmen somehow managing to edge the score towards the hundred mark, occasionally with judiciously pushed singles but quite often with the kind of four that Larkins sent flying high over Dujon's head when he tried to hook Ambrose. But soon after, Ambrose, looking almost as dangerous as he had done during his memorable match-winning spell in Barbados, found a more profitable edge and Hooper took a straight forward catch at second slip. Larkins had made a very uncharacteristic 30 in 181 minutes.

Ambrose continued to be unkind to his Northampton colleagues by hitting Lamb near the point of the elbow first ball. The England skipper retaliated immediately by driving a three, but then Laurie Brown had to race on with that high stepping run that used to have them on the go at Old Trafford in his Manchester United days and administer the spray.

Another injury to a front-line batsman was just what England could not afford and although he battled on through the biggest short-pitched blitz of the tour so far, Lamb could never find the rhythm that had brought him hundreds in Kingston and Barbados and Bailey often looked the more secure of the two. England, in fact, seemed to be fighting back well when both batsmen attacked Bishop and the Trinidadian's first over of his second spell cost 11 runs. At 143–2 there was a real promise of greater things, but the bouncers kept coming and little more than an hour later it was 167–5.

Bailey was the first to go and it was needless, too, because he slashed at a wide, short delivery from Bishop and gave Dujon a catch off the bottom edge. He had made 42, one short of his highest Test score, made against the West Indies at the Oval in 1988. He was furious with himself as he walked off. A 50 had been there for the taking.

Smith was soon exercising his back muscles as he leant further than that tower in Pisa to avoid the head-high thunderbolts that Bishop rained down on him in what could be described as a torrid over. But if the forty-eighth was bad, the forty-ninth proved lethal when a single to Lamb left Smith facing Walsh. A straight one that wasn't as short as the rest surprised Smith and caught him smack on the side of the chin. Logie and other West Indians crowded round, but Robin seemed as all right as anyone can be when struck in the face by a very hard object travelling at 90 m.p.h.

Smith survived another ten overs, twice letting Walsh know that if this was supposed to be intimidation, it wasn't working with lovely off side drives to the boundary. But there were more blows on the finger as the ball kept bouncing up off Andy Robert's tailor-made pitch and this harrowing examination of Smith's character and technique finally came to an end when he fell lbw on the back foot to Walsh, having faced forty balls for just 12 runs.

In the next over Ambrose found the edge of Lamb's bat and Richards clutched the catch to his stomach before charging off in the direction of the stands to our right where specatators found themselves being given the V sign by the West Indies captain. For a moment I thought he was gesticulating at the two-tier stand with the Union Jack draped over the balcony, but this did not seem to be the case as he veered more towards the little knot of Antiguan spectators who had been giving him a hard time early on over something or other. The feedback is instant and often irritating on this tour because eye-witnesses are always being second guessed by people watching television 3,000 miles away and reports were soon coming back from London suggesting Richards had been giving Lamb the V sign. I watched the whole incident and this was not true.

Before rain curtailed play for the day in the seventy-second over, England's plight was worsened when Bishop had Capel caught by Haynes, grabbing the ball as it bounced back off his chest. Capel, who had scored 11, had hit it hard and Haynes caught it well. So England's 203–6 was not nearly enough and so much less than it might have been. If some keen researcher wants a job, they can check back to find out the last occasion when the first four men in a batting order all passed 25 and all failed to reach 50 in a Test match. It doesn't happen very often because Test batsmen, once set, should go on to make a substantial score. Later than anyone imagined, England's inexperience was beginning to show.

While everyone drove over to the south-eastern side of the island to attend a splendid party at the St James' Club, one of Antigua's most sumptious resorts, stories of a bouncer war breaking out in the Caribbean were being sent back to London. Short-pitched bowling and V signs were supposed to have put the teams at each other's throats. Good story but unfortunately not quite true. Apart from some over-the-top sledging between Stewart and Haynes in Trinidad and a row that got a bit nasty between Greenidge and Small in Barbados, the teams have got along fine and it showed tonight as everyone mixed freely, chatting and cracking jokes as they lined up for the buffet and listened to the band out on the terrace.

Nor were there any complaints from the English team about short-pitched bowling. Their only surprise was that there had not been more of it sooner.

'If you're playing Test cricket out here, it's what you expect,' said Robin Smith, whose face looked much the same despite having Walsh's bouncer embedded in it. I asked him why, if he felt the need of a helmet, he didn't go the whole hog and use the grill as well.

'I just don't like the idea of having all that in front of my face,' he replied. 'It's the temple I want covered. That's the place to protect because if you get hit there, it can be lights out. Anywhere else and it just means your face might get reorganized like Gatt's did out here four years ago. I can handle that. Luckily it caught me on the side of the jaw today which is the best place if you are going to get hit in the face. I was doing pretty well swaying out of the way of most of them, but that one caught me by surprise.'

I found Jack Russell almost hidden behind a pillar near the bar and discovered that he had not had as much time as he would have liked to sketch the kind of sights he caught so evocatively with his drawings in India and Pakistan. Apart from a few days in Barbados, this had been a hard tour for the little wicket-keeper. But he wasn't complaining about that.

'It's been great keeping to these bowlers out here,' said Russell. 'There has been no comparison to the stuff I kept to handle during the summer. It's all line and length now, so much more disciplined.'

As no one is in a better position to judge, that was a well-earned accolade for England's pace attack. I also confirmed what I had suspected after watching Russell bat for so long in Barbados, namely that he has developed a superstition about touching a spot on the ground with his bat near short leg before every ball he receives.

'Yes, it's become a sort of superstition,' he laughed. 'It's something I started on this tour. I walk away to leg after every ball anyway and now I find myself looking for the middle hole of the stumps on an old wicket to touch with my bat. They've played so little on this ground this year, there weren't any stump marks so I had to make one for myself out there this evening.'

David Gower didn't stray very far from the bar and one couldn't blame him. David's debonair façade never allows too many deep feelings to show through, but it was not difficult to detect the extent of his disappointment.

'Yes, it was a bit of a blow,' he admitted with one of those wry smiles. 'I was definitely under the impression I was going to get a game this time. But there you are. Now I'm just going to piss off back home.'

The team management's handling of Gower has been the one black mark against them on this tour. I have tried not to draw too many comparisons between tennis and cricket in this book because the two sports inhabit such different worlds but, really, can you imagine the Swedish Davis Cup captain saying to Stefan Edberg, 'Look we've got Mats Wilander and three other players ranked around 100 in the world, but if you'll come along we'll see if we can get you a game.'

Edberg is about as polite and outwardly laid-back as Gower, but his reply to such a suggestion would, I can assure you, be very short and very sharp. The difference is that the Davis Cup is a very small part of a professional tennis player's money-spinning year while Test cricket is virtually everything to a cricketer. If Gower ever wants to reclaim his rightful place in the England team, he has little option but to place himself at the beck and call of those in charge. It is humiliating, but he has no choice. Of course it can be argued that he had two opportunities to remain in charge himself, but his failings as a captain make him no less deserving of respect as a great batsman and a thoroughly honourable human being. To have treated him as an errand boy was demeaning in the extreme. If he was not wanted, he should not have been asked. If he was asked he should have played.

For years I have been warning people in tennis that it was dangerous to underestimate Stefan Edberg just because of the image he projected. The well-mannered, soft-spoken and seemingly lackadaisical attitude was seen as being the persona of a man with no ambition and no heart. No-one lacking guts and ambition wins Wimbledon or comes even close to it. Now that Edberg is ranked No. 2 in the world, people are starting to realize that.

David Gower has suffered from the same misconceptions. No one scores 7,000 runs in Test cricket if they lack ambition. No one scores a hundred for England against the Australians at Lords, when their credibility and reputation are on the line, as Gower did last summer, if they are blessed with anything less than a very serious supply of guts and fighting spirit.

The challenge for the new regime that has achieved so much of what Gower was not able to achieve as captain is to realize that and find a way of harnessing David's exceptional talents and loyal commitment to the cause – a commitment he demonstrated

quite selflessly twice in three weeks out here – to the spirit that
now exists under Gooch's leadership and make them work for
the general good. If they don't, it will be their failure, not
Gower's.

Rest Day

13 April

Good Friday the 13th sounds like something of a contradiction and it may turn out to be anything but good for the state of relations between the West Indies and the British Press.

Looking for a rare hour of quiet relaxation on a beach, I joined Ian and Sarah Wooldridge and some of their friends for a drink at Halcyon Cove today and began hearing some extraordinary stories of a confrontation that has taken place between James Lawton, chief sports writer of the *Daily Express* and Viv Richards.

Lawton, who has been on perfectly good terms with Clive Lloyd and the West Indies players he has asked to interview on the tour to date, apparently walked up to Richards as the team meeting here at the hotel broke up and asked him, in his polite, low-key manner, if he would mind talking about the V signs Viv had directed at the crowd after he had caught Allan Lamb yesterday.

He was greeted by a stream of expletives which were quickly followed by repeated threats of physical violence. 'I'll whack you,' Richards snarled, using the word again and again. Before Lawton had a chance to say very much, Richards walked away and then came back to unleash another torrent of abuse at the reporter. By that time Paul Weaver, whose credentials in the West Indies should be quite good after being thrown out of South Africa, had joined Lawton and witnessed the second tirade.

'I was glad Paul arrived just at that moment, because I would have had trouble writing the story otherwise,' Lawton told me. 'Without a witness I might have had trouble making people believe what Richards said. It was a very unnerving experience.'

No one is suggesting that it was the sort of question that Richards would have been happy to have thrown at him on what he described as 'my day off', but I fail to see how Lawton had any option but to file the story to his newspaper. No one, much less Test captains, can threaten people with violence and expect to get away with it.

The Press and the West Indies are staying at Halcyon Cove while England are billeted at the Ramada Renaissance on the other side of St Johns. They must be quite pleased about that. Their day passed with a little beach cricket and a snooze in the sun. All very peaceful. It will be different tomorrow.

Fifth Test – Day Two

14 April

Just how different, I had not quite realized although England, thankfully, managed to stay insulated from the new and rather serious war that had broken out between Viv Richards and the Press.

About ten minutes before the start of play, I was hovering around at the back of the little press-box, wondering, with more hope than realism, if a seat might suddenly materialize, when I became aware of someone brushing past the back of me and advancing on Jim Lawton who was seated in the back row. It was Viv Richards and he was fit to bust.

Still wearing a black cap, black T-shirt and white track suit trousers, he was dripping sweat from the team's morning work out and nothing that happened in the following fifteen minutes was going to help cool him down.

'Are you Lawton?' Richards demanded standing in front of the desk with his back to the playing field. 'You the one who wrote the story in the *Express* today? Well, I tell you, man, it's not finished yet. One day someone is going to settle with you personally. It may not be me. I may give you a lot of ammunition, but he who laughs last laughs loudest. He laughs longest, you understand? Viv leaves things up to fate, but I will take things into my own hands if you hurt me enough. If you were a younger man, I might do something here and now.'

Another great splodge of sweat plopped down on to Lawton's Cable & Wireless notepad and Jim, who is short, pink faced, curly haired and rather cherubic in appearance, looked momentarily put out at the reference to his age, but was otherwise standing up to the barrage reasonably well. But even if a knock out was unlikely, he was not exactly winning on points.

'Viv, I approached you in a perfectly polite manner and all you had to do . . .'

'Don't say "had"!' Richards shot back. 'Don't use words like that to me. I don't have to do anything, understand? Somebody's going to get it. You make Vivvy angry. I'm bubbling.'

Indeed he was. Only the narrow corridor between the rows of desks was keeping him pinned to one place. All the body language suggested he wanted to break free and dance about as he spoke, like a boxer who had just climbed into the ring.

'You hurt a lot of people with the things you write,' he continued. 'You people write a lot of shit and when people are hurt, they get very angry.'

It began to get repetitious but, even as the tirade entered its tenth minute, Richards was never in danger of losing his audience. With the nearest notepad out of commission, reporters who could get within earshot – Richards was not really shouting and his voice, in any case, is not one that carries – were trying to scribble snippets on anything that came to hand and Karl Kershaw of the *People* compiled the most coherent account of what had become one of the most extraordinary scenes between the Press and a leading sports figure I had ever seen. Even John McEnroe had never done this – not, at any rate, five minutes before he was due on court.

And time was now Richards' main problem. He could have got away with this at the close of play, when deadlines were passed and stories written. The *Daily Express*, obviously, and the down-market tabloids would have run with it but, for the rest, it would have become a footnote to yesterday's news. But not only was all this going on under the nose of journalists who had been wondering what to file for their first editions, but it was happening at 10.05 a.m. on the second day of a Test match, the exact moment that Viv Richards was supposed to be leading his team out on to the field.

Downstairs in the West Indies dressing-room, no-one knew where he was. Desmond Haynes was told suddenly by Clive Lloyd to lead the team out with Brian Lara as twelfth man. Up in the press-box, Richards seemed quite oblivious to all this and even when his old Somerset team mate, Vic Marks, looking extremely embarrassed, leant over to tap him on the shoulder and point to the field, it did not seem to register. He was still rattling on about people being hurt and getting hurt. In reality he was hurting himself.

After he finally left at 10.10 a.m., just a couple of minutes before rain brought the players back in, Matthew Engel, who had just flown in from that genteel, green-jacketed world of Augusta, Georgia where those black men who do make it into the clubhouse tend not to raise their voice, held up the notepad that was now liberally splattered with the captain's sweat and asked, 'How much am I offered for this work of modern art?'

It helped break the ice because, frankly, most of us were a little stunned and Marks, as a former colleague, was not the only one who was embarrassed. It was not a happy sight to see one of the greatest cricketers one could ever hope to write about, lose control of himself in such a public manner.

Not that I did not sympathize with much of what he was feeling. Richards has always seen himself as an ambassador for his people and his concern for their feelings is genuine. When the tabloid press attacks Vivian Richards, it is attacking Antigua.

As his former county captain at Somerset, Peter Roebuck, has written, 'Viv rarely gives vent to his strong views; his innermost beliefs remain hidden from all but his small circle of friends. Consequently his anger at injustice and prejudice surprises those who only know his ready smile.'

Frank Tyson makes a similar point in his excellent book, *The Test Within*.

'Attitude played an important part in determining the way Richards approached his day-to-day delighting of the cricket public. There was always the serious underlying theme, which he once expressed when looking into the encircling sea of West Indian faces at the Oval Test in 1976: "We must not let these people down." When in an aggressive or vindictive mood, Richards was completely ruthless. He would bat with all the pent-up passion of a man determined to gain retribution for the centuries of slavery and oppression suffered by his people.'

The tragedy now, of course, lay in the fact that Richards had let his people down by failing, if only for a couple of minutes, to fulfil his obligations as West Indies captain. I couldn't help noticing, either, that he was attacking the wrong target, in a specific sense, just as so many people had vented their fury and frustration at the wrong targets during the previous three months. Jim Lawton had not been writing bad things about the West Indies. Richards should have turned around and addressed the press-box as a whole so that he could, at least, have included those reporters working for editors who demand stripped-down, unthinking, unexplained sensation on a daily basis.

I remembered Johnny Woodcock's comment in Verwoerdburg about stories like that creating so much unhappiness and, in his aggressive and slightly incoherent way, Richards had been trying to say the same thing. But try making that point to the editors of Britain's mass circulation newspapers and they will laugh in your face. Only when the circulation starts dropping faster than it already is will they listen. It is what one has to suffer for a free press, which is something, of course, that Antigua doesn't have to worry about.

Once Richards got himself back where he was supposed to be – at first slip and in charge of his team – England's attempt to make a passable first innings total was forced to rely on Hussain's dogged determination to prove he was right to play and DeFreitas' haphazard talents which, with the bat, always seem to fall infuriatingly short of fulfilment.

Russell barely had time to find his lucky spot out at short leg before he was undone by a vicious Bishop bouncer, touching a catch to Dujon off a flailing bat as he tried to protect himself. Russell's technique is now so sound that a bowler needs to find the exact spot – almost the only spot – that is going to pierce that West Country armour; just short of a length and rising fast to a point right between the eyes.

While Hussain nudged ones and two off his legs, DeFreitas let the bat swing through its full arc and amassed 21 runs in thirty minutes, including a lovely cut for four off Bishop – before the same bowler did him lbw as he tried to swing to leg.

Small was also lbw, giving Walsh his third wicket, and with Malcolm refusing a single so that Hussain could take the strike next over, the Essex youngster decided to push his luck and was caught by Dujon, flashing off Bishop for a brave 35. Malcolm, incidentally, refused a two in Barbados. When his career is over and someone is being unkind enough to cast aspersions on his competence as a Test batsman, he can always tell them about the shots he played for runs he didn't take!

A score of 260 on this wicket was at least 150 short of what England should have scored. Yet although West Indies had bowled with all the intimidating fire that had been expected right from the start there had been very little sign of panic amongst the top order batsmen. A couple had got out to shots that should have been reserved for a Sunday league match at Guildford which is a form of panic, I suppose, but, for the most part, they had coped well and that only made it all the more frustrating.

Not, however, as frustrating as the way England bowled at Greenidge and Haynes for the rest of the day. For the first time in the entire series, the four-pronged pace attack looked prongless and lifeless and no amount of chivvying from the busy Lamb could do anything about it. Greenidge and Haynes, who were going to come good together sooner or later in this series, proceeded to give a masterly exhibition of batsmanship and Greenidge, playing in his hundredth Test, was, appropriately, the first to reach his hundred which had come from a steady stream of effortless strokes off 134 balls with two sixes and eleven fours. Haynes followed him to three figures soon after – his second successive century after two noughts in three innings – and the celebrations in the frail looking two-tiered stand to the left of the pavilion threatened to bring it crashing to the ground. May Field, a local comedian who likes to dress up in frilly attire, was pirouetting off the edge of the balcony; canned music, switched on and off with the timing of a Greenidge cover drive by someone called Chicky, was inducing most of the spectators to leap up and move to the rhythm and if the entire stand was not swaying to the beat then my eyes were deceiving me.

By the time the final drinks interval arrived, the place was in bedlam, a state of affairs that was only enhanced when a local lady, endowed with a backside of what one could politely call generous proportions, stuck that part of her anatomy out over the balcony and seemed only too delighted to find May Field climbing aboard to engage in gyrations of a somewhat suggestive nature. How he didn't fall off was not immediately apparent but as an Antiguan insisted on telling me somewhat superfluously, 'We enjoy our cricket here, man!' No kidding.

By the close Greenidge and Haynes had enjoyed it so much that they had put on 228 of which Greenidge had scored 118 and Haynes 101.

15 April

Easter Sunday and it was England who needed the miracle of a resurrection. One comforting thing about the Recreation Ground, with a prison on one side and a church on the other, is that retribution and salvation are never much further apart than the distance between deep extra cover and the square leg boundary and that only looks a long way to a tired bowler being hit to both places in one over. This was the fate of most of the English attack as the West Indies opening pair, having registered the fourteen-century partnership of their careers, continued their assault on the record books as much as the bowling.

At the start of the day many feared that the world-record first wicket-stand set by Roy and Mankad for India against New Zealand in Madras in 1955–6 would be in danger. But as it turned out, Greenidge and Haynes had to be content with beating their own record of 296 against India on this very ground in 1982–3. Nevertheless Greenidge was far from content with the way it ended in the seventy-fourth over of the innings just before lunch. They had taken the score to 298 when Haynes called for what should have been two runs to Small at long leg. But while Haynes was sprinting back, Gladstone noticed Greenidge dawdling and threw down his stumps. Greenidge, who had made 149, was both furious and amazed, having been totally oblivious to the danger.

So history repeated itself. A surprise run out had sent Greenidge on his way in Kingston, precipitating an amazing West Indies batting collapse and exactly the same thing was about to happen now. Ten wickets fell for a mere 148 runs which would have been very handy indeed had the openers put on 98 instead of 298. I fear that the poor bowling performance yesterday afternoon has cost England the series and no amount of atonement today is going to make up for it. In fact, while keeping alive the highly unlikely possibility of an England victory, bowling out West Indies in such surprisingly short order has only enhanced the home team's chances of clinching the series. For Richards, being the sort of captain he is, would have wanted as many first innings runs as possible on the board and would therefore have reduced the amount of time available to bowl England out a second time. Now he has two full days to do it, unless Lamb cracks a very big hundred in very quick time.

There was still no sign of collapse while Haynes and Richardson were together, adding 59 jaunty runs, but then Russell picked up Richie off Malcolm and, after consulting his colleague at square leg to make sure it had carried, umpire Andrew Weekes put his finger up. Then it began. Hooper, still struggling to look like a Test batsman, had his off-stump knocked back by Capel for one and when Richards sauntered on, everyone held their breath. What manner of revenge did he have in mind? Was it Malcolm he had in his sights or Lawton? Maybe he was confused because, after taking a single off Capel, he completely mistimed a delivery from Malcolm and drove the ball tamely to Smith at cover. 'We want Malcolm!' the crowd had been chanting a few minutes before. As in Kingston, he had found the perfect way to silence them. Despite the mauling he had received from the West Indies captain in Barbados, he had still taken Richards' wicket three times out of four which, I reckon, sort of left him ahead on points.

After tea Lamb caught Logie off DeFreitas and immediately afterwards Small got one to pop and Haynes, half forward, edged it to Russell. And so a wonderful innings came to an end. The Bajan had scored 167 off 317 balls and hit twenty-three fours and a six.

Of the rest only Dujon threatened to delay England's revival, but he was also run out after scoring 25. Malcolm, wicketless for so long, had bounced back splendidly to take 4–126 and Capel had also worked hard for his reward of 2–118. But, once again, the West Indies batting had sprung a leak with alarming rapidity. What a difference Fraser might have made in these last two Tests.

Obviously England were desperate to survive the last half-hour without the loss of a wicket, but it was not to be. With the shadows moving across the pitch, Larkins stabbed at a ball from Ambrose and played it on to his stumps. It was the last ball of the day, as it happened, because as soon as Small appeared, the umpires offered the light. A cruel end to a surprisingly successful day that showed, yet again, what reserves of fighting spirit are contained in a team whose stature will not be diminished by defeat.

16 April

It was all over soon after 2.30 p.m. I sat in the section near where the players sit outside the entrance to their dressing-room and watched the procession. They came and went like men who had seen the mortar shells explode once too often. Cricket is not warfare, but after two solid weeks of ducking and diving or standing and taking it, the effects take sport as near as it can come to that point where the eyes sink into their sockets and the will to fight begins to falter in the face of sheer fatigue and loss of concentration. If we were really in the trenches, the Red Cross would be working overtime.

There were the mental casualties like Stewart who cut wildly at Bishop when he knew caution was the priority of the day and was caught by Richardson in the gully. And the even sadder case of Bailey who flashed at Bishop and was dropped by Dujon in the very act of throwing the ball skywards in celebration. As if hypnotized by his escape, Bailey did exactly the same thing next ball and Dujon, barely daring to believe his luck, let the ball settle very safely in his gloves. That made it 33–3 and when Small could not stop a riser from Ambrose rolling off his body on to the stumps it was 37–4. No matter what happens at the Wanderers, there are no sticky bails in Antigua.

So, once more unto the breach dear friends, came Lamb and Smith and who knows how long these two warriors from a far-off land might have held the flag aloft for Queen and adopted country had not Smith been speared on the fingers twice in an over from Walsh. Twice too many even for this doughty fighter for, as it was revealed later, Robin's finger had been broken on the first day – a fact which, amazingly, he had chosen to ignore by fielding throughout the West Indies innings. Now, on the advice of Laurie Brown, he could ignore it no longer and was led away after an on-pitch examination, retired hurt for 8, with an embryonic stand broken at 61 for 4 or, effectively, 5.

Lamb, of course, was not in much better shape himself with a cracked bone in his elbow and, after defiantly off driving Walsh for four, he was bowled off his pads by the persistent Baptiste for 35. It would have been difficult for the acting captain to have done more in this series to make up for the inexperience of others. In four Tests he has spent the better part of twenty hours at the crease. People probably received medals at Mafeking for doing less than that.

There was a casualty of another kind when Capel was run out for one after realizing too late that Hussain was not participating in a run. If it was Hussain's fault he did as much as any twenty-year-old could be expected to do to stem the remorseless tide, producing his best shot in Test cricket to date when he cover drove Baptiste for four. It brought up the 100 and when Russell began to look as if he might offer a repeat of his rearguard action in Barbados, optimists amongst the English supporters started searching the skies for rain. There was a little in the offing, but the West Indies knew nothing would deny them now and when Ambrose found that spot again, Russell's feet and bat were all in the wrong place and Richardson accepted a dolly at cover. Jack, once again outscoring several specialist batsmen, had scored 24.

DeFreitas lasted one ball before giving Ambrose his fourth wicket of the innings and his sixteenth in two Tests and then Hussain saved Malcolm any further examination of his batting technique by taking a swing at Bishop and giving Dujon, a weary and fallible keeper now, the satisfaction of taking the catch that won the series.

With the captain below decks, Gooch's ship had finally been scuttled. All out for 154 and defeated by an innings and 32 runs. But Admiral Nelson, who spent many years of his life stationed at the other end of this island at English Harbour, would have known, without the aid of a score card, just how difficult it is to negotiate these Caribbean waters.

After Chicky had finally been persuaded to turn down the music in the West Indies Oil Co. Stand, there was a little oiling of egos to be done in front of the pavilion. The sign that was to have proclaimed the central stand as Viv Richards' very own, was still covered over, the ceremony having been put off until a more suitable moment after the way Viv rocked the press-box which sits on top of it. Nevertheless it was still deemed appropriate to present him with the Antiguan Order of Merit, a decision which, I understand, would not have been universally approved of by members of the West Indies Board of Control.

Less controversially, Desmond Haynes was made Man of the Match and Curtly Ambrose, to the delight of his Antiguan fans, Man of the Series. As he had spent a good part of it making life rather unpleasant for four of his Northampton colleagues, he will no doubt face a fair bit of ribbing in the dressing-room when the county season starts. But Curtly is a lovely fellow when that hand is not wobbling around above his head and his spell in the final session in Barbados was as good a demonstration of how to win a Test match as one could wish to see.

Nevertheless, there was more than a little substance to the suggestion that Ezra Moseley became Man of the Series the moment he broke Graham Gooch's hand in Port of Spain. Sport is forever weighed down with 'What ifs' but in the context of England–West Indies cricket an inordinate number of them seem to swirl around the persons of Gooch and Gatting. What if Gatting's nose had not been smashed at the start of Gower's tour here four years ago? Would his presence have helped maintain team morale and lessen the disaster? What if Gooch had followed his instincts and been allowed to go home? Would that have been the end of his Test career? What if Ossie Wheatley, in a minority of one, had not overruled his fellow selectors and Gatting had been made captain for the series against Australia? Would he have survived to lead the team out here? And where would that have left Gooch? In South Africa, perhaps? It is all fuel for idle gossip on a rainy day at Chelmsford, but none of it matters much now except that *if* Gooch had managed to get his hand out of the way of a couple of deliveries from Moseley, there would have been a very real chance of England saving this series, if not actually winning it.

But in defeat, there is only one thing to do – applaud the victors. There was no doubt that the West Indies, their pride stung by events in Jamaica and Trinidad, got their act together in a big way during the last two weeks of the tour and that was enough. In retrospect, it is interesting to think back and realize that defeat in Kingston provided Richards with his finest moment of the tour. He was dignified in his statements then which should not be forgotten in the light of what has transpired since. But the warning had been clear enough. 'We will come back and win the series,' he had said. And they did. It doesn't leave much to argue about.

Within two minutes of the Cable & Wireless representative handing over the cheques, it rained. Not soon enough and not long enough for England, of course, but it was a nice reminder of how the fate of outdoor sport rests with the gods.

No sooner had all the dignitaries run for cover than May Field, attired in maroon mortar board and gown today, appeared and began doing handstands on the trestle table in the rain. Even some of the England team managed to laugh.

It was harder to raise a giggle at the way the press conferences were conducted outside the dressing-rooms a few minutes later. Although it is of small interest to the world at large, press conferences after Test matches are amongst the most chaotically organized gatherings I have ever attended. And I am not referring solely to the West Indies. The shambles I witnessed at the Sydney Cricket Ground when Australia finally managed a win over the West Indies in 1989 was beyond belief. Most of what Allan Border had to say was drowned out by a ghetto blaster turned up to full volume just a few feet away in the Australian dressing-room. I know we are spoiled by the organization that exists on the ATP Tour, where the tennis players are produced automatically in a proper conference room after every match (they are fined $1,000 if they do not appear), but, even so, cricket should really try to do a better job in this respect.

Here at the Recreation Ground about twenty of us tried to lean over the little railings to hear what Micky Stewart and Allan Lamb were saying and then we moved back over to where Clive Lloyd had appeared. His deep baritone is difficult enough to hear at the best of times, but no doubt the mini-recorders stuck under his moustache caught the gist of it. 'Good, hard series; England did well . . .' and more interestingly, confirmation that Richards had apologized to the team for his non-appearance. Everything would now depend on how the West Indies Board of Control viewed Lloyd's report.

After that Lloyd turned around and, spotting his captain, virtually ordered Richards to come over and have his say. For reasons that I will explain in a minute, I also found it difficult to get close enough to Viv, but agency reporters like David Lloyd and Geoffrey Deane have him quoted as saying:

'I'm not going to put my finger up and blame myself. I think we should blame certain instances and past words which have been used. We've all had our say, but the world didn't really hear Viv Richards, they heard what other people have had to say. I'd like to let sleeping dogs lie. I've got my future to think about and at the end of the day I think we have all been a little bit guilty about what has happened.'

I caught some of this but the difficulty in getting close enough was compounded by a young Antiguan, who was not a member of the local press corps, trying to push me aside as he elbowed his way into the throng.

'Excuse me,' I said in as mild a tone as I could muster, 'but this is supposed to be a press conference and if you do that I won't be able to take any notes.'

'This isn't South Africa!' he shot back. 'You can't tell me what to do here. This isn't South Africa.'

Lord, have mercy. It just won't go away, will it? That's what our wonderful world of mass communication does, even for a people who don't have a proper newspaper to read. They have the airwaves, though, with the ninety-second clips of white police beating up black demonstrators and their local politicians helping them to formulate a rather simplistic view of the world. So it only takes a white man to open his mouth for him to have South Africa shoved in his face. It is hardly surprising, really, but once again it was a case of wrong subject, wrong target.

Naturally the irony of this particular retort to this particular reporter passed my accuser by. But I think I managed to persuade him afterwards that South Africa really did have very little to do with whether or not I should be allowed enough elbow room to write down the utterances of his very own Antiguan hero, and we parted with a handshake. Patience, patience. It's been a long journey.

17 April

I have had a variety of taxi drivers on this trip and although they are the great journalistic cliché as a source of information, the very nature of their job makes them a better barometer than most people if they are talkative types.

The young Antiguan taking me to the airport last night turned out to be one of the most interesting of the lot. He had played football with Viv Richards on a team that ended up being called 'Vivvy's Supas'.

He was obviously a great admirer of Richards, who had also managed the team, so I was surprised when he went on to say, 'England disappointed me in this match. I wouldn't have minded England winning. I know a lot of people here who wouldn't have minded England winning.'

I must confess I hadn't noticed too many but, as we continued to talk, I realized where his true feelings lay. He insisted he liked the England team, but soon started complaining about the way the West Indies – with Bajans singled out for particular criticism – treated Antiguan players.

'They didn't want Curtly Ambrose in the side at the start of this tour and look how he's ended up Man of the Series,' he said. 'And Keith Arthurton – they put too much pressure on him, saying how many runs he has to make to keep his Test place. They should have just let him go out and play.'

My driver skirted a pot hole in the airport road and then, coming to the heart of the matter added, 'You know, Antigua could field a world team. Look at all the talent we have – Richards, Richardson, Ambrose, Baptiste, Benjamin. We could play Test cricket.'

The idea of each island fielding its own Test side has been bubbling around the Caribbean for a few years now but, for financial reasons if nothing else, is likely to be fiercely resisted by the West Indies Cricket Board of Control. Politically, too, it would be a great shame to disband the one unifying force that binds these very different islands.

Nevertheless, right now, the Leeward Islands, of which Antigua is a part, certainly have a formidable side and when one realizes England even managed to lose to the Windwards, the least of the Red Stripe Cup teams, the widespread strength of cricket in the Caribbean becomes evident.

If Richards does step down as captain in the near future, it would seem indelicate to choose another Antiguan to replace him. But men of real stature can rise above parochial pettiness and, from all I have heard, Richie Richardson, by his quiet demeanour as much as his flamboyant batting, is such a man. In Viv's absence, he captained the Leewards to their first-ever victory in the 1990 Red Stripe Cup and did so without diminishing the potency of his contribution as a batsman. In five matches, all of which were won, Richie averaged 70.16.

However, if he does eventually succeed the great Viv, Richie will need to be a diplomat as well, not only to maintain the unity within the West Indies team, but to convince young men like my taxi driver that independent Test playing islands are not a viable proposition in the long run.

In the meantime, however, my driver was not going to let the West Indies get away with anything. 'Your guys were unlucky not to save the Test in Barbados. The decision that gave Rob Bailey out, that was bad, man, bad.

'I took a look at it *that* close ten times on television,' he said, leaning forward to stick his nose to within one inch of his steering-wheel, 'and I tell you that was a tief decision, man, a *tief* decision!'

Viv Richards, of course, had strenuously denied that any

thieving went on over the Barker-Bailey (and ultimately Martin-Jenkins) Affair, but that had not, apparently, impressed the former member of 'Vivvy's Supas' who, in every sense, was a very independent-minded young man.

London

24 April

There was a little ceremony on the steps of the pavilion at a virtually deserted Lords Cricket Ground this evening. Middlesex had just beaten the Minor Counties in the first round of the Benson & Hedges Cup and John Emburey, Mike Gatting's co-marcher amidst the band of chanting Zulus in Pietermaritzburg, sat on one of the benches waiting to receive the winner's cheque from the sponsor's representative. Behind him, smartly attired in cricket whites and a blue Middlesex blazer, stood Viv Richards' deputy in a series that was still just eight days old, Desmond Haynes, the Man of the Match.

Elsewhere on this bright April day, Graham Gooch, batting with a hand healed two weeks too late, was scoring a hundred against Nottinghamshire at Chelmsford while at Edgbaston Richards himself, wearing Glamorgan colours for the first time, was facing a Warwickshire attack that included Gladstone Small.

The scars in cricket can heal quickly enough when necessity demands; the battles on far away fields, if not forgotten, cast aside as old allegiances are resumed in the yearly ritual of spring. There are no echoes of gunfire in the Long Room at Lords, just a familiar group of elderly members who have survived winter's frost picking up on conversations cut short last September, as they offer opinions on the performances of the troops who have returned from campaigns around the world.

The sameness of it all is comforting in a way, as is the realization that, despite all the hype pumped at the sporting public through the Press, the players are more than happy to switch blazers, accept the foe of yesterday as a friend today, and get on with the game. It is all part of being a professional.

Not that the arguments stop, heaven forbid. After Haynes had received his cheque, which he promptly handed to Emburey, from David Steele, I walked over to the Tavern where nine months before Mike Gatting, the man who said he knew nothing about apartheid, had told me of his decision to go to South Africa. I found him standing at the same corner of the bar buying pints of Guinness for a couple of Middlesex members, both of whom just happened to be black. Well, why not?

After a few minutes he came over to chat about some of the experiences we had shared. It was too early, he said, to know what was going to happen with the remainder of his South African contract.

'That depends on Ali Bacher,' he said. 'I wouldn't mind going back. I've learnt a hell of a lot and I really enjoyed seeing the country. I saw quite a lot in the end and got driven around Soweto one afternoon. I never realized it was so big. There are some homes that look pretty nice, too, which surprised me. It is not all poverty stricken.'

Soon we were joined by Emburey, who had been captaining Middlesex today because Gatt has a thigh strain, and Desmond Haynes, who always seems to have plenty to say for himself, even after what must have been an exhausting eight days. Apart from his 80 today, he had also been up to Old Trafford to score a century against Lancashire just five days after he had completed his 167 at the Recreation Ground in St Johns.

He was quite unrepentant about declaring so late while captaining Barbados against England in Bridgetown and swept aside suggestions that the public had been short changed.

'There was practically no one there,' he said. 'And anyway when Lamb won the toss and put us in on a good wicket, that signalled to me that England weren't interested in making a serious match of it. So why should I declare early and offer them extra batting practice when they hadn't taken the opportunity in the first place?'

Haynes wasn't about to concede anything on the bumper issue, either.

'Fast bowlers who sling it down all day should be able to take it themselves,' he declared. 'And that goes for our quicks as well as Devon Malcolm.'

'Hey, wait a minute, that's all very fine for someone who can bat,' Emburey interjected. 'But some No. 11s like Malcolm don't know what they're doing out there. And anyway you'll get them out far quicker by bowling straight at the off-stump. It won't take them long to miss.'

'We're all cricketers,' Haynes insisted. 'We all play the same game. If you dish it out, you should take it.'

He's a good man to argue with, is Dessie. He'll listen, but you're going to have to produce one that swings, seams and lifts before you get him to change his mind.

He was ready for the over rate issue, too. 'The people don't mind slow over rates if you're giving them good cricket,' he said. 'Did anyone complain in Kingston when England beat us in four days? The rate was only twelve an hour there, too. Listen, the West Indies play a lovely game of cricket, man, and it's only the Press and the administrators who want to meddle with it.'

So was it, I asked, 'A Tour of Hell' as the *Sun* suggested in a thrice-repeated headline across the top of Ian Todd's report?

'Of course not,' said Haynes. 'The teams got on fine. Viv was out of line in Antigua. I found myself leading the team out without knowing where the hell he was. But I think I know what got him so upset. Some of the papers suggested he had made the V sign at Allan Lamb and that really made him mad. He values his relationship with Lamby too much to have that kind of accusation flying around.'

The distortions of the tabloid press are becoming too danger-ous to ignore. Haynes has received life-threatening letters since he arrived in England from people who have been fed a diet of hate. If anything they had been reading in certain newspapers over the past three months bore any relation to the truth, how was it possible that Gatting, the white 'racist' and Haynes, the black 'cheat' – to use names they have been labelled with – were standing there having a perfectly friendly argument over a couple of beers at the start of a season that would see them backing each other to the hilt in the same county side? Having written for every newspaper in what used to be called Fleet Street over the past thirty-four years, I understand perfectly that the popular sections of the Press have to be colourful, vivid and controversial. But that in no way should give them the licence to stir up hatred by gross and untruthful distortion of the inevitable flare-ups that occur between highly competitive individuals in the sporting arena.

In pointing a finger at my own profession, I am in no way suggesting that volatile players like Richards and Haynes should escape criticism when they let their emotions run away with them. Quite apart from the press-box incident, Richards had no business making V signs at the crowd because it is unacceptable behaviour for a man in his position who knows that whatever he does is likely to be emulated by people who revere him as a demi-god. But we, in the Press, must also examine our role in the level of hysteria that is generated by these incidents. And, as John Emburey pointed out, it is not just the newspapers that are at fault here.

'The commentators on Sky Television made a big point of saying what a bad example Richards set for kids by making V signs,' said Emburey, 'and then they proceeded to go on showing it again and again and again all through the broadcast. They can't have it both ways. Show it a couple of times, but why make absolutely certain that every child then gets to see it by constant repetition?'

It is a fair question and no doubt Dave Hill at Sky and any other television executive would have ways of answering it from their end of the lens. But the responsibilities of the media is an issue that needs to be addressed before an exaggerated accent of venom and vitriol begins to poison the very essence of the games we play.

The issues that have erupted since I started this chronicle of two very different cricket tours have been, of course, many and varied and seldom less than fascinating. They will take time to digest. The world is on the move and cricket, that esoteric sport played by English speaking peoples to the bewilderment of everyone else, remains a strangely potent catalyst for so many of the world's problems. It binds independent West Indian islands while exacerbating old colonial sores; it divides people who should be batting on the same side in South Africa while still offering itself as a conduit for faster social change through sporting contact than might otherwise have been possible. It attracts demonstrations and delegations and spawns fledgling political movements as well as lifting people's passions to levels that, as we have seen, need to be tempered rather than inflamed. And all that for the symphony that rings out when bat meets ball.

It has been a long road from Springbok Park in Bloemfontein to the Recreation Ground in St Johns, Antigua, so where better to end it than in the Tavern with Mike Gatting, John Emburey and Desmond Haynes, two rebel tourists and the West Indies vice-captain, playing the same game on the same team under the watchful eye of Father Time as a new season dawns. That, I would suggest, is not a bad example of sporting harmony.

Summarized Scores of English Tours

ONE-DAY INTERNATIONALS

First one-day international, Verwoerdburg, 16/2
English XI 217 (M.W. Gatting 55, B.N. French 43; A.P. Kuiper 3/22, R.P. Snell 3/39). South Africa 218/5 (S.J. Cook 73, A.P. Kuiper 37, C.E.B. Rice not out 36). South Africa won by 5 wickets.

Second one-day international, Durban, 18/2
South Africa 219/5 (H.R. Fotheringham 51, C.E.B. Rice not out 43, T.R. Madsen 42 not out; K.J. Barnett 3/33. English XI 205/7 (K.J. Barnett 76, C.W.J. Athey 44). South Africa won by 14 runs.

Third one-day international, Bloemfontein, 20/2
South Africa 301/7 (A.P. Kuiper 117, S.J. Cook 73, P.N. Kirsten 40; M.W. Gatting 3/54). English XI 94 (C.W.J. Athey 50; A.A. Donald 3/11). South Africa won by 207 runs.

OTHER TOUR MATCHES

Combined Bowl XI v English XI, Kimberley, 26–28/1
English XI 305 (M.W. Gatting 75, B.N. French 55, C.W.J. Athey 43, P.W. Jarvis 35) and 206/4 decl (C.W.H. Athey 70, A.P. Wells 45 not out; H.C. Lindenberg 3/57). Bowl XI 152 (W.S. Truter 31, J.M. Arthur 30; D.A. Graveney 6/45, J.E. Emburey 3/47) and 105 (J.M. Arthur 38; J.E. Emburey 5/36, D.A. Graveney 4/20). English XI won by 245 runs.

SA Universities XI v English XI, Bloemfontein 30-31/1, 1/2
SAU XI 328/6 decl (W.J. Cronje 104, T.N. Lazard 87; P.W. Jarvis 3/58) and 160/9 decl (L.J. Wilkinson 40; N.A. Foster 5/37). English XI 212 (J.E. Emburey 57, B.C. Broad 37; S. Jacobs 5/29) and 75/4 (B.C. Broad 32). Match drawn.

SA Invitation XI v English XI, Pietermaritzburg, 3–5/2
SA XI 305/2 decl (M.W. Rushmere 154 not out, D.J. Cullinan 73 not out, R.F. Pienaar 63) and 315/2 decl (M.W. Rushmere 151 not out, R.F. Pienaar 81, P.G. Amm 65). English XI 292/5 decl (B.C. Broad 85, M.W. Gatting 71; O. Henry 3/115) and 198/5 (A.P. Wells 48, R.T. Robinson 41, B.C. Broad 36; O. Henry 3/76). Match drawn.

WEST INDIES v ENGLAND (1st One-Day International)

Played at Port of Spain on February 14, 1990. Match abandoned. Toss: England. Debuts: E.A. Moseley and C.C. Lewis

WEST INDIES

C.G. Greenidge	c Stewart b Capel	21	ENGLAND	O	M	R	W
D.L. Haynes	c Russell b Lewis	25	Small	10	1	41	2
R.B. Richardson	c Stewart b Fraser	51	Fraser	10	1	37	2
C.L. Hooper	c Smith b Hemmings	17	Capel	6	0	25	1
C.A. Best	c and b Gooch	6	Lewis	7	1	30	1
I.V.A. Richards*	b Small	32	Hemmings	9	0	41	1
E.A. Moseley	c Lewis b Fraser	2	Gooch	8	0	26	1
M.D. Marshall	b Small	9					
P.J.L. Dujon†	not out	15	**WEST INDIES**				
I.R. Bishop	not out	18	Marshall	6	1	12	1
C.A. Walsh	did not bat		Bishop	5	2	6	0
Extras	(b 4, lb 4, nb 1, w3)	12	Walsh	1	0	1	0
TOTAL	(50 overs) 8 wkts	208	Moseley	1	0	6	0

ENGLAND

G.A. Gooch*	not out	13	**FALL OF WICKETS**		
W. Larkins	c Best b Marshall	2		WI	E
R.A. Smith	not out	6	1st	49	9
A.J. Lamb			2nd	49	—
A.J. Stewart			3rd	89	—
D.J. Capel			4th	100	—
R.C. Russell†	did not bat		5th	155	—
C.C. Lewis			6th	162	—
G.C. Small			7th	172	—
E.E. Hemmings			8th	180	—
A.R.C Fraser			9th	—	—
Extras	(lb 1, nb 4)	5	10th	—	—
TOTAL	(13 overs) 1 wkt	26	Umpires: D.M. Archer and		
			C.E. Cumberbatch		

WEST INDIES v ENGLAND (2nd One-Day International)

Played at Port of Spain on February 17, 1990. Match abandoned. Toss: England.

WEST INDIES 13/0 (5.5 overs) (Greenidge 8*, Haynes 4*; Small 3–1–7–0, Fraser 2.5–0–5–0).
Teams and umpires as for first match.

WEST INDIES v ENGLAND (3rd One-Day International)

Played at Kingston on March 3, 1990. West Indies won by 3 wickets. Toss: England. Award: R.B. Richardson.

ENGLAND			WEST INDIES	O	M	R	W
G.A. Gooch*	b Bishop	2	Marshall	10	1	39	1
W. Larkins	b Walsh	33	Bishop	10	1	28	4
R.A. Smith	c Marshall b Hooper	43	Walsh	6	0	38	1
A.J. Lamb	b Bishop	66	Moseley	6	1	15	0
A.J. Stewart	c Dujon b Hooper	0	Richards	9	0	32	0
D.J. Capel	c Dujon b Bishop	28	Hooper	9	0	34	2
R.C. Russell†	b Marshall	2	**ENGLAND**				
P.A.J. DeFreitas	not out	3	Small	9	0	37	2
G.C. Small	b Bishop	0	DeFreitas	10	2	29	1
E.E. Hemmings	did not bat		Capel	9	1	47	0
A.R.C Fraser	did not bat		Fraser	10	0	41	1
Extras	(b 3, lb 25, nb 3, w 6)	37	Hemmings	10	0	31	3
TOTAL	(80 overs) 8 wkts	214	Gooch	2	0	15	0

WEST INDIES			FALL OF WICKETS		
D.L. Haynes	c Smith b DeFreitas	8			
C.A. Best	b Small	4		**E**	**WI**
R.B. Richardson	not out	108	1st	20	11
C.L. Hooper	b Hemmings	20	2nd	71	23
I.V.A. Richards*	c Small b Hemmings	25	3rd	117	74
K.L.T. Arthurton	c Russell b Hemmings	0	4th	117	158
P.J.L. Dujon†	c Smith b Small	27	5th	185	158
E.A. Moseley	c Gooch b Fraser	0	6th	206	204
I.R. Bishop	not out	6	7th	212	210
M.D. Marshall	did not bat		8th	214	—
C.A. Walsh	did not bat		9th	—	—
Extras	(b 12, lb 4, nb 1, w 1)	18	10th	—	—
TOTAL	(50 overs) 7 wkts	216			

Umpires: L.H. Barker and S. Bucknor

WEST INDIES v ENGLAND (4th One-Day International)

Played at Georgetown on March 7, 1990. West Indies won by 6 wickets. Toss: West Indies. Award: C.A. Best.

ENGLAND				WEST INDIES	O	M	R	W
G.A. Gooch*	b Moseley		33	Bishop	10	1	42	2
W. Larkins	c Richards b Moseley		34	Walsh	10	1	33	2
R.A. Smith	c Hooper b Walsh		18	Baptiste	9	3	29	0
A.J. Lamb	c Dujon b Bishop		21	Moseley	9	0	44	2
A.J. Stewart	c Dujon b Walsh		0	Hooper	10	0	31	1
D.J. Capel	b Hooper		1					
R.C. Russell†	b Bishop		28	**ENGLAND**				
P.A.J. DeFreitas	run out		11	DeFreitas	7	1	32	0
G.C. Small	not out		18	Small	9.2	1	43	0
E.E. Hemmings	not out		0	Capel	9	2	39	1
A.R.C Fraser	did not bat			Fraser	10	1	42	1
Extras	(lb 9, nb 8, w 7)		24	Hemmings	10	1	33	1
TOTAL	(48 overs) 8 wkts		188					

WEST INDIES			FALL OF WICKETS		
D.L. Haynes	c DeFreitas b Hemmings	50			
C.A. Best	run out	100		E	WI
R.B. Richardson	c Russell b Capel	19	1st	71	113
C.L. Hooper	not out	16	2nd	88	155
I.V.A. Richards*	c DeFreitas b Fraser	2	3rd	109	179
K.L.T. Arthurton	not out	0	4th	109	182
P.J.L. Dujon†			5th	112	—
E.A.E. Baptiste			6th	132	—
E.A. Moseley	did not bat		7th	156	—
I.R. Bishop			8th	181	—
C.A. Walsh			9th	—	—
Extras	(lb 2, nb 1, w 1)	4	10th	—	—
TOTAL	(45.2 overs) 4 wkts	191			

Umpires: D.M. Archer and C. Duncan

WEST INDIES v ENGLAND
(Additional One-Day International)

Played at Georgetown on March 15, 1990. West Indies won by 7 wickets. Toss: West Indies. Debut: C.B. Lambert.

ENGLAND

G.A. Gooch*	b Hooper	42
W. Larkins	c & b Bishop	1
R.A. Smith	c Dujon b Bishop	1
A.J. Lamb	c Best b Moseley	9
A.J. Stewart	b Hooper	13
R.J. Bailey	c & b Ambrose	42
D.J. Capel	c Dujon b Ambrose	7
R.C. Russell†	c Best b Ambrose	19
G.C. Small	c Dujon b Ambrose	0
E.E. Hemmings	not out	3
A.R.C Fraser	not out	3
Extras	(b 2, lb 9, nb 3, w 12)	26
TOTAL	(49 overs) 9 wkts	166

WEST INDIES

	O	M	R	W
Bishop	7	2	22	2
Ambrose	9	1	19	4
Moseley	10	1	48	1
Baptiste	10	1	30	0
Hooper	10	0	28	2
Best	3	0	8	0

ENGLAND

	O	M	R	W
Capel	9	1	41	0
Small	7	0	32	1
Fraser	9.2	1	33	1
Gooch	5	1	22	0
Hemmings	10	1	37	1

WEST INDIES

C.G. Greenidge	lbw b Fraser	77
C.B. Lambert	b Hemmings	48
R.B. Richardson	c Capel b Small	7
C.L. Hooper	not out	19
C.A. Best	not out	7
K.L.T. Arthurton		
P.J.L. Dujon*†		
E.A.E. Baptiste	did not bat	
E.A. Moseley		
I.R. Bishop		
C.E.L. Ambrose		
Extras	(lb 2, nb 3, w 4)	9
TOTAL	(40.2 overs) 3 wkts	167

Umpires: D.M. Archer and C. Duncan

FALL OF WICKETS

	E	WI
1st	13	88
2nd	18	105
3rd	47	152
4th	86	—
5th	89	—
6th	103	—
7th	150	—
8th	151	—
9th	161	—
10th	—	—

OTHER TOUR MATCHES

February 2,3,4,5
ST KITTS: Leeward Islands drew with England XI
England XI 444/6 dec (Wayne Larkins (107 – England's first first-class 100 in WI since 1981) added 96 for 1st wicket with Graham Gooch (46) and 124 for 2nd wicket with Alec Stewart (125); Stewart and Robin Smith (71) then added 144 for 3rd wicket. Nasser Hussain 42; Noel Guishard 3 for 160); **and 213/6 dec** (Gooch 50, Smith 37, Jack Russell 32*; Guishard 3 for 71); **Leeward Islands 256** (Richie Richardson 83, Eldine Baptiste 61; Gladstone Small 4 for 75, Devon Malcolm 3 for 86) **and 301/5** (target of 402 in 66 overs – S. Bassue 57; Keith Arthurton 86, Ralston Otto 51*, Livingstone Harris 54* – chase called off with 12 overs left).

February 9,10,11,12
ST LUCIA: Windward Islands beat England XI by one wicket.
Windward Islands 317 (Lance John 83, Dawnley Joseph 59. Julian Charles 39; Phil DeFreitas 3 for 87) **and 139/9** (Darwin Telamaque 43; Eddie Hemmings 4 for 41, Keith Medlycott 4 for 36 – collapsed from 82 for two to 132 for nine); **England XI 126** (Wayne Larkins 31; Mervin Durand 7 for 15 on first-class debut) **and 326** (following on – Alec Stewart (77) and Allan Lamb (83) added 183 for 3rd wicket, David Capel 65; Ian Allen 3 for 55, Thomas Kentish 3 for 92 – last four wickets fell for 18).

February 19,20,21
KINGSTON: Jamaica drew with England XI.
England XI 405 (Graham Gooch 239 – highest score for England – opening stand of 145 with Wayne Larkins (45), Allan Lamb 31; Robert Haynes 3 for 118, Delroy Morgan 4 for 31) **and 248/4 dec** (Wayne Larkins 124 retired hurt – opening stand of 137 with Alec Stewart (39); Clive Banton 3 for 64); **Jamaica 311** (Robert Haynes career best 98; Angus Fraser 3 for 78) **and 44/2**.

March 17,18,19,20
POINT A PIERRE: President's XI lost to England XI by 113 runs
England XI 252 (Graham Gooch 66, Robert Bailey 52; Eldine Baptiste 4 for 91) **and 278** (Gooch 61, Robin Smith 99; Robert Haynes 6 for 90, Ken Benjamin 6 for 90); **President's XI 294** (Brian Lara (134) and Gus Logie (40) added 131 for 4th wicket; Devon Malcolm 3 for 60, Phil DeFreitas 3 for 89) **and 123** (needed 237 to win – collapsed to 26 for 6 – Haynes 30; Malcolm 3 for 29, Phil DeFreitas 4 for 54).

FINAL TEST MATCH AVERAGES

England batting and fielding

	M	I	NO	Runs	HS	Avge	100	50	Ct
A.J. Lamb	4	7	0	390	132	55.71	2	—	7
G.A. Gooch	2	4	1	128	84	42.66	—	1	2
R.A. Smith	4	7	2	186	62	37.20	—	2	2
W. Larkins	4	8	1	176	54	25.14	—	1	4
A.J. Stewart	4	8	1	170	45	24.28	—	—	2
R.C. Russell	4	7	1	139	55	23.16	—	1	14
N. Hussain	3	5	0	100	35	20.00	—	—	1
D.J. Capel	4	7	1	81	40	13.50	—	—	2
A.R.C. Fraser	2	2	1	13	11	13.00	—	—	—
R.J. Bailey	3	6	0	73	42	12.16	—	—	—
P.A.J. DeFreitas	2	4	0	45	24	11.25	—	—	1
D.E. Malcolm	4	6	3	17	12	5.66	—	—	1
G.C. Small	4	6	1	17	8	3.40	—	—	3

Bowling

	O	M	R	W	Avge	BB	5i	10m
A.R.C. Fraser	71.1	19	161	11	14.63	5-28	1	—
G.C. Small	161	33	505	17	29.70	4-58	—	—
D.E. Malcolm	161.4	22	577	19	30.36	6-77	1	1
P.A.J. DeFreitas	78.5	12	242	6	40.33	3-69	—	—
D.J. Capel	124	17	436	9	48.44	3-88	—	—

West Indies batting and fielding

	M	I	NO	Runs	HS	Avge	100	50	Ct
D.L. Haynes	4	7	0	371	167	53.00	2	—	1
C.A. Best	3	5	0	242	164	48.40	1	1	3
C.G. Greenidge	4	7	0	308	149	44.00	1	—	3
A.L. Logie	3	5	0	212	98	42.40	—	1	1
I.V.A. Richards	3	5	0	141	70	28.20	—	1	4
R.B. Richardson	4	7	0	195	45	27.85	—	—	4
P.J.L. Dujon	4	7	2	109	31	21.80	—	—	15
I.R. Bishop	4	7	3	69	16	17.25	—	—	1
C.L. Hooper	3	5	0	71	32	14.20	—	—	3
C.E.L. Ambrose	3	5	1	51	20*	12.75	—	—	1
E.A. Moseley	2	4	0	37	26	9.25	—	—	1
C.A. Walsh	3	5	1	25	8*	6.25	—	—	—
M.D. Marshall	2	4	1	17	8*	5.66	—	—	—

PLAYED IN ONE MATCH: E.A.E. Baptiste, 9; B.P. Patterson, 2, 0.

Bowling

	O	M	R	W	Avge	BB	5i	10m
C.E.L. Ambrose	132	33	307	20	15.35	8-45	1	1
I.R. Bishop	162.1	37	419	21	19.95	5-84	1	—
C.A. Walsh	93.2	14	243	12	20.25	5-68	1	—
E.A. Moseley	87	14	261	6	43.50	2-70	—	—
M.D. Marshall	59	17	132	3	44.00	2-55	—	—

ALSO BOWLED: E.A.E. Baptiste 23-5-77-1; B.P. Patterson 21-3-85-1; R.B. Richardson 2-1-3-0; C.A. Best 4-0-19-0; I.V.A. Richards 28-10-47-0; C.L. Hooper 24-5-54-0.

FINAL ENGLAND TEST AVERAGES

England batting and fielding

	M	I	NO	Runs	HS	Avge	100	50	Ct/st
G.A. Gooch	6	11	1	616	239	61.60	1	4	6
A.J. Lamb	7	12	0	549	132	45.75	2	1	9
W. Larkins	8	16	2	524	124*	37.42	2	1	4
R.A. Smith	9	16	3	477	99*	36.69	—	4	5
A.J. Stewart	9	18	1	516	125	30.35	1	1	4
N. Hussain	6	10	1	260	70*	28.88	—	1	2
R.C. Russell	8	15	5	269	55	26.90	—	1	24/2
D.J. Capel	8	15	3	245	65	20.41	—	2	5
R.J. Bailey	6	12	1	177	52	16.09	—	1	3
P.A.J. DeFreitas	6	11	4	108	24	15.42	—	—	2
C.C. Lewis	2	3	0	33	21	11.00	—	—	1
K.T. Medlycott	3	3	0	24	21	8.00	—	—	1
D.E. Malcolm	7	9	3	29	12	4.83	—	—	3
A.R.C. Fraser	4	5	1	17	11	4.25	—	—	2
G.C. Small	5	6	1	17	8	3.40	—	—	4
E.E. Hemmings	4	6	1	13	6	2.60	—	—	2

PLAYED IN ONE MATCH: D.I. Gower, 4.

Bowling

	O	M	R	W	Avge	BB	5i	10m
E.E. Hemmings	108.1	30	301	15	20.06	5-77	1	—
A.R.C. Fraser	122.2	28	353	17	20.76	5-28	1	—
G.C. Small	201	40	644	23	28.00	4-58	—	—
D.E. Malcolm	258.4	38	948	32	29.62	6-77	1	1
K.T. Medlycott	100.2	11	425	13	32.69	4-36	—	—
P.A.J. DeFreitas	196.4	27	697	21	33.19	4-54	—	—
D.J. Capel	201	26	733	14	52.35	3-88	—	—
C.C. Lewis	35	6	128	2	64.00	2-30	—	—

ALSO BOWLED: G.A. Gooch 3-0-6-1.

Index

Birmingham, Alabama, 44
Bishop, Ian, 94, 97–8, 100–1,
  116, 121, 128, 135–6, 145–6,
  171–3, 206–7
Black, Johnny, 117–18
Bloomfield, Andrew, 188–9
Bloomfield, Sue, 188–9
Border, Allan, 11, 98, 159, 168,
  223
Botha, P.W., 25, 55–6, 65–6, 88
Botham, Ian, 75, 96, 113, 168,
  204
Boycott, Geoff, 137, 158–9, 168,
  198
Braithwaite, Vere, 190–91
Brearley, Mike, 83
Brink, André, 58
British Airways, 44, 88, 91, 93,
  175, 199–200
Broad, Chris, 22, 47, 74, 77
Brokaw, Tom, 56
Brown, Laurie, 142, 205
Bryden, Colin, 14
Burke, Doug, 70
Business Day, Johannesburg, 70
Butcher, Roland, 8–9, 70
Buthelezi, Mangosuthu, 40
Butts, Clyde, 171

Cable & Wireless, 160, 195, 214,
  223
Camacho, Steve, 188–9
Cambridge University, 80, 111,
  148
Cape Town, 54, 57–8, 81, 83,
  87
Capel, David, 93–4, 119, 128–9,
  136, 146–7, 167, 170, 196, 207
CARE, 70
Carib Brewery, Trinidad, 138
Carillo, Mary, 133
Carlisle, John, 48
CBS Television, 47
Celliers, Peter, 48–9
Centurion Park, Verwoerdburg,
  73–4
Chelmsford, Essex, 223, 228

Churchill, Winston, 38
Clark, David, 104
Clarke, Nina, 159
Close, Brian, 100
Cockerell, Michael, 34
Colonial Office, 188
Compton, Denis, 156
Conservative Party, South
  Africa, 84
Constantine, Leary, 164
Cook, Jimmy, 41, 48, 52, 76–7
Cook, Nick, 99
Corneal, Alvin, 138
Cowdrey, Chris, 8, 45, 76, 132
Cowdrey, Colin, 95, 158, 175
Cozier, Tony, 112, 131, 137,
  152–4
Craven, Danie, 2
Cricketer, The, 181
Croft, Colin, 103, 189
Cronje, Hangie, 16
Crook Town CC, 127
Cry, The Beloved Country, 17
Cumberbatch, C.E., 139, 145
Curren, Kevin, 64

Daily Express, 6, 211, 213–14
Daily Mirror, 20, 44, 70, 72
Daily Nation, Barbados, 152–3,
  190
Daily Telegraph, 26
Dakin, Geoff, 80, 86
Daniel, Wayne, 171
Davis Cup, 2, 4, 152, 209
Deane, Geoffrey, 224
DeFreitas, Philip, 8–9, 12, 93,
  112, 118, 144, 163, 167, 170,
  176–8, 216
de Klerk, F.W., 4, 18, 25–6, 32,
  50, 56, 66, 69, 81, 88–9, 134
de Klerk, Vimpy, 26
de Lisle, Tim, 138
Denness, Mike, 132
Derbyshire CCC, 106
Dexter, Ted, 10, 125, 137
Diep Kloof, Soweto, 63
Dilley, Graham, 16, 45, 76–7

Dimbleby, David, 56
d'Oliviera, Basil, 40
Donald, Allan, 15, 47
Dube, Ethan, 187
Dublin *Sunday Tribune*, 35
Dujon, Jeffrey, 98, 107–8, 115,
    120–21, 127, 139, 163, 170,
    174, 195, 199, 219–20
Duke of Norfolk's XI, 132
Dutch Reform Church, 25
du Toit, Hempies, 88–9

Eagles Club, Bloemfontein, 14
Eastern Province CC, 41, 51, 74
Edberg, Stefan, 209
Edgbaston, 175, 228
Edmonds, Frances, 105
Edmonds, Phil, 80, 96, 100,
    103–5
Edrich, Bill, 111
Elcock, Richard, 92–3
Elizabeth Hotel, Durban, 38
Ellison, Richard, 41, 52, 77, 83
Emburey, John, 13, 18–22, 32,
    34, 228–32
Engel, Matthew, 215
English Harbour, Antigua, 222
ESPN Television, 133
Essex CCC, 9, 113, 131, 149, 174
Etheridge, John, 20, 27, 137
Evans, Godfrey, 110
Evening Standard, 96
Evenwood CC, County Durham,
    127
Everton FC, 84
Ezell, Bill, 112

Feeney, Paddy, 35
Fellows-Smith, 'Pom-Pom', 41
Felton, Nigel, 12
Field, May, 217–18, 223
Fletcher, Keith, 9
Flinders Park, Melbourne, 3, 64,
    111
FNB Stadium, Soweto, 64
Folley, Malcolm, 6, 20

Forbes, Frances, 4–5, 44, 51
Forbes, Gordon, 4–5, 44, 51, 56,
    64–6, 85
Forbes, Jamie, 51
Foster, Maurice, 190
Foster, Neil, 16, 41, 45, 48, 52
Fotheringham, Henry, 41, 48, 52
Francis, Bruce, 66–7, 71
Fraser, Angus, 93–4, 111–12,
    121, 127, 136, 140–41, 144,
    163, 165, 167, 204
'Freedom in Sport', 47, 48–9
Freeman, Tich, 151
French, Bruce, 45, 74

Gandhi, Mahatma, 39
Garner, Joel, 189
Gatting, Mike, 3, 7–13, 19–22,
    31–5, 40–41, 47, 58–9, 70–72,
    74–8, 82–3, 86, 92, 99, 105,
    115, 151, 159, 171, 180–82,
    185–6, 197, 204, 222, 228–30,
    232
Gavaskar, Sunil, 168
Genghis Khan, 39
Georgetown, Guyana, 116, 122,
    130, 142, 192
Glamorgan CCC, 228
Gleneagles Declaration, 67
Goddard, John, 175
Goddard, Trevor, 47
Gomez, Gerry, 131–2
Gooch, Graham, 9–11, 18, 47,
    92–4, 104, 109, 112–14, 123–7,
    133–6, 141–3, 147, 149, 165,
    169–71, 174, 181–2, 203, 204,
    222–3, 228
Gorbachev, Mikhail, 14
Gower, David, 8, 22, 91, 96,
    109–10, 112, 149–50, 157–9,
    161, 182, 200, 203–4, 208–10
Graveney, David, 20, 26, 32, 34,
    41, 45, 58
Greenidge, Gordon, 93, 102,
    115–16, 139, 157, 167, 199,
    207, 217–19
Greenset Courts, 5

On Sport) 31, 36
SACU (South African Cricket Union), 26, 45, 58–9, 71, 80–81, 83, 86
Sanchez, Emilio, 133
Sandham, Andy, 101
Sandton Holiday Inn, 43
Sandton Sun Hotel, Johannesburg, 13
Scargill, Arthur, 2
SCG (Sydney Cricket Ground), 146, 223
Segal, Abe, 5
Selvey, Mike, 96, 137
Shaw, Tim, 74, 77
Sheffield Wednesday FC, 78
Shepherd, David, 97, 108
Sky Television, 41, 75, 97, 121, 127, 143, 198, 200, 231
Small, Gladstone, 93–4, 107–8, 127, 140–41, 162–3, 167, 170, 179, 204, 207, 218–19, 228
Smith, David, 149, 161–3, 165, 182, 200, 204
Smith, Robin, 98–101, 112, 123, 135, 173–6, 195–7, 207–8, 221
Snell, Richard, 48, 74
Snow, John, 94, 159, 170
Sobers, Gary, 137–8, 163, 168, 189
Sogoneco, John, 20
Somerset CCC, 215
Soweto, 60–64, 75, 229
Sparrow, 199
Springbok Park, Bloemfontein, 13–14, 82, 232
Springer, Henderson, 157
Sri Lanka, 12, 18, 186, 196
Stanmore CC, 111
Steele, David, 229
Stellenbosch University, 87–8
St James' Club, Antigua, 207
St Kitts, West Indies, 92
St Lucia, West Indies, 47
Stewart, Alex, 94, 112, 127, 133, 143, 145–6, 162, 172–3, 194, 204, 207, 220
Stewart, Micky, 10, 92–3, 104, 114, 145, 147, 149–50, 163, 180–87, 193, 203, 224
Stollmeyer, Jeffrey, 132
Streeton, Richard, 21, 26, 187
Sugar Circuit, South Africa, 68
Sun, 8, 20, 107, 191, 230
Sun City, Bophuthatswana, 5, 31
Sunday Correspondent, 170
Sunday Star, Johannesburg, 52
Sunday Times, Johannesburg, 38
Sunday Times, The, 110
Surrey CCC, 150, 156, 183
Sussex CCC, 111, 150
Suzman, Helen, 3, 60, 64–6, 83
Swanton, E.W., 132
Swiss Red Cross, 79
Sydney, Australia, 4, 7, 142

Takeba, Herman, 61–3
Tavern, The, 11–12, 229, 232
Taylor, Bob, 159
TCCB (Test & County Cricket Board), 11, 75, 134, 181–2
Test Match Special, 131
The Test Within, 215
Texaco, 115
Thatcher, Margaret, 2–3, 65
Thicknesse, John, 96, 132
Thomas, Greg, 12, 41, 45, 50–51
Thule Awastasia, 79
The Times, 2, 21, 59, 75, 88–9, 96, 109, 176
Today, 20, 43
Todd, Ian, 107, 230
Toshiba, 85
Toyota, 85
Trenty Bridge, 7, 10, 152
Trinidad *Guardian*, 130, 137, 139
Trinidad Hilton, 122, 130, 137
Twickenham Rugby Ground, 78
Tyson, Frank, 142, 215

United Nations, 85
USSR, 68
Uxbridge, Middlesex, 10, 33, 180